"Do we really misread Scripture with individuali[s]
question to rest . . . yes, we do! If collectivist thin[k]
even unbiblical, this book can bring clarity. It is not only practical, it's a page-turner. Its
scriptural insights are gems and its stories illuminating. The authors demonstrate the
significance of collectivist thinking both in the Bible and our contemporary world,
making this book a vital resource for missionaries, theologians, and biblical scholars. At
the same time, the book's down-to-earth style will make it popular for a broader audience."
Jackson W., theologian-in-residence with Mission One, author of *Reading Romans with
Eastern Eyes*

"What an illuminating book! Richards and James take us on a delightful journey
through the biblical world of collectivist culture. They make concepts like kinship,
honor and shame, patronage, and brokerage come to life by illustrating them richly
from both Scripture and their own life experiences. Their fresh readings of biblical
stories alone are worth the price of the book. But Western Christians also should
prepare to be unsettled. The authors expose how often our individualist readings of
texts lead us to miss the point. Beautifully written and highly accessible, the book not
only shows how Scripture reflects collective values but also how the gospel reshapes
and redeems those values. Please read this book. Be challenged by it. You may never
read the Bible the same way again!"
Dean Flemming, MidAmerica Nazarene University, author of *Contextualization in the
New Testament*

"Richards and James are master storytellers who bring to life the world of the Bible. By
explaining the implicit cultural backdrop to biblical stories, the authors paint a
rainbow of color on the black and white pages of Scripture. *Misreading Scripture with
Individualist Eyes* draws on decades of international experience living in non-Western
cultures and on vast biblical knowledge. Readers gain a deep and clear understanding
of the Bible's stories and characters, plus a rich appreciation for the global church
today. Profound insights and fun to read—this book delights the heart and mind!"
Lynn H. Cohick, Provost/Dean, Denver Seminary

"The best biblical studies address two horizons at once: behind the text and in front of
the text. This book does exactly that. It deals seriously with a constellation of complex
cultural dynamics from the biblical world in a way that invites readers to reflect on
their own cultural assumptions. The result is a fresh engagement with familiar texts
and profound implications for a range of topics from soteriology to discipleship."
Brandon J. O'Brien, Redeemer City to City, coauthor of *Misreading Scripture with Western Eyes*

"Like seasoned travelers to a foreign land, Randy and Rich help us understand the culture of the biblical world as they take us on a trip through the Scriptures. Since we are Westerners born and bred in a world that celebrates our individualism, it doesn't take long for us to realize that the people of the Bible don't think like us, act like us, share our social convictions, or claim the same worldview. That's when our expert tour guides step up to answer the question, 'Why do they do that?,' keeping us from misreading Scripture with individualist eyes."

Rodney Reeves, senior pastor of First Baptist Church, Jonesboro, Arkansas

"Without bashing modern scholarship or Western individualism, Richards and James show us the major benefits of reading Scripture from a collectivist cultural model, a model much closer to the original readers and writers of the Bible. What they make abundantly clear in every example and illustration is that we (individualists) take so much for granted and miss so much in the process. Entertaining. Enlightening. Inspired."

David B. Capes, senior research fellow, Lanier Theological Library, editor, *Word Biblical Commentary*

"Everyone reads the Bible through their own cultural framework. It just so happens that Westerners do so through an individualist one, which is foreign to the collectivist worldview of the biblical authors. Richards and James argue winsomely that understanding social values such as patronage, honor, and shame will make us better readers of the Bible. Their book should be on every hermeneutics reading list!"

Miguel Echevarria, assistant professor of New Testament and Greek, director of Hispanic Leadership Development , Southeastern Baptist Theological Seminary

MISREADING

SCRIPTURE WITH

INDIVIDUALIST EYES

PATRONAGE, HONOR, AND
SHAME IN THE BIBLICAL WORLD

E. RANDOLPH RICHARDS
AND RICHARD JAMES

IVP
Academic
An imprint of InterVarsity Press
Downers Grove, Illinois

InterVarsity Press
P.O. Box 1400, Downers Grove, IL 60515-1426
ivpress.com
email@ivpress.com

InterVarsity Press® is the book-publishing division of InterVarsity Christian Fellowship/USA®, a movement of students and faculty active on campus at hundreds of universities, colleges, and schools of nursing in the United States of America, and a member movement of the International Fellowship of Evangelical Students. For information about local and regional activities, visit intervarsity.org.

All Scripture quotations, unless otherwise indicated, are taken from The Holy Bible, New International Version®, NIV®. Copyright © 1973, 1978, 1984, 2011 by Biblica, Inc.™ Used by permission of Zondervan. All rights reserved worldwide. www. zondervan.com. The "NIV" and "New International Version" are trademarks registered in the United States Patent and Trademark Office by Biblica, Inc.™

While any stories in this book are true, some names and identifying information may have been changed to protect the privacy of individuals.

Cover design and image composite: Cindy Kiple
Interior design: Jeanna Wiggins
Image: portrait of a man: © Ana Paula Biondetti / EyEm / Getty Images

ISBN 978-0-8308-5275-8 (print)
ISBN 978-0-8308-4379-4 (digital)

Printed in the United States of America ♾

InterVarsity Press is committed to ecological stewardship and to the conservation of natural resources in all our operations. This book was printed using sustainably sourced paper.

Library of Congress Cataloging-in-Publication Data
A catalog record for this book is available from the Library of Congress.

P	25	24	23	22	21	20	19	18	17	16	15	14	13	12	11	10	9	8	7	6	5	4	3	2	1
Y	41	40	39	38	37	36	35	34	33	32	31	30	29	28	27	26	25	24	23	22	21	20

For my daughter-in-law
Savanna, who brings
such joy to our family.
—Randy

For my amazing wife, Judy,
and our two children,
who continue to teach me
the importance of family.
—Rich

CONTENTS

PREFACE

THERE IS A LOT OF INTEREST these days in how the East is different from the West. There is always a need to read the Bible better. These two topics intersect for students of the Bible, since the Bible is an Eastern book.

One of the big differences between East and West is that modern Western (a.k.a., American and European) societies are individualist. Almost all Eastern and African, as well as most Middle Eastern and South American, societies are collectivist. Collectivist? Here we go. We have already gotten technical and the book hasn't even started. We will try to avoid technical terms. When we do need to use a term, such as *collectivism*, we'll work to explain it and—more importantly—to illustrate it until you are comfortable with it. If Western culture can be generalized as *individualistic*, then Eastern culture can be generalized as *collectivistic*. The rest of this book will unpack a few key aspects. We think to understand ancient Mediterranean (and most modern Eastern) collectivist cultures, you need to understand six basic ingredients: kinship, patronage, brokerage, honor, shame, and boundaries.

Like an earlier book, *Misreading Scripture with Western Eyes,* this book is a guide, an introduction, to some foundational aspects of collectivist cultures. It is not another one of those tired books that bash the West, meaning mainly criticizing America and England. We're sick of those books, and not just because one of us is American and the other is English. Both the West and the East are God's creation—warped by the fall, sure, but God's hand is evident in all the cultures. There is plenty of room around God's table for all of us and that every believer deserves an equal seat at the table. We think the West has contributed much to the work of God's kingdom (and we're not done); the East is where it began. It is not an either-or but a both/and. Which wing of an airplane is more important? The challenge for many of us is that one side doesn't understand the other well.

This understanding gap is important because the Bible arose in an Eastern, collectivist context. Although it is God's Word, an essential element of an orthodox (or evangelical, if you like) understanding of inspiration is that the personalities and cultures of the writers still come through. Jesus spoke with a Galilean accent (Mt 26:73); Paul got angry, and God used his anger to fuel a letter such as Galatians.[1] Jeremiah wrote like an eighth-century Hebrew-speaking prophet, while John wrote like a first-century Greek-speaking evangelist.

Rather than highlight those differences, though, we want to dig further down to the more basic elements that tie Jeremiah with John: ancient Mediterranean culture. *In a culture, the most important things usually go without being said.* We Westerners don't talk all the time about being individualists or about the importance of efficiency or why we prefer youth over old age. Those values just go without being said. Yet to the discerning eye, they are in the undercurrents of billboards and commercials and even influence our everyday decisions. In Paul's world, there were also things that went without being said. Caesar promised peace and security.[2] When Jesus said he didn't bring peace like the world did (Jn 14:27), he didn't need to connect the dots. It went without being said what he meant. Caesar promised peace, but so did Jesus. They were kings offering competing kingdoms.

It can be helpful to take what goes without being said and place it up on the table for examination. This book examines some unspoken foundational social structures and tools used in the biblical world. Since they

---

[1]See, for example, E. Randolph Richards and Brandon J. O'Brien, *Paul Behaving Badly* (Downers Grove, IL: InterVarsity Press, 2016).

[2]Jeffrey Weima argues it was a common Roman slogan. See Weima, "'Peace and Security' (1 Thess 5.3): Prophetic Warning or Political Propaganda?," *New Testament Studies* 58 (2012): 331-59, esp. 332. Clearly Rome promised both peace and security, usually not together. Paul may have meant "peace" and "security"; see Joel R. White, "'Peace and Security' (1 Thessalonians 5.3): Is It Really a Roman Slogan?," *New Testament Studies* 59 (2013): 382-95.

operated in the background, they aren't clearly printed in Scripture. They were obvious to the original audiences. Everyone knows *that*. Yet we don't. These dynamics are not obvious to modern Western readers. That's why some of the biblical stories seem confusing, as if some essential piece were missing. Often pieces *are* missing, because some cultural aspects go without being said. We think collectivism is a major piece, a key cultural given, and that understanding it better will help us understand the Bible better. Moreover, we hope that understanding the Bible better will help us live more faithfully as Christians in the world.

A preface should introduce the authors. You have noticed by now that we use the word *we*. Two good friends, Randy and Rich, joined together to write this book. Randy has studied the topic from a technical, anthropological, and biblical perspective, and Rich has studied it from an experiential, practical-ministry perspective. Randy has written or cowritten other books on related topics, including *Misreading Scripture with Western Eyes*, and Rich has lived about a decade in the Middle East. He is fluent in Arabic and has a keen interest in how collectivism works in modern Middle Eastern societies and how that intersects with the biblical narrative.

Don't look, though, for which chapters or sections Randy wrote versus the ones Rich wrote. We did not collect independently written essays. One of us began a chapter by jotting down some ideas, then the other tossed half of them out, rearranged the rest, and otherwise began to mold the clay that became each chapter. We wrote on top of each other. We discussed every section and each paragraph, and sometimes argued over words in video conferences and debated in personal visits. We rewrote together endless times. Thus, the book is in the end an inseparable weld of both of us. We would not be able to separate out who was responsible for the wording on any given sentence.

Our modern stories are often based on real people and real events. We often changed names; sometimes we simplified events or conflated stories to protect the person or to make the illustration simpler, but we believe we maintained the integrity of the cultural story. An illustration from the

Middle East usually began with Rich, while stories from the Far East began with Randy, but we decided not to try to clarify which author first told that story. This book isn't about us but about helping you to read the Bible better.

Authors often end their prefaces by thanking their spouse. In this instance, we need to offer extra appreciation to Stacia Richards. Randy was leading a Bible conference in Istanbul when he met Rich. Stacia, who was also there, kept insisting, "You should get Rich to write that honor-shame book with you." I pointed out that someone living in Florida who happened to bump into someone living in Beirut during a conference in Istanbul would likely never meet again. After bumping into each other in a ~~chance encounter~~ *divine appointment* in another location far from both our homes, Stacia said, "See!" I am often amazed at how frequently God speaks in a soprano voice.

We are thankful to InterVarsity Press for accepting the idea, to various conferences for inviting us to speak on the topic, and to Kevin Boyle, a promising young scholar, for the arduous task of tying up loose ends and preparing the indexes. Last, I (Randy) am thankful to my dear friend and oft cowriter, Brandon O'Brien, an accomplished theologian and skilled wordsmith, for giving the manuscript a thorough scrubbing. It is a much better book because of him.

Does an understanding of the unspoken social systems of the ancient Mediterranean help us to read the Bible better? We think so and invite you to read the book and to decide for yourself. Come explore with us the collective biblical world of kinship, patronage, brokerage, and honor.

INTRODUCTION

"It's wrong to shame someone!" the student asserted, with clear pain in her eyes. Just to be clear, I hadn't done anything, but she seemed to be talking about some personal experience. "Is it always wrong to shame someone?" I asked. "Absolutely," she and some others insisted.

Well, in my college student's defense, shaming is almost universally condemned in modern Christian discussions. Terms such as *body shaming, mom shaming, pet shaming,* and others leap to mind. The clear implication is that shaming others is sinful.

Yet Jesus practiced shaming. Jesus shamed those who objected when he healed a suffering woman: "When he said this, all his opponents were put to shame" (Lk 13:17 NRSV). It was Jesus' goal to shame them. At least twice, Paul shames the Corinthians to urge them toward proper actions. We know he intended to do this because he says so—"I say this to shame you" (1 Cor 6:5; 15:34). Wow, even God does it: "But God chose the foolish things of the world to shame the wise; God chose the weak things of the world to shame the strong" (1 Cor 1:27).

Shame can be used to do a lot of harm. But it can also be used to do good. We need to deepen our understanding of how shame is used (and abused) by people today. According to the New Testament, shaming others (appropriately) was a virtuous thing to do. Is it possible that our modern practice is the *misuse* of shaming? Shame was a powerful tool in the biblical world. Sometimes it was used well and restored. Other times it was abused and hurt. We can overlook the positive uses of shame, or misunderstand them completely, when we read the Bible as members of individualist cultures. The biblical cultures were just *very* different from ours.

In fact, there are multiple aspects of collectivist cultures that are often misread by modern Western individualists (like me). Remember, *the most important things in a culture usually go without being said.* Since the Bible was written in a collectivist context by writers who were all collectivists, I am at risk of misreading Scripture with my individualist eyes. We'll explain what we mean about collectivist and individualist culture soon, but first let's see another example of how collectivists are different.

"So how long have you been married?" asked the taxi driver as we sat in the usual Middle Eastern traffic. "About three years," I said. He smiled. "How many kids have you got?" I replied, "Oh, we don't have any children yet." He looked sad. "We had the same problem," he said. He opened the glove box and shuffled through all his papers. "I know a really good fertility doctor. I think I have his card here somewhere."

My wife and I waited a few years before having children. I hadn't said we had problems conceiving, but the taxi driver "knew" that's what I meant. My wife and I had similar conversations with a number of people. After all, in Middle Eastern culture, it went without being said that people marry to start a family. Whenever I went on to explain that waiting was a choice we had made, they were totally confused. "Why did you get married, if you didn't want to have children?" Why choose to leave your family to start a new family and then not try to have children? It seems bizarre, like registering for college with no intention to attend, or buying groceries with no intention of cooking.

Not every single Middle Easterner thinks like that taxi driver did, but his perspective is very common. I like to say that *generalizations are always wrong and usually helpful.* This general statement is itself a great example. When we try to lump together the various societies of the modern or ancient Mediterranean world and draw some conclusions, we must generalize. Just like the West, the Mediterranean is made up of many cultures and languages. There is a lot of diversity. This was also the case in the ancient Mediterranean world. Yet, it will still be helpful to generalize because the foundational unspoken values are often so very different from our own unspoken modern individualist values.

"When Abram came to Egypt, the Egyptians saw that Sarai was a very beautiful woman" (Gen 12:14). What is considered beautiful is one of those things that often goes without being said. Sarah was about sixty-five years old—a long way from a contestant for Miss America.[1] As Christians, we like to say, "Everyone is beautiful." Yet Miss America beauty pageants aren't filled with senior adults. Right or wrong, clearly our society has defined beauty by associating it with youth. If we had seen Sarah (in the days before dentists, braces, makeup, and hair products), it is unlikely we would have described her as a beautiful woman. Why did people then? There is not just a different view of beauty from ours but something else is going on.

There is scarcely a story more foundational to the Bible than the story of Abraham. He leaves his homeland to start a family but has no children. So Sarah, his wife, offers to let Abraham sleep with her servant to produce a child. Western readers find this arrangement unthinkable, yet this is the part of the story the Bible assumes we all understand. This is one of the "obvious" parts that are supposed to explain the mysterious parts about God. The writers of Scripture assume we share the same values. So, there are things he left unsaid because "everybody knows that." Understanding these values will help us understand the story, which will then help us to understand God.

Abraham was born and raised a polytheist. In Abraham's world, people believed there were many gods, who were each good at certain things. Some sent rain; others ensured flocks multiplied. People believed these gods often lived in and governed a certain region. This is the context for the beginning of Abraham's story. Leaving one's homeland meant leaving one's god(s) behind. Abraham is following a new, unnamed god. How does one even refer to a god with no name? Well, he's called Abraham's god, Isaac's god, Jacob's god (Ex 3:15). That's not much of a name, but it was all they had at the time. What is this god good at—a god of rain, a god of healing, a god who keeps bread from burning, a god of a particular river

---

[1] That line may offend, and we apologize, but in this book we will need to speak plainly about cultural values, recognizing that one culture's values may violate another's. Note that the biblical text records the shift in her name from Sarai to Sarah. Name changes were important, but we will use the one name "Sarah" here to simplify the story.

or mountain? He initially describes himself as none of those. This new, unnamed god has promised to give Abraham an heir. We need to be careful not to read the Bible backwards. *We* know he is the God of the universe, Creator, Sustainer, Savior, and so on, but Abraham didn't know any of that. There was no Bible yet.

What was obvious and went without being said to those who believed in multiple gods was that Abraham's previous god(s) had not provided Abraham with an heir. When Abraham's family is introduced in Genesis 11, the reader is told about people and their children. It is noted, however, "Now Sarai was childless because she was not able to conceive" (Gen 11:30). While as a modern Westerner, I might read past that detail as just another piece of information about the family, the author expected us to find this standalone sentence dramatic.[2] Abraham's marriage was a failure.

In much of the world today, people get married to have children. This is counter to our individualist culture, in which individuals marry because they are "in love." Love rarely had anything to do with ancient marriage. When we read the biblical story, we assume Abraham and Sarah loved each other. I don't know whether they did—I kind of hope they did, since I am a good individualist. But we certainly shouldn't superimpose our motives back onto them. Ancients married in order to have children, to cement alliances, and to gain strategic relationships. When Solomon married Pharaoh's daughter (1 Kings 7:8), it wasn't because they had fallen in love at some royal ball. When we superimpose our values back on these ancient characters, we will miss something in the biblical story, sometimes the main point of the story. The Bible has a clear purpose for telling us Solomon married *Pharaoh's* daughter. We will get to that story later.

Men married to become fathers. Abraham would have been seen as the father of the group he was leading; yet, he wasn't really a father. This would have been shameful to him. Sarah had failed to give him children; this would have been shameful to her. This unnamed god had offered them an heir, a source of joy and a way out of their shame—but at a high price

---

[2]Martin Kessler and Karel Deurloo, *A Commentary on Genesis: The Book of Beginnings* (New York: Paulist, 2004), 99.

(leaving their homeland and gods). They decided it was worth it to take this unknown god's offer. When no child came, their shame probably increased. Abraham had seemed so confident. In this context, Sarah offers her servant Hagar to Abraham. This is potentially a way out of shame for herself, a way to share the blame with Abraham, a way to satisfy the hopes of the rest of their group for someone to care for them, and a way to build a family for herself. There is no absence of strong cultural reasons why Sarah would do what she did. It would have made sense to people in her culture. No one would have scratched their head wondering why she did it.

Obviously, there is a lot going on in the story that we are expected to know. For many Western readers, this story can be somewhat puzzling. "What kind of wife offers to let her husband sleep with the maid?" We might wonder, "Was that okay in her culture?" More than that, if the goal was for Hagar to get pregnant, then why in the world is Sarah angry when it happens? These are the parts of the story the original readers were expected to understand without explanation—which is why the Bible doesn't explain it. The problem is not with the Bible. It was inspired by God and written by people in a culture. It was clear to the original audience. But we live in a very different time, in a very different culture. There are cultural gaps between the biblical world and our own. We are puzzled because we don't have the right cultural pieces to put in the gaps. Worse, when we don't understand, we often automatically fill the gaps by trying to squeeze in pieces from our culture, where they don't fit. Recognizing these cultural gaps and the pieces that go into them helps us to understand the Bible better. This helps us to apply it to our lives and our culture better. We hope this book will provide you with a few pieces of ancient culture to help you fill in some of these cultural gaps.

TREES ARE TREES, RIGHT?

Perhaps it is helpful to think of culture as being like a tree. Just as different trees produce different fruit—you don't get apples from orange trees—different (often unspoken) cultural values cause people in different cultures to act in different ways. Too often people in one culture judge the way other people dress, talk, and act, without thinking much about the culture that shaped them and certainly not the deep values that shaped the culture. We view their behavior as if those people are just branches off *our* same tree. In other words, we note the behaviors are different but assume the parts we haven't noticed are the same between "us" and "them." We often act as if deep down inside, everybody is the same. Deep down inside is where people are the most different.

The difference between collectivist and individualist cultures is not a surface value, such as "some people eat more rice than we do." Individualism and collectivism describe two very different ways people relate, interact, and live together, but much more too, such as how they view themselves, the way they think, the emotions they feel, the way they make decisions and why, and what motivates them to behave the way they do.[3] Let's picture these two cultural worldviews like apple trees and orange trees; they are really quite different. They are not technically polar opposites.[4] They are better described as different kinds of tree.

Just as individualist societies are not all the same, likewise with collectivist cultures. Not every orange tree is identical, either. There are multiple kinds of oranges: Navel, Cara Cara, Valencia, blood, clementine, and so many more, without even discussing the other kinds of citrus. Similarly, when we compare one collectivist culture with another, we can see all kinds of differences between them.[5] A Far East Asian and Middle Eastern culture can both be collectivist, but there are significant differences between them.[6] The United States and Britain are individualist cultures. Let's

---

[3] Geert Hofstede, *Culture's Consequences: Comparing Values, Behaviors, Institutions, and Organizations Across Nations*, 2nd ed. (Thousand Oaks, CA: Sage, 2001), 210.

[4] M. Kim, "Culture-Based Conversational Constraints Theory," in *Theorizing About Intercultural Communication*, ed. William B. Gudykunst (Thousand Oaks, CA: Sage, 2005), 108.

[5] S. Ting-Toomey, "Managing Identity Issues in Intercultural Conflict Communication: Developing a Multicultural Identity Attunement Lens," in *The Oxford Handbook of Multicultural Identity: Basic and Applied Psychological Perspectives*, ed. Veronica Benet-Martinez and Ying-Yi Hong (New York: Oxford University Press, 2014), 493.

[6] Even the phrase "Middle Eastern culture" is somewhat awkward, for a number of reasons. East of where? It is to the east of Europe, but to the south of Russia, to the north of Africa, and to the west of Asia. The region lays in the "middle" rather than east. As such, there is significant cultural, ethnic, and linguistic diversity in the region, far more than most people realize. We will stick with *Middle East* because it's what most people are familiar with, even though it is awkward.

say they are both apple trees, but they are not the same. What's more, not everyone in the United States is the same! They may all be apples, but there are dozens of varieties, including Red Delicious, Granny Smith, Gala, McIntosh, Honeycrisp, Cortland, and more. When a country is multicultural, like the United States, then different ethnicities complicate the formula.[7] Nonetheless, we can still speak in *general* terms of an apple or an orange, *and more importantly* we can say that oranges and apples have significant differences. The same is true of collectivist and individualist societies. We will say it again: generalizations are always wrong and usually helpful.

Thus, we are not proposing some overly simplistic approach to cultures, today or in the biblical times. We are well aware that the culture of Galilee differed considerably from that of Corinth. Nevertheless, we can speak of the orange trees of ancient Mediterranean culture when comparing it to the apple trees of modern Western culture. The biblical cultures of the Mediterranean world were all collectivist societies and, as we shall see, had a lot of foundational elements in common.

WHY LEARN ABOUT THESE FOUNDATIONAL SOCIAL STRUCTURES OF THE BIBLICAL WORLD?

When we tell a story, a lot goes without being explained. For example, I might say, "After I finished speaking, I looked at the audience. They were all smiling. Someone in the back shot me a big okay." If you are from my culture, you would conclude the speech went well. The exact same response in Indonesia signals a disaster. They smile when embarrassed. Our okay symbol is obscene in Indonesia. Same words, but what goes without being said differs. It is the standard cultural gap. It's the fun (and mischief) of crosscultural travels. Jayson Georges illustrates this well:

> Consider the meaning of these words: *He whistled at her, and she winked back.* This sentence probably brought to mind an image of two people

---

[7]Many times it becomes even more complicated. Asian and Hispanic Americans (for example) may be individualists because they are Americans, but perhaps less individualistic and more collectivistic in some ways, because of their heritage. One of my Asian friends (a grandparent) was complaining about how his grandson didn't understand and value "the old ways," and I recognized it was really that his grandson was thinking like an individualistic American.

flirting. Your mind intuitively used cultural assumptions to interpret the facial gestures as innuendos. But depending on your cultural context, winking could mean something entirely different: in Asia, it is an offensive gesture; in West Africa, parents wink at children as a signal for them to leave the room. Interpretation is based on cultural assumptions, so we must recognize that the cultural gap between the biblical world and us may cause different interpretations . . . Every writer assumes the reader can "read between the lines," so there is no need to state the obvious. . . . But when people from two *different* cultures try to communicate, meaning gets lost in translation. This explains why readers today might misinterpret aspects of the Bible—we don't share a common culture.[8]

Add to that cultural gap thousands of years and a jump from collectivism to individualism, and we have real potential for misreading the Bible.

The Bible is a series of books and letters written by people in collective societies, about the lives of people in collective societies, which they intended people of collective cultures to read. This is part of the beauty of the Bible, and an important part of the doctrine of inspiration. The authors assumed their audiences would see collective social systems in the texts. It was the air they breathed. Rarely are they mentioned, and even more rarely explicitly noted and explained. Yet, these values are there in the background, influencing the actions and decisions of the characters. Some of these values include loyalty based in blood, collective decision making, reciprocity, obligation, inequality, hierarchy, dependence, shame, and the enforcing of cultural boundaries. These are hardly the values of our individualist society. They are the fruit of a different tree.

In this book, we are going to explore what went without being said. That some things go without being said should not make us feel uncomfortable. We should not take it as a sign the biblical writers failed. Such feelings would be the result of another cultural value we hold. We individualists generally belong to what anthropologists term *low-context* cultures. That means that when we communicate, we assume a *low* level of

---

[8]Jayson Georges, "Series Introduction," in *James: An Honor-Shame Paraphrase*, ed. Daniel K. Eng (Edinburgh: Timē Press, 2018), 6.

shared information. We therefore assume it is good communication to spell things out. Not everyone thinks this way. The Bible was written in *high-context* cultures. People in these cultures assume there's a *high* level of shared information between them and their audiences. This means they don't feel the need to state everything explicitly. They take it as a given that everyone knows how things worked—and at the time, they did. This is not a sign they were bad low-context communicators, but rather that they were very good high-context communicators.

In part one, we will explore some of the deep-level social structures of cultures in the biblical world: kinship, patronage, and brokerage. In part two, we will examine some of the key social tools collective people used to maintain, enforce, and reinforce their societal values. These structures and tools are foundation stones buried deep in collective cultures. They are in the background of much of the biblical texts. But we can miss them and some of the significance of what the biblical writers were saying in their culture. In part three, we will apply these things to our individualist lives.

To help you grasp this, we are going to do two things throughout. First, to try to help you see how these aspects of collective culture work, we will bring illustrations from how people live (and think) in collective cultures today. We will share examples from South American, Asian, and most often Mediterranean cultures. But we are *not* suggesting for a moment that these cultures are somehow the same as the biblical world. There are many differences, and we cannot simply read the Bible on the basis of how collectives think today. We are wary of people simply reading modern Middle Eastern cultural values into the biblical text and saying, "That's what Paul meant." Sometimes a modern collective pattern seems to have ancestors in the biblical text, but often it does not. So, perhaps there is a parallel, but we should not simply assume it. You will see that when we exegete (explain) the biblical text, our exegesis comes from standard hermeneutics (methods to interpret) and is based in what the texts say. We use stories from the culture around the text at times to help explore what they meant by what they said. These are taken from the language and culture around the time of the Bible, not today. We also use an awareness of how our individualist culture could be leading us to assumptions—to fill in the gaps with pieces of our individualist culture—when there is a gap because something from collective culture was assumed by the writers. As you have already seen, we tell modern stories to add color and help you grasp the way collectives think, and to see these things are about real people, not just theories. We do, however, want to underline that these modern stories are illustrations and *not* the basis for our exegesis.

Second, to help you see how these collective values work in the text, these deep cultural values will be separated out, disassembled, and explained, with lots of stories to illustrate them. We will show how they work in some modern collectivist cultures and then in the biblical world. We will then show how these provide more context and help us read some biblical passages even better. The more individualists understand the Bible was about collective people, the better we will read it. We hope these illustrations will cause an "Aha!" or two when you read the biblical text.

For example, in my culture there is an American success story. It often goes without being said explicitly, but it is common in our movies and our literature. The plot is usually like this: A small-town boy leaves home (alone). He moves to the big city and after lots of plot twists eventually strikes it big, but he never forgets his small-town values. If we can add to the story that the boy was forced to leave town, overcame lots of adversity, and his family ultimately admires his success, then it is even better. The story of the patriarch Joseph (with his multicolored coat) has a lot that went without being said. Since many Western readers don't know that culture, we tend to fill in the gaps. The result is that we can inadvertently turn the Joseph story into the American success story. I grew up as an individualist and thought the pinnacle of Joseph's story was when he became second only to Pharaoh. The small-town boy had made it big. I also admired Joseph for actions that the biblical author expected me to be appalled over, as we'll see in the next chapter. Let's start our exploration of the social systems of the biblical world.

PART 1

SOCIAL STRUCTURES OF THE BIBLICAL WORLD

EVERYONE LOVES THE STORY of the patriarch Joseph, with his multi-colored coat. I as an individualist often think of the story as if it were all about Joseph. Potiphar's wife and Joseph's brothers (and later his fellow slaves) are just supporting cast in the background of the play. The way we often tell the story goes from Joseph-in-Jacob's-tent to Joseph-in-Pharaoh's-palace. There are some crazy details about cups and contraband. People come and go, and after a long and protracted process Joseph's dad shows up and then dies. The later chapters, when Joseph is ruling in Egypt and his brothers show up, feel like a kind of epilogue. They are so anti-climactic to us. I was stunned to learn these are the chapters my collec-tivist friends love the most. Those chapters are not anticlimactic; they are not an epilogue but the grand finale. To my Mediterranean friends, this is where the story really gets exciting. They are on the edge of their seats.

This is because the entire story of Joseph is actually about Joseph's *family* and how God reconciled them. For collectivists, it is *not* a story about how God advanced Joseph's career. It is not an urban-migration success story. Rather, Joseph angered his brothers, who respond badly, and Joseph be-comes estranged from the family. Some collectivists might say it is *Joseph's* fault. He should have known better than to anger his brothers. My Mediter-ranean friends who are careful readers of the Bible place the blame some-where else. Not on the brothers, not on Joseph. To them, most of the blame lies squarely with their father, Jacob. He is the father of *all* the brothers. As the head of the (ancient) household, it would have been his job to sort out disagreements and tensions like this one. Joseph is young. Fathers are supposed to correct arrogant young sons. The brothers were angry. Jacob should have raised his sons to care for one another even when Joseph was arrogant. Did Jacob even notice the problem? He could, and should, have reconciled the tensions. Instead, he exacerbates them. He gives Joseph a special robe and allows him to stay home while the others have to work. There are a lot of problems in the family. But, never fear, God overcomes (all their) sin. The end of the story is good, because it is about how Jacob, Joseph, and all the brothers are reconciled.

My individualist culture constantly gives me signposts that point me to focus on individuals and their interests. I often miss or underplay collective groups and their collective interests. These same individualist signposts can also cause me to misread the story of Joseph. I easily assume the whole story is about him, almost turning it into a fable about how a young man left home, overcame adversity, and found success. Worse, the way I read the story had the Bible reinforcing capitalism and the American dream. When I do this, I miss a lot of what the Bible is saying. I think I know the story. Joseph is Jacob's favorite son, and Jacob gives him a gift. Right there, I have focused on two individuals. This is actually a kinship (family) story.

Jacob has two wives, Leah and Rachel. At this point in Genesis, we know Jacob prefers the younger wife, Rachel. The Bible tells us the story of Rachel first. Jacob asks (inappropriately) to marry Rachel when her older sister is still unmarried (Gen 29). This matches a pattern in Jacob's behavior of not respecting relatives, including his own brother (Gen 25:29-34). For Laban to arrange the marriage of the younger before the elder sister might doom Leah to spinsterhood. Jacob ends up married to both sisters but loves only Rachel (Gen 29:30-33). Things get worse. Leah, the older sister, bears sons aplenty, but Rachel "was not bearing Jacob any children" (Gen 30:1). As a modern individualist, I see this as a personal matter, perhaps a personal tragedy, because whether one has children is an individual matter. Every part of my last sentence contradicts the values of the ancient Mediterranean world. Children are not a choice. Children are not an individual, personal matter. Children determine inheritance, who owns the flocks. They are a gift and a blessing from God (to the family).

Eventually, God helps Rachel give birth to a son of her own, Joseph (Gen 30:25). As an individualist I note (with a proper frown) that Jacob plays favorites and prefers Joseph over his brothers. I fail to note, though, very important kinship factors in the story. *All* the other brothers in the story are sons of Leah. When Jacob gives the multicolored coat (or full-length robe) to Joseph, this isn't just a matter of Joseph getting a nicer Christmas gift than the other brothers. It isn't merely Jacob showing he loves Joseph more. Jacob is indicating who will be the *heir*. Reuben is the oldest son—but the oldest son *of Leah*. Joseph is the oldest son of *Rachel*. Jacob is indicating that the inheritance will run through Rachel's side of the family, the wife he loves. The Bible states it plainly, albeit in ways that go without being said. Joseph is given higher status. We note that Jacob keeps Joseph *home with him* while the other brothers are out shepherding in the *field* (Gen 37:12-14). What went without being said is that Jacob is giving Joseph more than just an easier job. Joseph is in the manager's office, while the brothers are on the factory floor. Jacob even sends Joseph out to give instructions to the *older* brothers.

Couldn't the other brothers have just gotten on with their own lives? Inheritance wasn't just a father-son relationship issue. If Joseph inherits, then the sons of the noninheriting wife are out. These sons, Joseph's half-brothers, have their own families to consider. What will happen to them and their children? In the ancient world, the noninheriting counted on the inheritor. Joseph's brothers should be able to count on their *brother*. Joseph should look after them and treat them fairly. They are, after all, family.

Well, one would expect a man to treat his brothers well. Yet, Joseph's attitude about inheriting has already been made clear to them: "Listen to this dream I had: We were binding sheaves of grain out in the field when suddenly my sheaf rose and stood upright, while your sheaves gathered around mine and bowed down to it" (Gen 37:6-7). If God gave him that dream (which the Bible doesn't say God did), Joseph is under no obligation to share it with his brothers. Yet, his attitude has already been made clear. Joseph has already tattled on them (Gen 37:2), and now he is bragging he will lord it over them, flaunting that he is to inherit and not them.

Alienating his brothers is a bad idea. The ancient world had no police force. Your *family* was the one to protect you from wandering caravans. Yet, Joseph's brothers don't protect him. Instead they are the very ones who sell him to the caravan. They very likely reason that removing the favored son of Rachel will ensure that Reuben will inherit and thus guarantee a better future for all their *families*. Later Jewish texts emphasize this by saying that the brothers use the money to buy shoes for their families.[1]

Yet, with all this family dysfunction, God still fulfills his promise to Abraham. God watches over Joseph; God does not abandon those who sin. Joseph is not sold to some unknown farmer. He ends up at a country estate of a high-ranking Egyptian official, Potiphar, the captain of the guard.

At this point, a bit of Egyptian history will help us—another thing that went without being said. Egypt had been ruled by Egyptians (of course). But in the 1700s BC a group of Asiatics from the region of Canaan and beyond moved into Egypt and began to seize land. By 1720 BC they had established a capital in the eastern Nile Delta at Avaris. These rulers were called the Hyksos (Rulers of Foreign Lands).[2] These Hyksos were of the same general ethnic group as Joseph. If the Pharaoh was Hyksos, then likely Potiphar was as well. His wife's family may have been Egyptian. Her marriage to a high-ranking Hyksos would help provide security for her family and the estate in those turbulent days. When we read the story carefully, we can see she makes racist comments about Joseph: "She called her household servants. 'Look,' she said to them, 'this Hebrew has been brought to us to make sport of us!'" (Gen 39:14). She aligns herself with the slaves against this outside Hebrew—an ethnic marker. This is us versus them language. All cultures have racism, but us-them language strikes a particular nerve for collectives, as we will see later.

---

[1]Testament of Zebulun 3.1-3: "But Simeon and Gad and six other brothers of ours, taking the price of Joseph, bought sandals for themselves, their wives, and their children."

[2]Ancient Egyptian history is always debated, but many biblical scholars place Joseph's arrival and rise to power during the Hyksos period.

We return to the story. Potiphar's wife—note that she is never named, because this part of the story is about Joseph and Potiphar—takes a shine to Joseph and invites him to bed. Joseph refuses. Good for him, but we should note why. (There aren't Ten Commandments yet.) Joseph states: "'With me in charge,' he told her, 'my master does not concern himself with anything in the house; everything he owns he has entrusted to my care. No one is greater in this house than I am. My master has withheld nothing from me except you, because you are his wife. How then could I do such a wicked thing and sin against God?'" (Gen 39:8-9). Joseph states he is the greatest person in the house and Potiphar has put everything (including her) into Joseph's hand. We are supposed to notice that Joseph has placed himself above her as well as above all the other slaves. They are his new household unit, but the same arrogance he had with his brothers he has here.

Of course, Potiphar is going to know what happened. Slaves see what's going on, and someone will pass the word to Potiphar.[3] She lies to Potiphar and says that Joseph tried to seduce (or rape) her. Potiphar is enraged. We should be careful not to simply read our modern individualist values into this story. We have no idea whether Potiphar loved this wife, but he would have cared about the dishonor and the lack of loyalty shown to him by either his wife or his favored servant. He has two choices:

1. He publicly supports his wife's story: a slave has attacked her. The punishment was routine. The slave would be executed.

2. He publicly supports his head slave and disgraces his wife. The result was routine. He would divorce her.

It seems that whatever Potiphar decides to do, he loses. He clearly doesn't believe his wife's story, because Joseph isn't executed. But if he sides with his wife, then he loses the best estate manager he has ever had (Gen 39:2-3). An honest and successful manager was hard to find. Jesus told

---

[3]The wife of the estate owner would probably never have been left unattended. Individualists value privacy. Many languages in collective cultures don't even have a word for privacy. At the very least a handmaiden would be there. If one slave knew, they would all know. It is quite possible the slaves knew what really happened. If so, then Joseph's alienation of them is even more poignant: they won't come to his rescue.

several parables about lousy servant-managers on estates (Lk 12; 16). On the other hand, if he sides with Joseph, then he must divorce his wife. Since she hasn't committed adultery (at least according to the story he got), if he divorces her the bridal price, almost certainly the estate, will go back to her family. Thus, Potiphar can keep the estate and lose his manager, or he can keep the manager and lose the estate. Potiphar is furious that Joseph has put him in this mess.

Potiphar decides to keep ~~the estate~~ his wife. But we are to notice that not only is Joseph not executed, but he is placed in the best prison in Egypt, the one where the king's servants are placed. We think of prisons as solitary places, but Joseph is given a new community. Yet again, Joseph rises to prominence in his community. But something is different. This time, for the first time, Joseph doesn't alienate his new community. He hit rock bottom, but he has at last learned how to live as a member of a community. Finally, Joseph is ready to be used by God to be put in charge of another community: Egypt.

But this is not the climactic end of the story. This is only part one in the restoration story. The happy ending where we celebrate the saving work of God comes at the end, when Joseph and his brothers and father are restored (Gen 45). Joseph uses his status to care for his family. He provides for all his brothers' families as he should have done at the beginning. More than that, they are relationally restored as brothers who care for one another (Gen 45:14-15). The dysfunctional family is restored. Sin is overcome.

Clearly, kinship plays a very important role throughout the story. It starts with a family and ends with a family. The part that is all about Joseph on his own is not the good part but the bad part. We haven't highlighted it, but Joseph was also supposed to be his brothers' patron, someone expected to use his status to protect and care for others. Joseph fails to fulfill this role initially, but then he does at the end. Potiphar was Joseph's patron, as was Pharaoh. (If you don't understand the term *patron* now, don't worry. We're going to explore this important social structure in chaps. 3–5). Several times, we see a broker—a middleman or a mediator—working to join two parties in the story. Reuben attempts to mediate or broker several times for Joseph with the other brothers. Someone may have been able to mediate with Potiphar or his wife. Joseph asks the cupbearer to broker for him with Pharaoh.

Kinship, patronage, and brokerage are key social structures in the story. The author assumes his intended audience knows these social structures. They surely did; they were collectives and lived in such cultures. They would have recognized how these values were at play. Equally important (or perhaps even more so), the audience is expected to notice when these values should be in play but are not. To ancient hearers (and many modern collective ears), it is obvious that Joseph's arrogance played a role in his being separated from his community, as did his father's passivity and his brothers' fear and jealousy. Collectivists recognize immediately that this is a story about a family (as are all the patriarchal stories). When Joseph needs his community's help, it often doesn't come. The plights of Joseph were the obvious consequences for someone who cut himself off from his community. Thankfully, salvation is a family matter in the story. God has promised much to Abraham and his descendants (Gen 12:1-4). Despite the broken family and failings, God is faithful. He is the star of the story.

ME VERSUS WE

We have been tossing the word *collectivist* around. What do we mean? Doesn't everyone else basically think the same way I do? Actually, like we said above, deep down is where we are the most different. One of my biggest shocks from living abroad came when I realized other people's way of thinking about a topic was just completely different from mine.

Allow me a favorite story to illustrate. I was teaching in Indonesia. I was surprised by how many students left test questions unmarked, even multiple-choice questions. As I handed back graded exams, I commented to a student, "Why didn't you select an answer on question number three?" He looked up and said, "I didn't know the answer." "You should have at least guessed," I replied. He was appalled. "What if I accidentally guessed the correct answer? I would be implying I knew the answer when I didn't. That would be dishonest!" Now it was my turn to be surprised. Blessedly, before I responded, I realized I was about to argue him to a lower standard. My American pragmatism had urged me onward. My Christian standard of honesty had remained oddly silent. Somehow, honesty had not seemed to apply in this situation (when clearly it did). My seminary students today initially don't enjoy this story—because they still want to guess answers. Nonetheless, after I share this story in class I often see exams with unanswered multiple-choice questions, sometimes with a smiley face next to them.[4]

Many things in our cultures are so deep down that we never even think about them. In fact, the most important things in our cultures are usually buried the deepest, way below anything we are really aware of and yet influencing everything above them. The collectivist and individualist distinction is one of these things. We are usually not aware of it, and so in both collective and individualist cultures, this orientation almost always goes without being said. In Britain, it's more and more common to hear people grumbling about individualism. Yet, while we may grumble about some of the effects of individualism, we rarely talk about the core assumptions that underpin them. I don't grumble that I think of myself as an "I." I don't even think about it. Likewise, collectives can grumble about their cultures. It's common to hear collectives grumbling, "People always think they have a right to get involved in my life and give me their opinions," or, "I always have to follow the expectations of others in my family, not what I want to do." But, I haven't heard them grumble about seeing themselves as "we." This is because it is buried very deeply.

We all assume it is simply the way the world is. While we don't like some of this, we can't imagine another way of thinking about it. Even if we can sometimes see some fruit (both good and bad) in our cultures, we rarely imagine there is another tree entirely.

Naturally then, when we see other cultures acting differently, we assume our culture is the norm, the baseline, the standard. This makes their way different and quite strange. We Western individualists might be surprised

---

[4]This story and other examples of Western values are discussed in E. Randolph Richards and Brandon J. O'Brien, *Misreading Scripture with Western Eyes* (Downers Grove, IL: InterVarsity Press, 2012).

to learn that our modern Western culture is the less common view. Dutch social psychologist Geert Hofstede measured individualism and collectivism across people from fifty-three nations. He found the three most individualistic nations in the world were the United States, Australia, and Great Britain. Their scores weren't just the furthest left of the global norm; they were actually more than *double* it.[5] In other words, the global normal or the baseline, the standard, is more similar to the ancient and modern Mediterranean cultures than our Western culture.

WHY DOES THIS MATTER?

This is nothing to panic over. Western culture is not a plague on the world. We are just a different tree. I can go through life quite successfully as an apple tree without needing to know anything about orange trees, unless I interact with one. I don't have to know anything about how my culture compares with ancient biblical cultures unless I want to read the Bible better. Our Scriptures arose in a collectivist world, a world of orange trees, so it would help us to learn a bit about collectivist cultures. Collectivism is so deep in the culture of the biblical writers that they rarely say so directly. It goes without being said, so we can miss it. To exacerbate the scenario, we often fill in what went without being said in their world (collectivism) with what goes without being said in ours (individualism).

We saw how this plays out in the Old Testament story of Joseph and his family. Let's look at a briefer illustration from the New Testament. In this one, collectivism is clearly stated, but I read my individualism right over the top of it. In the modern Western world, I write letters (or emails) as an individual. I sit alone and compose my letter. We often assume New Testament writers did the same. Thus, we assume Paul as an individual wrote his letters. In fact, I grew up calling them "Paul's letters." But the Bible actually tells us differently. The opening of the letter to the Thessalonians tells

---

[5]Geert Hofstede, *Culture's Consequences: Comparing Values, Behaviors, Institutions, and Organizations Across Nations*, 2nd ed. (Thousand Oaks, CA: Sage, 2001), 215. It is easy to critique a sweeping generalization, but we think his research provides some helpful broad brushstrokes.

us: "Paul, Silas and Timothy, to the church of the Thessalonians in God the Father and the Lord Jesus Christ: Grace and peace to you" (1 Thess 1:1).

As a Western individualist, I immediately dismiss this. Paul couldn't really mean that they worked together to write the letter. Western scholars suggest that it just means Silas and Timothy are sending their greetings. Yet, when Timothy sends greetings, it is at the end of a letter: "Timothy, my co-worker, sends his greetings to you, as do Lucius, Jason and Sosipater, my fellow Jews" (Rom 16:21). Other scholars suggest Paul is just being humble. Yet, why wasn't he humble to the Romans, Galatians, or Ephesians?[6] For Western individualists, coauthorship isn't even considered an option. The thought never occurred to us. We read "Paul, Silas and Timothy," but we never really *see* it.

Likewise, as an individualist, I think the Bible was written to *me*. I "forget" that the opening of the letter tells us it was written to a group of people: "Paul, Silas and Timothy, to the church of the Thessalonians in God the Father and the Lord Jesus Christ: Grace and Peace to *you* [plural]" (1 Thess 1:1).

I grew up reading the letter as if Paul (an individual) were speaking to me (an individual). Thus, at the end of the letter, when Paul writes, "Rejoice always, pray continually, give thanks in all circumstances; for this is God's will for you in Christ Jesus" (1 Thess 5:16-18), I imagine Paul telling me to do those things. I sit in my bedroom (alone) and think about how to apply those commands to my life. Yet the *you* in the passage is plural; the commands are plural: *you all rejoice*. Since the church would have been assembled and listening as a group to Paul's letter as it was read aloud to them, they most likely discussed together how Paul's command for them (as a group) to rejoice, pray, and give thanks should shape their community life. Why does this matter? We think that recognizing the collective nature of the biblical world helps us to be better readers of the Bible, and crucially, better able to apply it to our lives and to help *each other* apply the Scriptures to *our* lives.

---

[6]See the argument in E. Randolph Richards, *Paul and First-Century Letter Writing* (Downers Grove, IL: InterVarsity Press, 2004), 32-36.

THE COLLECTIVE SELF: WHO TELLS ME WHO I AM?

When I introduce myself to someone, I usually say my name and occupation. In the collective culture of the Middle East, I can sometimes talk to someone for over an hour before they ask me my first name. The first question they ask is, "Where are you from?" They ask about my job, my family, my age, my children, and my religion. That tells them a lot more about me than my first name. I am the sum of my group. To know me means to know who my group is, or more accurately said, to know my group is to know me.

Collectivism and individualism primarily describe the way people identify and think about the self.[7] People in individualist societies, such as me and most likely you, think of ourselves as an individual person: I am me, and the rest are they. Members of an individualist culture such as me think of my identity as comprising my individual attributes, personality traits, and what I have achieved in my life. As an individualist, these things define the way I see myself as a person and how I see others. I focus on fulfilling my own potential. I was taught in college I should want to be self-actualized. I should seek to be independent and autonomous, and only be expected to look after myself and my immediate family.[8] I can hear my dad saying, "Be your own man. Don't follow the herd." My old anthropology professor worked as an American in a collectivist culture. They nicknamed him "Man Who Needs No One." His mom would have been proud, but they didn't intend it as a compliment. I make independent decisions for myself and bear the responsibility alone. We in individualist societies see ourselves this way. This is very deep down and often goes without being said. As an individualist, nothing struck me as odd when A. A. Milne, the author of *Winnie the Pooh*, had Piglet say, "The thinks that make me different are the thinks that make me ME."[9]

---

[7]Hofstede, *Culture's Consequences*, 210.

[8]Hofstede, *Culture's Consequences*, 225.

[9]Interestingly, Pooh is quite individualistic, but in the story he also needs his friends. See Fredrica Harris Thompsett, *We Are Theologians: Strengthening the People of the Episcopal Church* (Cambridge: Cowley, 1989), 95.

Collectivist people find Piglet's statement confusing in more than just grammar. Collectivist people define who they are in relation to others. I might say, "I'm an honest guy." A collectivist friend would reply, "Says who?"[10] As an individualist (from Texas), such a reply sounds to me like a challenge, maybe even fighting words. My collectivist friend was just wondering who decided that I was an honest guy. If the community that thought I was an honest guy was a community whose opinion my friend valued, then I would be accepted by him and his community as honest. And it wouldn't just be token acceptance. The community would be willing to entrust valuables to me because I was *proven* honest. In my individualist culture, I might need to demonstrate my honesty individually or get a personal reference (by an *individual* he knows).

Individualist societies tend to think of community as being the sum of the individuals. We bring our individual identities, characteristics, values, and talents, and the sum of this becomes our community. Individuals gather to make a community. In collectivist societies, however, the individual is the sum of the community. The community identity, characteristics, values, and talents form the identity of those who all belong to that community. Collectives are defined by the things they share with others, things such as shared blood, shared interests, shared history, shared land, and shared loyalty. They define their core identity as being part of a group, in distinction to other groups.

This is what we mean by collectivism. Collectivist people understand their identity from the group they are part of. It is about identity, which is why people in collective societies live their lives oriented toward their group. They seek to make personal decisions in the interest of their group. They value interdependence, social harmony, and the group welfare. They make collective decisions as a group. To an individualist, that may sound dreadful or disempowering, but there are upsides. Responsibility is shared corporately. It is never just my fault. In fact, I admit that many times as an individualist I have asked others to help me make a decision. I wanted

---

[10]This phraseology was inspired by some of the work of Harry C. Triandis, "Individualism-Collectivism and Personality," *Journal of Personality* 69 (2001): 907-24.

their wisdom, but I also wanted to socialize blame. Yet, this was my (individual) strategy. Collective people do it because they think they *are* the group. They don't see themselves as an individual in a group. Given that people in collective societies see themselves this way, they also see others this way too.[11]

COLLECTIVE DECISIONS: WE WILL HELP YOU DECIDE

"I'd like to buy a set of curtains, please." One of my British friends was moving into a new apartment in Beirut. Before she went to the curtain shop, she spent some time carefully measuring her window and thinking about what color fabric suited the room, and then went to the shop. Her new landlord, his wife, and the staff in the curtain shop looked shocked when she gave them the dimensions. "Those dimensions aren't right," said the shopkeeper. "They are too short. You need full-length curtains." My friend politely said that actually she preferred window-length curtains because she had placed a dining table beside the window. The shopkeeper replied, "No." Surprised, my friend looked to her new landlord for support to deal with this uncooperative shopkeeper. Instead, the landlord replied, "He's right. You want full-length curtains." When she objected, saying she had made the decision already based on the table, both he and his wife replied, "We know best. You don't know. You're not from here." The shopkeeper joined in, saying, "Everyone does it this way." After fifteen minutes of trying to object, with them responding more and more strongly, our friend finally had to accept. She got full-length curtains and had to pay the price for them too. She was upset because she felt that no one had listened to her. She didn't get what she wanted. Actually, it was deeper than that. She believed she had the *individual right* to choose her own curtains for her own house. They had not respected her right. She had expected to be able to make the decision based on what *she* preferred. The community, however, was frustrated. She hadn't listened to wisdom. They expected her to make the decision based on what the *community* preferred. After all, she

---

[11]Uichol Kim, *Individualism and Collectivism: A Psychological, Cultural and Ecological Analysis*, NIAS Reports 21 (Copenhagen: NIAS, 2001), 46-47.

wouldn't want every guest who entered her house to think her curtains were too short, would she? It was their responsibility to make the decision for her, as her new landlords, neighbors, and friends. Everybody was oblivious to what was really going on. It wasn't really about curtains. That was the surface symptom, but all the real activity was occurring deep down in the social structures of their cultures.

These social structures are foundational to the biblical worldview. In order to explain them, we will need to oversimplify. Worse than that, we will treat these social structures in collective cultures—kinship, patronage, and brokerage—as if they were separate or distinct from one another. Like most of life, it is never so neat and clean. Often these roles overlap or are mixed, muddled, or switched partway through a story.

For example, in the story of Abraham and Sarah, Abraham is the one responsible to lead, care for, and protect the large group he is leading. He is described as their father, but not by blood or marriage. He is a patron of the group. The issues of Abraham and Sarah's marriage are problems of kinship (in our eyes, a personal matter); yet, how that gets worked out affects everyone else in the group. If Eliezer of Damascus becomes the designated heir (Gen 15:2), then the status of everyone else in the group could be dramatically altered. Eliezer could choose to have others as his clients, rather than them. These people have left their own homeland— their own fathers and gods—and now could be fatherless. There is a lot at stake. Sarah's actions to resolve her own shame would have been viewed as acceptable because of the positive effects for the rest of the group. If Abraham has an heir, everyone in his care will still have a father. So Sarah acts on her own family's behalf to restore her own and her family's honor, but she is also a broker (mediator) between Abraham and the rest of the group.

The roles of father, patron, and broker are all a bit jumbled. There is no contradiction in this. Ancient writers mixed their images because they were confident their readers could follow. These were, after all, basic ideas that *everyone* understood. They reflected real life. When we understand the roles of a patron, client, honor, shame, and family, then we can then put all the pieces back together to see how they overlap in key Bible texts, often for purposeful reasons, as in Abraham's story and the promises God made to his family.

My friend's argument was over curtains, but the deeper issue was a conflict between individualism and collectivism. Her new friends thought they were helping her, and she thought they were interfering. If collectivists expect the community to be involved in making a decision over something as minor as curtains, what about really important decisions, such as marriage or religion? As long as Westerners stay in the West and Easterners stay in the East, there aren't problems—everyone knows what isn't being said. When people move crossculturally, the misunderstandings start. When an individualist like me picks up the Bible, an ancient book written in a collective world, misreadings happen.

1

KINSHIP

Being in a Family

"**How long are you vacationing in Lebanon?**" the owner of the local cafe asked, when she realized I spoke Arabic. "I live here," I replied. "Oh, so you have *qaraybeen* here." Arabs use *qaraybeen* ("close people") to mean members of an extended family, including parents, siblings, grandparents, uncles and aunts, first cousins, and sometimes more distantly removed relatives. I said, "No, just me, my wife, and our son." Perplexed, she asked, "Why would you live alone as a family?" In Arab culture, a person's family provides her with support, care, protection, and identity. She couldn't understand why we would want to live like orphans, apart from the support of our (extended) family. What a way to start a conversation. A friendly waitress back home would have asked, "What's your name?" That's because in individualist cultures we view a person as a unique entity. We feel we need to get to know the unique things about them, such as their name, hobbies, and personal interests. These things help us get to know who they are. Isn't it interesting, though, that these things help us to get to know their individual preferences, the most unique things about them? These supposedly unique preferences are not actually the most foundational aspects of who they are. Like decorations on a cake, these things can easily change.

One of our Syrian friends is currently a refugee. Because her family fled quickly, they had to leave most things behind. Among the few treasures they packed was a book of their family tree. In Britain, many people trace their family trees. I have seen some that go back hundreds of years. But I'd never heard of one that went back thousands of years until our Syrian friend told us about hers. They have family records that go back to within a few generations of Abraham. They chose to bring it with them because it embodied so many generations' effort to record names. They carried their family tree, though, for another reason: their family tree defined *who* they were. This was especially important now they had become refugees.

Her story illustrates that in many ways in the East today, as in the biblical world, the family is the basic building block of society.[1] People live with their extended family. They look out for and care for their family. They rely on their family, and they make their personal decisions as a family. They do this because they see themselves as "we" (our family) rather than "me."

The writer of 1–2 Chronicles introduces Mahalath as "the daughter of David's son Jerimoth and of Abihail, the daughter of Jesse's son Eliab" (2 Chron 11:18). The Bible introduces people this way so often it might feel to us like some Bible-ese way of speaking. It is actually the language of collectivism. This way of describing people is integral to the style of the Bible. The biblical authors think that introducing someone requires explaining their family. Even today in many Arab countries, a person's identity card includes their own name, their father's name, and their grandfather's name. The reason it is written on their identity card is that it is their identity. People are always perplexed my identity card does not mention my grandfather's name, let alone my father's name. They wonder, *What kind of identity card is that?*

Kinship formed the basic building block of communities all across the ancient world. People's identity, actions, decisions, and loyalties were shaped by family. Most family reunions remind us how complex family lines and relationships can be. The biblical family lines are just as much or more complicated. Kinship dynamics play an important role in stories

---

[1]Halim Barakat, *The Arab World: Society, Culture, and State* (Berkeley: University of California Press, 1993), 97.

throughout the Bible. Some of these dynamics are clear, but others go without being said. When we see how ancient families worked, how they were organized, how people joined them, and how people remained in them, then we will become even better readers of the Bible.

BLOOD IS THICKER THAN WATER

What an odd expression. Of course, blood is more viscous than water, but that is scarcely what we mean. When I say it, I am explaining why an extra effort was made, extra grace was extended, extra loyalty was given. Ancient people would have agreed with the sentiment. When Abimelek makes his case to become leader of Shechem, he says, "Ask all the citizens of Shechem, 'Which is better for you: to have all seventy of Jerub-Baal's sons rule over you, or just one man?' Remember, I am your flesh and blood" (Judg 9:2). Abimelek thinks this is a strong claim. After all, blood was the social glue of society—and he shares blood with them. Abimelek is right. His argument, based on sharing family ties, persuades them, "When the brothers repeated all this to the citizens of Shechem, they were inclined to follow Abimelek, for they said, 'He is related to us'" (Judg 9:3).

In the West, we have another odd saying, "You can pick your friends, but you can't pick your family." My Eastern friends would completely agree. But we mean *very* different things. As a Westerner, this saying suggests friends are to be preferred because they are chosen. My Eastern friends draw the opposite conclusion, pointing out this saying means family is far more permanent than choice.

For individualists, the smallest family unit is often termed the nuclear family. It is a mom, dad, and immediate children. Today, that family unit can be blended, have a single parent, or have a number of other variations, but it is still premised on that basic model. In the ancient Mediterranean, the smallest family unit was called the father's household. We might think this is just a more paternalistic way, of saying the same thing as a nuclear family. But in the biblical world, the father's household included the father, his wife (or wives), his married sons and their wives and children, and all his unmarried daughters. When God tells Noah to take his family into the ark, we are told, "Noah and his sons and his wife and his sons' wives entered the ark" (Gen 7:7). This was the basic family unit. Noah had one wife, but when polygamy was practiced, the father's household could be quite large, since it included half-brothers and half-sisters.

We are still not done counting members of the father's household. There were also household and field servants (Ex 20:10). Although the father of the household was not the biological father (or even the adoptive father) of all these people, he was termed the *father* of the household.

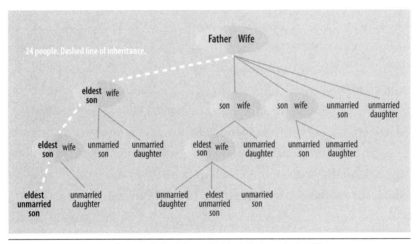

Figure 1.1. An example of what a father's household might have looked like

The father was the eldest male, responsible for their welfare and their protection. The household respected his decisions as the head of the household, even if they themselves were adults. Moses was elderly when God spoke to him at the burning bush; yet he still went to ask his father in law, the head of the household, to let him go to Egypt (Ex 4:18). In Hebrew culture, a father's household generally included three generations. This could have included as many as thirty people.[2] Later, in the Greco-Roman world, people used the words *oikos* (Greek) and *familia* (Latin) to mean all the people under the legal authority of the head of household. This included his wife, children, and potentially other blood relatives he was

---

[2]Sandra L. Richter, *The Epic of Eden: A Christian Entry into the Old Testament* (Downers Grove, IL: IVP Academic, 2008), 26.

legally responsible for, as well as any slaves he owned.[3] We should note that slavery was widespread in the Greco-Roman world, and so slaves were part of many families. It was fairly common for families to comprise about four or five blood relatives. The number of slaves a family included often accounted for the difference in family sizes.[4] Wealthier families would be larger usually because the family included a larger number of slaves. Both the Hebrew and the Greco-Roman conceptions of family were different from the modern American family of a mom, dad, and 2.5 children. When the father of a household died, his eldest son would inherit the responsibility of caring for everyone in the household. This is part of the reason why Deuteronomy 21:15-17 gives eldest sons a double portion of the inheritance. He needed it to care for the others. Eventually, when a household grew too large for one man to care for everyone, it divided and began separate households.

The father's household was the smallest unit of kinship. When God tells Abraham, "Go from your country, your people and your father's household to the land I will show you" (Gen 12:1), it meant more than someone leaving home for university or taking a job in another town. It meant leaving the basic building block and protections in one's culture: his father's house, his people, and his land. This profound call exposed Abraham to all kinds of risks. That's what is remarkable, that Abraham trusted God. When Abraham left his father's household, he didn't go alone. "Of course," we might add, "Abraham was *married*." But he didn't just take Sarah. By leaving his father's household, Abraham becomes responsible for his own household. Although Abraham had no children, his household is quite large. The Bible never says how large, but on one

---

[3]Halvor Moxnes, "What Is Family? Problems in Constructing Early Christian Families," in *Constructing Early Christian Families: Family as Social Reality and Metaphor*, ed. Halvor Moxnes (New York: Routledge, 1997), 20-21.

[4]Census records from Roman Egypt (AD 12–259) show that in urban environments, an average of 4.04 blood relatives lived together. Some of these people were extended families and multiple generations. The mortality rate partly explains this number because grandparents often did not survive to live alongside their grandchildren. Larger numbers lived together in the countryside. Households commonly included slaves in addition to these blood relatives. See Roger S. Bagnall and Bruce W. Frier, *The Demography of Roman Egypt* (Cambridge: Cambridge University Press, 1994), 68, table 3.3.

occasion, Abraham assembles the men in his household who have been trained to fight, and they numbered 318 (Gen 14:14).

The father's household did not include everyone ancients considered kinfolk. It was the *smallest* family unit. Next in size was the clan, a collection of multiple households. These households were joined by sharing blood lineage back to the same ancestor. This shared lineage could go back multiple generations, and so clans included many more people than we might consider our relatives today. When we talk about our own flesh and blood, we usually mean members of our nuclear family and maybe as far as our cousins. When Abimelek says this, he means everybody in his mother's clan (Judg 9:1-2).[5] Clans generally governed themselves, maintaining justice and religious life and practices (Ex 12:21; 1 Sam 20:6; 2 Sam 14:7).[6] Clans were too large for one person to lead, so fathers of households in the clan formed a group of elders. Land came to be divided and possessed by clans, and so often a number of villages or even a town belonged to a single clan (e.g., Josh 19:16, 23, 31). As a result, sometimes the names of clans and towns could be used interchangeably; hence the town of Bethlehem is also called a clan of Judah (Mic 5:2).[7]

Then there were the tribes, which were even larger groups of people who shared blood lineage back to a common (even more) distant male ancestor. Often tribes are called "the sons of [that ancestor]." In Joshua 13, when land is divided among the tribes, we read about the sons of Reuben and the sons of Gad and the sons of Manasseh receiving land. By "the sons of" the writer is talking about whole tribes. This wasn't just some poetic way of speaking—a tribe understood itself to be "sons" of the same (distant) father. They shared blood, the glue of the ancient kinship world. So, they carried a sense of solidarity (albeit more diluted than that of the clan). This is one reason why we see so many genealogical lists in the Bible. The lists don't just work to outline histories; they define identities. They

---

[5]See Roland De Vaux, *Ancient Israel: Its Life and Instructions* (Grand Rapids, MI: Eerdmans, 1997), 5.
[6]Daniel I. Block, "Marriage and Family in Ancient Israel," in *Marriage and Family in the Biblical World*, ed. Ken M. Campbell (Downers Grove, IL: InterVarsity Press, 2003), 37-38.
[7]Christopher J. H. Wright, *God's People in God's Land: Family, Land, and Property in the Old Testament* (Grand Rapids, MI: Eerdmans, 1990), 50.

define to whom you belong and who belongs to you. Genealogies could define access to land, grazing rights, and water, since these resources were often owned by tribes.[8] One of the reasons our Syrian friend kept her family tree was that is worked to define *who* they are as a family. It mattered even more to her now that they had left their land.

The Old Testament refers to the *tribes* of Israel, as well as the entire *nation* Israel. We tend to think the various groups identified primarily as Israelites, and it is just a bit of an historical curiosity that there were twelve tribes. But a careful reading of Old Testament texts shows that people's loyalty was often first to their family, then clan, then tribe. God wants them to unite as one people (the people of God), but they rarely do. We cite as the norm what are actually the few occasions (under Moses, Joshua, David, Solomon) when they are one united people. When these figures die, the people quickly dissolve back into tribes—who often don't get along well. Part of the book of Judges is tribal disunity. At times, the tribes are united briefly under a judge, a military leader with charisma. Yet, after this leader dies, unity dissolves (Judg 5:16-17; 20:13-14; 21:24-25). The tribes never lost their identities; this aspect was strong. The problem was their larger identity as a nation of *united* tribes was less strong. Even when the tribes are supposedly united under Moses or Joshua or David, we commonly see cracks in the unity. When David first becomes king, he is king only over one tribe, Judah. One of Saul's sons, named Ish-bosheth, is also proclaimed king, and for two years rules over the other eleven tribes (2 Sam 2:1-11).

After Solomon's death, his son Rehoboam becomes king. The people are weary of the oppressive reign of Solomon and ask Rehoboam for relief. He refuses. Note the kinship language in how Scripture recounts their revolt:

> When all Israel *saw* that the king refused to listen to them, they answered the king:
>
> "What share do we have in David,
>> what part in Jesse's son?
> To your tents, Israel!
>> Look after your own house, David!" (1 Kings 12:16)

---

[8]De Vaux, *Ancient Israel*, 9.

The language is *tribal:* "the son of Jesse" and "the house of David." The other tribes say they have no connection to the tribe of Judah. When Rehoboam wants to go to battle, the prophet of God emphasizes that they share kinship: "This is what the LORD says: Do not go up to fight against your brothers, the Israelites. Go home, every one of you, for this is my doing" (1 Kings 12:24). God underlines their kinship as his people (Israel). They, on the other hand, see no kinship but separate tribes. They break along tribal lines: ten tribes in the north unite under Jeroboam, while only two tribes in the south remain loyal to the son of David. It was all about kinship.

JOINING THE FAMILY

Much of our Western societies are not intrinsically ordered around kinship.[9] Families are important, sure, but for the most part, access to state institutions, rights, and jobs is not built on family. In fact, I can throw kinship terms around rather freely without real meaning. When frustrated with a student the other day who had not been using his head, I exclaimed, "Son, what were you thinking?" I was not claiming kinship or responsibility for him. It was an affectation, just as the expression "She is like a daughter to me" can be used a bit generously in some parts of America. Sometimes we have close friends whom our children call "aunt" and "uncle," but they are not really family. In the biblical world, kinship terms were not tossed about as casually because kinship ordered society. Across the ancient Mediterranean world, one entered into a family, a clan, a tribe by birth, adoption, or marriage. This seems straightforward, but we are going to spend some time outlining how this worked in their world. You will find this adds some pieces of the puzzle to some well-known biblical stories.

Birth. Joining a family by birth seems fairly simple. The main purpose of marriage in Abraham's time was to maintain the family. Sarah appeared barren. Ancients weren't stupid. They understood it took two to tango.

---

[9]Individualism appears more strongly among white Americans and Europeans and less so among certain other ethnicities. Some subcultures in the West are actually quite collectivist. Forgive our generalization here.

They knew the problem could have been Abraham. Sarah, though, took cultural responsibility. Women were often blamed for the lack of children. They would say, "The Lord has closed her womb." Sometimes the Bible means the Lord has actually intervened in a particular woman's life to miraculously close or open a womb. Usually, though, it is meant in the sense that the Lord is the Creator of all and thus responsible for all (Rom 9:20-22). In any case, Abraham and Sarah have no children, and this is a problem for the entire household. Once Abraham is old, Sarah offers her handmaiden Hagar to Abraham, "The LORD has kept me from having children. Go, sleep with my slave; perhaps I can build a family through her" (Gen 16:2). Sarah (like everyone) is thinking about the problem of who will inherit their family. Polygamy was common in Abraham's time, and so was having female concubines. We are not accustomed to polygamy and concubines, and we can be so shocked by what Sarah thinks is normal that we miss the point in this verse. Sarah makes the suggestion because she is thinking of *herself* and the *family*. She is not a strangely submissive wife who is willing to live with injustice so her husband can have an heir. Sarah wants to build a family for herself through Hagar. Hagar is just a pawn in Sarah's (perhaps selfish) plan.

My Mediterranean friends read the story of Sarah differently from how I learned it in Vacation Bible School. They urged me to look at the rest of the picture Genesis gives us of Sarah. "She is a harsh woman," they explained. Every time Sarah speaks to someone, she is harsh. Furthermore, she doesn't seem to be a model wife.[10] Hospitality was important in the ancient Mediterranean. When Abraham sees three visitors (one of whom is the Lord), he runs and bows down before them. He implores them to enjoy his household's hospitality: "So Abraham hurried into the tent to Sarah. 'Quick,' he said, 'get three seahs of the finest flour and knead it and bake some bread'" (Gen 18:6). We are then told Abraham brings some

---

[10]First Peter paints Sarah as a submissive wife, using the image of Sarah from the Testament of Abraham, where she calls Abraham "lord" five times, something she does not do in Genesis. See Peter H. Davids, "A Silent Witness in Marriage," in *Discovering Biblical Equality: Complementarity Without Hierarchy*, 2nd ed., ed. Ronald W. Pierce, Rebecca Merrill Groothuis, and Gordon D. Fee (Downers Grove, IL: IVP Academic, 2005), 232.

curds, milk, and the calf he has prepared and sets them before his guests. I must confess I then missed what went without being said until my Mediterranean friends pointed it out to me: there is no bread. It seems Sarah hadn't bothered to make it. As they eat, his visitors point out that Sarah is missing, "Where is your wife Sarah?" (Gen 18:9). Abraham responds, "There in the tent" (Gen 18:9). Sarah has not honored their guests. Amazingly, one of them responds by saying, "I will surely return to you about this time next year, and Sarah your wife will have a son" (Gen 18:10). God is showing great grace to Sarah.

Abraham isn't portrayed well either. When Sarah suggests that he sleep with Hagar to produce an heir, he simply follows her command. Abraham doesn't show any leadership in the decision. When Hagar becomes pregnant, the Bible tells us Sarah begins to despise Hagar. Sarah's response is characteristically harsh. Despite it all being her plan, she blames Abraham: "You are responsible for the wrong I am suffering. I put my slave in your arms, and now that she knows she is pregnant, she despises me. May the LORD judge between you and me" (Gen 16:5).[11] Again, Abraham shirks his responsibility. Fathers were supposed to govern their families and offer guidance, care, and protection (for everyone in his household); yet Abraham doesn't protect Hagar. "'Your slave is in your hands. . . . Do with her whatever *you* think best.' Then Sarai mistreated Hagar; so she fled from her" (Gen 16:6). Hagar is part of Abraham's household, and he is not caring for those under his responsibility. We are supposed to notice the only one who acts with care and compassion in the entire story is God. God takes care of all three of them. He blesses Abraham with an heir, removes Sarah's shame, and rescues Hagar in the desert.[12]

---

[11]Her plan was likely that Hagar would remain childless. After all, Abraham was quite old. Nonetheless, with Hagar also childless, it would at least raise some doubt as to who was to blame for the lack of children. When Hagar becomes pregnant, there is no doubt that Sarah is responsible. Hagar despises her as particularly barren.

[12]When we view children as an individual gift from God and the product of a loving relationship (as we do in the West), God appears a bit of a monster in Gen 22, when he asks Abraham to sacrifice Isaac. But if everyone's primary concern is inheritance, Abraham does in fact show great faith by being willing to sacrifice his only heir. Ultimately, God is vindicated either way.

We then move to the story of Jacob. Esau is described as the firstborn. This is more than a statement about birth order. In the ancient world, *firstborn* was a title (earned initially by being born first). Firstborn was about inheritance. Isaac is the firstborn and inherits from Abraham the responsibility for the household. He will become the next "father." Usually, this would have meant he also inherited responsibility for land, except that Abraham didn't own any. Abraham's god had promised his family vast lands, but so far, nothing. Esau is Isaac's firstborn, and so now Esau will inherit this promised land from an unknown and unnamed god (Ex 3:6). At this point, the promise seems a little thin. They are wandering shepherds with no land. In fact, the inheritance doesn't seem worth much. Esau has his possessions by this point, as does Jacob. All that is left to inherit as the firstborn is the promised land. What is that promise worth? That depended on how much you trust an old promise that your grandfather said some god had made him. Esau doesn't seem to think that promise is worth much. He sells it for a bowl of beans.

We all know the story, and it seems a sad state all the way around. Jacob's brother is hungry. Brothers should look out for each other, so when Esau is hungry, Jacob should help him. Instead Jacob offers to sell his help. Let's read the story:

> Jacob replied, "First sell me your birthright."
>
> "Look, I am about to die," Esau said. "What good is the birthright to me?"
>
> But Jacob said, "Swear to me first." So he swore an oath to him, selling his birthright to Jacob.
>
> Then Jacob gave Esau some bread and lentil stew. He ate and drank, and then got up and left.
>
> So Esau despised his birthright. (Gen 25:31-34)

Esau *despises* his birthright because he considers the promise of God to be worthless. It has become a joke between brothers. But God takes it seriously, even when no one else does. God honors the sale. He later identifies himself to Moses by saying, "I am the God of your father, the God of Abraham, the God of Isaac, and the God of Jacob" (Ex 3:6). He doesn't say, "the God of Abraham, the God of Isaac, and the God of Esau." Jacob is now the firstborn. The title had been sold. It is not an issue of chronology. The title belonged to Esau by birth, but Jacob gains the title in a rather dubious manner. Firstborn wasn't a title to indicate birth order but rather to identify who would inherit and take on responsibility for the family. In the New Testament we see that Jesus is given the title of firstborn (Col 1:15), which also has nothing to do with being born first. It means, as it did with Jacob, Jesus is the inheritor (Rev 5).[13]

The story of Joseph and his coat of many colors is also a story where being firstborn isn't determined by chronology. Jacob had two wives. Joseph was the eldest son of the second wife, Rachel. He was younger than Reuben, who was the eldest son of the first wife, Leah. The coat shows that Jacob is choosing the firstborn of the *second* wife as the inheritor. This is more than merely insulting the first wife, although it certainly does that. It could threaten the well-being of all the children of the first wife, as we saw in the story. They would depend on their half-brother, and we have seen how he treated them arrogantly. This is one of the reasons why the Bible is careful to tell the full story and show how the sons of Leah are not discarded.

Birth was not just a matter of biology, though it included that. Birth was the way ancients received their identity. Their blood, their family, their place in their family, all determined who they were and where they stood in society. Birth was not something you chose. If you were born high or born low (1 Cor 1:26), this was almost always the place you would remain throughout life. Likewise, if you were designated the firstborn, you received more inheritance and also more responsibility for the rest of your life. Your blood determined where you lived. Birth carried all sorts of practical and relational connotations. When Jesus says to Nicodemus, "Very truly I tell you, no one can see the kingdom of God unless they are born again" (Jn 3:3), he is saying something very profound. To see the kingdom of God, you need to belong to a new family.

Adoption. Birth (blood) was the most common way someone gained their place in a family in the ancient world, but adoption was also practiced.

---

[13]See E. Randolph Richards, "Scrolls, Books and Seals," *The Biblical Illustrator* (Summer 2015): 90-92.

In the New Testament, we read an interesting exchange between Paul and the Roman commander who had arrested him:

> The commander went to Paul and asked, "Tell me, are you a Roman citizen?"
> "Yes, I am," he answered.
> Then the commander said, "I had to pay a lot of money for my citizenship."
> "But I was born a citizen," Paul replied. (Acts 22:27-28)

The commander notes he had purchased his citizenship. Roman citizenship came generally by birth or by a gift of Caesar, such as to retired soldiers. Technically, citizenship could not be purchased. A Roman could adopt someone, granting them citizenship. Sometimes this was done solely for money, even though the empire frowned on the practice. Paul notes that he was *born* a citizen, indicating his entire family was citizens. Hearing Paul was a Roman citizen causes the commander to pause: *Hmmm, a Roman citizen, and even more so, he was born a Roman. Perhaps he also comes from a prominent family?* The commander wisely delays any beatings or brash actions.

Although in the Greco-Roman world, the setting of the New Testament, adoption was a fairly common practice, people's motivation for adopting was quite different from ours. Modern Westerners usually adopt so that they (the family) can care for the (young) child. In the ancient biblical world, people adopted so that the adopted son could care for the family.[14] In the following passage, a man recounts how and why he was adopted by an elder relative named Apollodorus:

> Now Apollodorus had a son whom he brought up and dearly cherished, as indeed was only natural. As long as this child lived, he hoped to make him heir to his property; but when he [his son] fell ill and died in the month of Maemacterion of last year, Apollodorus, depressed by his misfortunes and viewing his advanced age with regret . . . came to my mother, his own sister,

---

[14]Most attention has been given to Athenian adoption because we have lots of evidence. The way adoption functioned in the Greco-Roman world varied between city-states. However, we should not overexaggerate these differences. See James M. Scott, *Adoption as Sons of God: An Exegetical Investigation into the Background of ΥΙΟΘΕΣΙΑ in the Pauline Corpus*, Wissenschaftliche Untersuchungen zum Neuen Testament 2/48 (Tübingen: Mohr Siebeck, 1992), 3-4. Adoption was only frowned on where it was used to sell Roman citizenship. Otherwise, it was honored.

for whom he had a greater regard than for anyone else, and expressed a wish to adopt me and asked her permission, which was granted. He was so determined to act with all possible haste that he straightaway took me to his own house and entrusted me with the direction of all his affairs.[15]

Apollodorus adopted someone who already had a family. The adopted son was brought into the family and given responsibility for the estate. (Remember how family didn't mean blood relations but people who were legally under the authority of the head.) Apollodorus adopted him to sonship to ensure his estate was well managed, since his own biological son had died.

Part of the reason for adoption was high child mortality; perhaps more than 50 percent of children (of those who survived childbirth) died by age ten. This often led to a lack of males to inherit estates and carry the responsibility of leading and protecting their families. Families chose a man to adopt as a son because they deemed him worthy of caring for the family. This is why they adopted an adult, not a child.[16] He was proven for the task—and had survived childhood. (Women were not adopted for this purpose because a woman's inheritance would transfer to her husband's family.)[17] Thus adoption for this purpose was commonly called "adoption to sonship."[18]

Stepping back in time to the world of the Old Testament, we find that the process of adoption was not as formalized, but families faced the same problem of having no son to inherit and care for them. This is exactly the situation Abraham and Sarah were in. Given their world was based just as much or more strongly around family and protection by the father of the household, the lack of a male heir was just as serious a problem. So those

---

[15]*Isaeus* 7.14-15, trans. E. S. Fortster, Loeb Classical Library (Cambridge, MA: Harvard University Press, 1962), 259. For this and other texts, see also James C. Walters, "Paul, Adoption and Inheritance," in *Paul in the Greco-Roman World: A Handbook*, ed. J. Paul Sampley (New York: Bloomsbury T&T Clark, 2016), 1:42.

[16]Maureen Carroll, *Infancy and Earliest Childhood in the Roman World, "A Fragment of Time"* (New York: Oxford University Press, 2018), 147; Walters, "Paul, Adoption and Inheritance," 34; Scott, *Adoption as Sons*, 4-5.

[17]Hugh Lindsay, *Adoption in the Roman World* (New York: Cambridge University Press, 2009), 57.

[18]Greeks used a number of terms to talk about adoption. The most common term was *huiothesia*, which normally meant "adoption as son(s)" (see Scott, *Adoption as Sons*, 267).

with no children might have chosen a relative or trusted servant to designate as the heir. Thus we see Abraham in Genesis 15. God promised him uncountable offspring, and yet he has no heir and expects his estate will be inherited by Eliezer of Damascus, a servant in his own household. As he is wrestling with this, the word of the Lord comes to him: "'This man will not be your heir, but a son who is your own *flesh and blood* will be your heir.' He took him outside and said, 'Look up at the sky and count the stars—if indeed you can count them.' Then he said to him, 'So shall your offspring be'" (Gen 15:4-5). Again, Abraham demonstrates faith by waiting on God.

When Jacob is on his deathbed, Joseph comes with his sons Manasseh and Ephraim. Jacob recounts to Joseph how God had appeared to him and blessed him and said to him, "I am going to make you fruitful and increase your numbers. I will make you a community of peoples, and I will give this land as an everlasting possession to your descendants after you" (Gen 48:4). Jacob then says to Joseph, "Now then, your two sons born to you in Egypt before I came to you here will be reckoned as mine; Ephraim and Manasseh will be mine, just as Reuben and Simeon are mine. Any children born to you after them will be yours; in the territory they inherit they will be reckoned under the names of their brothers" (Gen 48:5-6). Jacob adopts Manasseh and Ephraim even though their father, Joseph, is alive. Why? The context is inheritance and land. Future lists of the twelve sons of Judah generally include Manasseh and Ephraim in the place of Joseph (Num 26:1-51).[19] Adoption in the biblical world carried very real implications for the kinship of those adopted and the families they joined. The adopted members were placed into the family, they inherited in the family, and these realities shaped their lives and the lives of the family's descendants. When Paul wrote to the Ephesians that God "predestined us for adoption to sonship through Jesus Christ, in accordance with his pleasure and will," (Eph 1:5), there would have been a gasp from those who heard the letter read. The family of God was growing, and this had very real implications for the lives of those involved; they were about to join a new

---

[19]Bill T. Arnold, *Encountering the Book of Genesis* (Grand Rapids, MI: Baker, 1998), 162.

family with new siblings. Gentiles and Jews were co-inheritors with equal honor and standing in the family of God. Their identity was brothers and sisters. Likewise, slaveowners and slaves were now brothers and sisters. They all had the same honor: co-heirs. For example, Philemon had a slave called Onesimus, who ran away. Somehow Onesimus and Paul meet in Rome, and during this time Onesimus comes to faith in Christ. Paul wants to reconcile Onesimus with Philemon his owner. Paul writes:

> I appeal to you for my child Onesimus, whom I have begotten in my imprisonment. . . . For perhaps he was for this reason separated from you for a while, that you would have him back forever, no longer as a slave, but *more than a slave, a beloved brother*, especially to me, but how much more to you, both in the flesh and in the Lord. (Philem 10, 15-16)

Marriage. In addition to birth and adoption, one joined a family in the ancient world through marriage. When we read about marriages in Scripture, we should remember the collective kinship implications involved. The Bible assumes that we understand that marriage forged kinship links between many more people than just the husband and wife. Solomon married the daughter of Pharaoh (2 Chron 8:11) in order to solidify a treaty between the countries. Marriages cemented treaties: "We can't fight anymore because we are family." Incidentally, the Chronicler doesn't tell us details about Solomon's other wives. He has special motives for speaking about Solomon's marriage to Pharaoh's daughter. Although Solomon's actions were normal, even expected, the Chronicler intends his readers to be scandalized. He expects us to remember the warning Moses gave in Deuteronomy 17:

> When you enter the land the LORD your God is giving you and have taken possession of it and settled in it, and you say, "Let us set a king over us like all the nations around us," be sure to appoint over you a king the LORD your God chooses. He must be from among your fellow Israelites. Do not place a foreigner over you, one who is not an Israelite. The king, moreover, *must not acquire great numbers of horses* for himself or make the people return to Egypt to get more of them, for the LORD has told you, "You are not to go back that way again." *He must not take many wives*, or his heart will be led astray. *He must not accumulate large amounts of silver and gold.* (Deut 17:14-17)

The Chronicler knows the whole story (since he wrote it). He knows the fate of the temple at the end of the book when he starts writing at the beginning. He knows the son of David who sits on the throne will eventually be overthrown by the Babylonians and that Solomon's temple will be destroyed (2 Chron 36:18-19). He knows Solomon won't be the Son of David promised by Nathan the prophet (1 Chron 17:1-15). Solomon didn't establish a kingdom that would last, and he didn't build a house for God's name that would last. Nor did any of his sons. So, when the Chronicler is describing Solomon, he paints him as the kind of king that Moses warned against. The Chronicler carefully describes Solomon as breaking *every one* of the commands from Moses.[20] Solomon gathers up horses, wives (from Egypt!), and gold. As a result (unsurprisingly), Solomon's heart is led astray. In fact, the Chronicler paints a picture of Solomon turning into Pharaoh. Pharaoh uses the foreigners in his midst (the Hebrews) as forced labor to build cities for himself (Ex 1:11); so also Solomon uses the foreigners in his midst as forced labor to build cities for himself (2 Chron 8:7-10). The Chronicler is trying to underscore dramatically that Solomon is not the one who will fulfil Nathan's prophecy. The promised Son of David has not yet come. (Christians believe Jesus is that promised Son of David.)[21] So the Chronicler has quite the theological agenda in mentioning that Solomon married Pharaoh's daughter. Nonetheless, we shouldn't lose sight of our most basic point. Solomon arranged the marriage for political reasons, to cement ties with Egypt by becoming kinsmen with Pharaoh.

The way people chose whom to marry was also very different from how I do it in my individualist world today. In the biblical world, marriages

---

[20]Even when the text seems to be complimenting Solomon, it really isn't. Notice the very significant "except" in this verse: "Solomon showed his love for the LORD by walking according to the instructions given him by his father David, except that he offered sacrifices and burned incense on the high places" (1 Kings 3:3). How is worshiping other gods okay? See J. Daniel Hays, "Has the Narrator Come to Praise Solomon or to Bury Him? Narrative Subtlety in 1 Kings 1-11," *Journal for the Study of the Old Testament* 28 (2003): 149-74.

[21]Jesus does establish a kingdom that lasts forever. He also builds a house for the name. For this reason both Paul (Eph 2:21) and Peter describe the church using temple language. Peter is very explicit: "You also, like living stones, are being built into a spiritual house to be a holy priesthood, offering spiritual sacrifices acceptable to God through Jesus Christ" (1 Pet 2:5).

were most commonly arranged. This usually offends our Western sense of individualism. *I alone* should choose whom *I* marry. While a noble sentiment, it doesn't work out as well as we might like. Randy is surrounded by college students who are often at the life phase of choosing a spouse. What Christian advice do we offer? "This is the most important decision you can make as a Christian. It will have implications for the rest of your life. Now go out there and choose wisely." That's a lot of pressure without any real help.

Ancients made such decisions collectively. Parents and other relatives were deeply involved. We would not, though, want to paint a rosy and hassle-free image of arranged marriages. In a fallen world, both cultures have flaws. When Jacob wants to marry Rachel, her father, Laban, is very much involved. He agrees that Jacob can only marry Rachel after seven years' work. Then, it seems he gets Jacob drunk at a feast and gives him Leah, his other daughter, instead.

> When morning came, there was Leah! So Jacob said to Laban, "What is this you have done to me? I served you for Rachel, didn't I? Why have you deceived me?"
>
> Laban replied, "It is not our custom here to give the younger daughter in marriage before the older one. Finish this daughter's bridal week; then we will give you the younger one also, in return for another seven years of work." (Gen 29:25-27)

Laban could have argued he was thinking collectively and caring for both his daughters. He does ensure his older daughter is married first, though to a man who does not want to marry her. We're told that Jacob's "love for Rachel was greater than his love for Leah" (Gen 29:30). Laban's plan, which may have seemed very pragmatic to him, leads to serious difficulties for Jacob, Leah, and Rachel. Laban doesn't help them make a good decision. He put the family (collective) interests too far above the individual interests of his daughters, a common pitfall in collective cultures. Parents have very valuable and wise counsel, but they must remember that however good their pragmatic reasoning, their children are the ones who actually have to live out the marriage.

It appears that no culture has this marriage thing worked out flawlessly. Living in a fallen world, filled with broken humanity, leaves no part of the world, individualist or collectivist, untouched by sin. Nonetheless, we should note these basic ideas. Families are important in collective and individualist cultures, but they are different and work differently. We individualists should not presume those in the Bible thought about family in the same way we do. Although someone could join a family in the ancient Mediterranean world in much the same way as today, by birth, adoption, and marriage, their world had many collective implications for those involved that went without being said.

CONCLUSION

There was a Christian organization in Lebanon with staff from ten different Middle Eastern ethnic groups. Their ethnic groups share a long history, and much of it is not good. In fact, sometimes one group had oppressed another, sometimes they had had battles, sometimes they had stolen each other's land or power. While the staff members worked together, they didn't feel they *belonged* together. It wasn't just that they felt a sense of being different from one another. It was much stronger than that. They remembered the conflicts in the historical relationship between their peoples as if it had happened during their lifetimes, between each other. Some felt victimized, while others reflected traditional views of superiority, and so they found themselves continually clashing. Some small action by one member of the group was interpreted through the grid of their peoples' histories, as just another example of this long story. As Americans, our memories are very short. My college students aren't still angry with the Japanese over Pearl Harbor. It's ancient history, after all. When my college students say, "That's history," they mean it doesn't matter. For collectives, their family history matters very much indeed. It made them who they are today. When they say, "That's history," they mean that it is of great importance and relevant right now.

This Christian organization brought in a Western mediation expert to help. During a session, she asked, "Can we forgive before we forget?"

While this seemed a simple question to this Westerner, it offended *all* the staff members. One stood up and began shouting: "What was done to us we will never forget. *They* killed *my* ancestors. The blood that was in my ancestor's bodies, which 'they' shed, is the blood in my veins. [Notice the kinship language.] What gives me the right to forget my ancestors, to betray them, to act as a friend of these people?" He was sobbing. To him, he was being asked to dishonor his family and ancestors, to declare their deaths didn't matter, for the sake of some acquaintances at the office. This is *not* at all what my American college students are thinking when they say World War II is history. My students are not dismissing the death of a grandfather in World War II. Somehow our connection to our family lineage isn't usually strong enough to make us yell and weep. This is an example of where some minorities in America feel their collectivist roots. As a white American, antebellum slavery is "ancient history," and many white Christians feel no complicity in past atrocities, but many of my black friends feel solidarity with their ancestors, similarly to my Lebanese friends: "The blood that flows in my veins was the blood shed by the slaveowner's whip."

When Israelites recount the story of the exodus, it is the story of how God delivered *us* out of Egypt. They tell the story as if they themselves were there. Sure, as individualists, we can all point to shared stories that help join us together with others into some kind of group, such as our family story, or our friendship group's story, or our church story, or even our national story. For individualists, while these stories shape our identity, we tend not to place as much in these stories as collectives do. For example, do you personally feel pain from what happened to your great-grand-parents in the First World War? My collective friends do. There are slogans spray-painted all over the walls in one neighborhood of Beirut saying things such as, "Never forget. Never forgive." These slogans remind the community there of the harm their ancestors experienced at the hands of another people during the First World War. These slogans were not sprayed by centenarians but by young people. They share their ancestors' story, they share their ancestors' pain, and want to remind others there about how "we" were treated—and so how "we" should treat that people group in response. From their perspective, our collective stories create powerful expectations among our kin about how we are to behave toward other peoples.[22] It shows us the collective context for our actions today.

Paul writes to the divided and disunited church in Corinth to call them into unity. In a carefully composed passage in 1 Corinthians 10, Paul reminds them of the exodus story.[23] Helping the church remember and understand this story in Christ is part of his pastoral concerns. Paul reminds them of their ancestors going through the desert. He draws a link between the cloud, passing through the sea, and baptism. All the Israelites ate and drank the same spiritual food together. The rock that accompanied them and sustained them, Paul says, was Christ. They were unfaithful and divided. They committed idolatry and adultery. They grumbled against God (1 Cor 10:1-10). But, like in the exodus story, Paul reminds them, "God is faithful; he will not let you be tempted beyond what you can bear" (1 Cor 10:13). Paul uses this story as a metaphor, but he is doing so because he was speaking in a collective world. Family history gives them good and bad examples, and they should never forget.

Paul argues that the exodus story is now the story of the Corinthians' spiritual ancestors. Lest we forget, the Corinthians were mostly Gentiles! These Gentiles, by believing in Christ, have now become part of this collective family (adopted). What goes without being said is why Paul is troubling to make this point. By making the exodus story the story of their ancestors, Paul is using collective pressure on them. Just as their ancestors got in trouble for immorality, for testing Christ, and for grumbling, then they should be warned: "Now these things occurred as examples to keep us from setting our hearts on evil things as they did" (1 Cor 10:6). Why should the Corinthians escape judgment, if their "ancestors" did not? I can

---

[22]James C. Miller, "Paul and His Ethnicity: Reframing the Categories," in *Paul as Missionary: Identity, Activity, Theology, and Practice*, ed. Trevor J. Burke and Brian S. Rosner (London: T&T Clark, 2011), 42.

[23]The level and style of composition in this passage suggests it may have been a sermon Paul taught and had decided to draw on in this letter. See Anthony C. Thiselton, *The First Epistle to the Corinthians*, New International Greek Testament Commentary (Grand Rapids, MI: Eerdmans, 2000), 741.

overlook these collective dimensions of shared kinship and shared history when I read stories in the Bible through my individualist eyes. The better I understand this, the better I can remember what "my ancestors" experienced in the exodus. Like the Corinthians, this Gentile now has a new family history. I need to see spray-painted on my walls "Never forget" what happened to my ancestors in the desert.

When Paul writes his first letter to the Thessalonian church, he uses all kinds of family language that would have made sense to both Jewish and Gentile family settings.[24] He calls them "brothers and sisters loved by God" (1 Thess 1:4). Paul speaks of them as brothers and sisters many times in the letter. Paul says he feels like any father would "being separated from you for a short time (in person, not in thought)" and that he feels "intense longing" to see them (1 Thess 2:17). As their father, he cares for them and knows the responsibility of writing to guide and instruct them (1 Thess 5:12-22). He speaks of himself as a nursing mother who has gently nurtured these young believers as his children (1 Thess 2:7). He also expects them to follow his instructions, as they would a parent.

Paul mentions how the Thessalonians "love all of God's family throughout Macedonia. Yet we urge you, brothers and sisters, to do so more and more." By emphasizing the kinship connections, he seeks to exhort them to continue to love and support one another, like families do. He also warns them not to be "idle and disruptive" brothers and sisters (1 Thess 5:14). Now that they are part of God's family, beloved by God, he expects this new identity to shape the way they treat one another. We don't *act* like family; we *are* a family, and this shows in the way we act. Elsewhere Paul talks about the way we are to treat older men as fathers, older women as mothers, and younger believers as sisters and brothers (1 Tim 5:1-2). We are to remember the church is a family, not an organization.

Moreover, we don't choose our family; we are born into it. We share the same blood (Christ's blood), and we are joined together by it. In consumerist cultures, fads and fashions can blow through cultures, and oftentimes

---

[24]Trevor Burke, *Family Matters: A Socio-historical Study of Kinship Metaphors in 1 Thessalonians* (New York: T&T Clark International, 2003), 250.

styles, dress, language, and music can seem to drive generations apart. The same trends can blow through church life too, and we can be susceptible to walking away from family too easily for the latest trend or celebrity. Paul reminds us the church is not a cultural group, not a subculture, not an organization, not an event, but a family of brothers and sisters joined by adoption by one father. My sister used to like music I didn't, but I accepted her as my sister. After all, my mom and dad taught us to do that. As a church, grasping that we *are* brothers and sisters and being family is what joins us together, helps us to weather the cultural storms that blow through, and also gives us a solid foundation on which to embrace and accept diversity in our church family.

2

KINSHIP

Staying in a Family

"**My role as a parent is done**," an American friend said with a heavy sigh. He had just dropped off his daughter to start college. Our Asian friend who had joined us for guys' night out looked shocked and said, "I am so deeply saddened for your loss." I started laughing, which made them both upset with me. When my American friend explained, our Asian friend was relieved no one had died. He then added, "We would never abandon our children like that," which now mortified my other friend. For my Asian friend, it was cruel to abandon parenting. He believes people in their twenties still need wise guides who love them, especially as they learn to live and work and prepare to get married.

Years ago, I was sitting in a grass hut in Papua surrounded by men wearing only gourds. This group of church elders was interested in how Christian elders in America help their young people lead godly lives. "Is it true in America," one elder asked, a bit worried that it was just foolish gossip, "that if two Christian young people like each other, they will go out at night by themselves?" I nodded. "We call it dating." All the elders started wagging their heads and clucking their tongues. The lead elder remarked, "American Christian young people must be amazing. If two of our young people did that, one of them would likely become pregnant!" I retained my poker face and said, "Well, yes, American teenagers are indeed paragons of virtue." These Papuans used a different metaphor, but basically their view was that if you put sodium and chloride together, you would likely get salt. It wasn't the fault of either the sodium or the chloride. For that reason, these Papuan elders felt it was necessary to provide chaperones for Christian young people. They thought that it was normal for young people who liked each other to struggle to keep their hands off each other. Parents then were to protect their children because they loved them.

In American Christian churches, we also recognize this struggle, but the only help we usually offer is to mandate self-control. We tell them, "Don't do anything." We offer no communal help. These young people have only their individual self-control. It always seemed to me that self-control works best the less you like someone. Perhaps American Christian young people should only date people they don't like. We are kidding, of course, but the point is that in our individualist world, this dating problem is an individual problem. My Papuan friends thought this was a collective problem and that the community should help these young people.

LEAVING OR REMAINING IN A COLLECTIVE FAMILY

We saw in chapter one that joining a family in the biblical world happened through birth, adoption, and marriage. In this chapter we are going to look at how people in the biblical world remained in (or left) kinship groups. The ways this worked were very different from our individualist societies. In such actions, then and now, a lot can go without being said.

Marrying your brother-in-law (levirate marriage). The Sadducees ask Jesus a question that to our modern ears might sound like a joke, certainly a hyperbole: "Now there were seven brothers. The first one married a woman and died childless. The second and then the third married her, and in the same way the seven died, leaving no children. Finally, the woman died too. Now then, at the resurrection whose wife will she be, since the seven were married to her?" (Lk 20:29-33). While this kind of situation sounds crazy to us, they were describing a plausible scenario. Dying young was common in the ancient world. Being widowed young was very common. Certainly in older times but even as late as the New Testament, Judaism maintained the practice of marrying a brother's widow (or at least talked as if they should). As the Sadducees themselves say to Jesus, this

practice was based in the teachings of Moses.[1] Their aim was not to ridicule the practice or to set up a hypothetical question. What they were
ridiculing was the concept of a life after death through resurrection. Jesus
does not dismiss their question as silly. He points out that there is life after
death; there is a resurrection, but there will be no marriages in heaven.

Given that the father's household was the basic unity of society, the law
addressed what to do if a woman's husband died before a child (an heir)
could be born: "If brothers are living together and one of them dies
without a son, his widow must not marry outside the family. Her husband's brother shall take her and marry her and fulfill the duty of a brother-
in-law to her" (Deut 25:5). We are appalled at this practice because our
perspective is individualist: "What if she doesn't *like* the brother-in-law?"
(She may not have liked the original husband.) Moses' solution resolved
several potential crises for her and the family in their collective society.
First, the widow remains within the protective environment of the father's
household. (Remember, marriages weren't for love but for security and
provision.) Second, if the widow marries outside the family, that share of
the land passes out of the family's possession. Third, "The first son she
bears shall carry on the name of the dead brother so that his name will not
be blotted out from Israel" (Deut 25:6). This was not simply to avoid
forgetting the father's name. It protected the organization of inheritance
in the family. As his eldest son, the newborn baby had inheritance rights
to the land and property of his *deceased* father. Moreover, the widow is
protected because her deceased husband's lands were passed on to her
firstborn son. It is interesting that the law provides regress for the widow
if the man refuses: "However, if a man does not want to marry his brother's
wife, she shall go to the elders at the town gate and say, 'My husband's
brother refuses to carry on his brother's name in Israel. He will not fulfill
the duty of a brother-in-law to me'" (Deut 25:7). We might wonder why
a widow would *insist* on being married to a man who didn't want to be her

---

[1]See, e.g., Dvora E. Weisberg, *Levirate Marriage and the Family in Ancient Judaism* (Waltham, MA:
Brandeis University Press, 2009), esp. 167-94, where she notes that rabbis were well aware of how
problematic this practice was by New Testament times.

husband. Again, we are viewing this from our modern individualist lens, and we have missed what went without being said. Let's use an Old Testament story to unpack it.

Judah and Tamar. The story of Judah and Tamar in Genesis 38 is hard to make sense of as a modern individualist. We wouldn't usually praise a woman who deceives her father-in-law into sleeping with her. We don't expect the father-in-law to praise the daughter-in-law as righteous. But that's what happens.

In Genesis 38, Judah marries the daughter of a Canaanite. She joins his household and gives birth to three sons, Er, Onan, and Shelah. Er, the firstborn, marries Tamar and brings her into his father's (Judah's) household. Then Er dies without bearing a son. According to the levirate marriage laws in Deuteronomy, Tamar should become the wife of Er's brother—Judah's second son, Onan. This means she remains in Judah's household and protection. The firstborn son who resulted from her marriage to Onan would carry the name of Er, her first husband. Er's name and inheritance rights would be "remembered." Onan is happy to sleep with Tamar but purposefully prevents her from getting pregnant because he knows the son will not carry his own name—but rather the name of his late brother (Gen 38:9).

More than just naming rights are in play here. Without an heir to Er, Onan becomes the firstborn, and he gains a larger inheritance. He is keeping the firstborn's share for himself. Onan's greed shames Tamar—she appears to be barren—and Onan shames his dead brother, Er, by stealing his birthright (by not providing Er an heir). The Bible considers Onan's actions wicked in the Lord's eyes. God puts Onan to death. Judah, the head of the household, then tells Tamar, "Live as a widow in *your* father's household until my son Shelah grows up" (Gen 38:11). Tamar should continue to live in *Judah's* household. Judah is failing in his responsibility to her. Why does he do this? Ancient people (and many modern ones) were very superstitious. Two dead husbands seem too much for a coincidence. Judah may believe she is the reason his first two sons died. (Genesis tells us she is not, so we know she's innocent.)

Being put out of Judah's household leaves Tamar nowhere else to go. She returns to her household, where she no longer has any rights, any place, or any inheritance. She is a sojourner, because she now belongs in Judah's household. She waits. When Shelah grows up, Judah doesn't arrange the marriage to Shelah. The text expects us to shake our heads in dismay over Judah's decision. He is the father of the household and has left Tamar homeless and inheritance-less. He also dishonors his eldest son, Er. None of this is stated explicitly in the story, because it went without being said. "When Tamar was told, 'Your father-in-law is on his way to Timnah to shear his sheep,' she took off her widow's clothes, covered herself with a veil to disguise herself, and then sat down at the entrance to Enaim, which is on the road to Timnah. For she saw that, though Shelah had now grown up, she had not been given to him as his wife" (Gen 38:13-14).

Tamar covers her face so Judah thinks she is a shrine prostitute. He asks her to sleep with him and agrees to give her a goat as payment. Tamar asks him to give her his seal, its cord, and his staff as a guarantee in the meantime (Gen 18:18). Tamar becomes pregnant. Three months later, Judah is told, "Your daughter-in-law Tamar is guilty of prostitution, and as a result she is now pregnant." Judah says, "Bring her out and have her burned to death!" (Gen 38:24). Temple prostitution (or any other kind) was not acceptable behavior for a daughter-in-law. The community, though, is shaming Judah, not Tamar, by noting his failed responsibilities: *your* daughter-in-law is guilty of prostitution, which was done in the ancient world as a means to survive. As the father of her household, Judah has responsibility for Tamar—to provide her with protection, support, and moral guidance. He also failed as the father of his household because he didn't give Tamar her rightful inheritance (through Shelah). Next, Judah uses his authority to call for Tamar to be killed, since he feels she hasn't been faithful. What about Judah's faithfulness to her? It seems this is the first time he has shown any interest in Tamar.

> As she was being brought out, she sent a message to her father-in-law. "I am pregnant by the man who owns these," she said. And she added, "See if you recognize whose seal and cord and staff these are.'"

> Judah recognized them and said, "She is more righteous than I, since I wouldn't give her to my son Shelah." (Gen 38:25-26)

As individualists, we can misread this story. We can view Tamar as the bad character in the story. This is because we read our way of doing family into the story. Certainly, Tamar should not have slept with Judah, but he carried responsibility for her, responsibility he did not provide. Judah acted unjustly by not giving Tamar to his third son, which was her right. Judah excluded her from his household and his protection. Tamar didn't have many, if any, other options. Without a household, she was vulnerable and disempowered. The very one who should have stood up for her, defended her, was Judah. Yet, he is the one who wrongs her at the beginning and end of the story. Disempowered, she was the object of all the actions but the subject of none.[2] Her family had failed her. Tamar seized on a way to gain the protection she deserved. When Judah sees what he had done, he confesses his sin and repents. He praises Tamar for being "more righteous" than himself. The Bible doesn't claim she is righteous. Even Judah doesn't say she is righteous. Instead, Judah says she is more righteous than him (which doesn't take much). Incidentally, the superstition is also proven wrong. Judah doesn't die from sleeping with her, and she is clearly not barren. The Bible uses this story to show that Judah had not acted honorably toward his family, his dead sons, or his widowed daughter-in-law.

LEAVING A COLLECTIVE FAMILY: DIVORCE

Not all marriages endured. Divorce was common by New Testament times, and just as marriage was a collective matter, so was divorce. In the West, we sometimes pretend that divorce affects only the couple and it is a private, individual matter. The children of divorced parents might well dispute that claim. Their parents' divorce affects them. The parents' divorce also affect grandparents. Divorce is a family matter. In the biblical world, divorce severed the relationship and responsibilities between a man and wife and those kinship ties between their two families. Land and

---

[2]Andy McCullough, *Global Humility* (Welwyn Garden City, UK: Malcolm Down, 2018), 19.

other benefits had to be reorganized between the kinship groups involved so they were no longer joined. When a woman was divorced, she had to be given a certificate and was then free to remarry.

It appears that most Jews of Jesus' day followed the teachings of Rabbi Hillel, who allowed a man to divorce his wife for any reason (Josephus, *Jewish War* 1.432). Sometimes the reasons were not even that the marriage relationship was bad. For example, Herod the Great divorced his wife Doris for political reasons. He wanted to marry Mariamme the Hasmonean to form an alliance with a Hasmonean priestly family and so build his honor and status. He divorced Doris and banished her son Antipater to strengthen his allegiance by avoiding questions about which of them was queen and which son would inherit. A minority of Jews followed the teachings of Rabbi Shammai, who allowed divorce only for serious transgressions.[3] Jesus of course says that a man cannot divorce his wife except for sexual immorality (Mt 19:9).

The Samaritan woman at the well. Divorce is often mentioned in commentaries on the story of the Samaritan woman in John 4. Christians over the centuries have not been kind to this woman, often painting her as "a promiscuous vixen bent on seducing unsuspecting men, and who therefore becomes the village pariah."[4] We can't be so sure, especially when we take into account her world rather than ours. First, the story never says she is immoral, and she is certainly not portrayed as a pariah. In fact, the villagers accept her word as trustworthy (Jn 4:42). Second, there are no ancient texts that suggest a woman appearing at a well alone at noon meant anything other than someone needing water. Third, her previous five marriages were likely ended by a combination of widowhood and divorce. John 4 does not suggest she was a young woman, and the Herodian princess Berenice was widowed twice with two children by age twenty-two. Women often married in their early to late teens, allowing for lots of young widows.

---

[3]K. C. Hanson and Douglas E. Oakman, *Palestine in the Time of Jesus: Social Structures and Social Conflicts* (Minneapolis: Fortress, 2008), 41; Bruce K. Waltke and Charles Yu, *An Old Testament Theology: An Exegetical, Canonical and Thematic Approach* (Grand Rapids, MI: Zondervan, 2007), 430.

[4]See the wonderful discussion in Lynn H. Cohick, *Women in the World of the Earliest Christians* (Grand Rapids, MI: Baker Academic, 2009), 123-28.

Fourth, we import our modern situations. A story today of a woman divorced five times often has moral overtones. Yet, divorce was more commonly initiated by the husband. If she is the victim of multiple divorces, she is not to blame. Barrenness was a common reason for divorce. If she were guilty of immorality, who would have married her the third or fourth time? As we just read, Hillel allowed any reason for divorce.

Fifth, what of the statement, "The man you now have is not your husband" (Jn 4:18)? There were lots of ancient explanations. If there were no dowry involved, villagers often didn't file (and pay for) official marriage papers.[5] This practice persisted in America until fairly recently; it was called a common-law marriage. Indonesians in the more remote islands still practice it.

There were also several kinds of Greco-Roman marriage that Jews did not recognize as legitimate. She could have been a second wife. She could have been a concubine. If her husband had Roman citizenship, he might not have been allowed by his family to marry someone of lower rank. Romans had marriages where the property of each remained with their respective families. This was more common when older adults married. Their children from a previous marriage inherited family property and didn't want the property subdivided further by future children from a different marriage. In other words, there were several kinds of marriage that Jesus as a Jew would consider "not your husband." As Lynn Cohick concludes, "The Samaritan is a woman of her times." While our presumptions may slander her character, John's Gospel does not. It is good for us to be cautious of simply assuming she was immoral.[6]

---

[5]See the explanation of a Salome Komaïse type of marriage, where a couple lived together for years but filed for an official marriage only once she inherited property (Papyri Yadin 15), in Cohick, *Women in the World*, 125-26.

[6]Cohick, *Women in the World*, 128. Modern readers often paint her immoral and also as not particularly bright. Yet John's story portrays a smart woman. In fact (as is common in John's Gospel), the unnamed disciples are the heroes; John's stories often have two levels. In their history, Samaritans were described as worshiping five gods and also worshiping Yahweh but as a golden calf (1 Kings 17:24-33). It was common for Israel's prophets to describe the worship of idols as unfaithfulness to Yahweh (see, e.g., Jer 3:6-10). If so, then she isn't changing the subject when she says, "Sir, I can see that you are a prophet. Our ancestors worshiped on this mountain, but you Jews claim that the place where we must worship is in Jerusalem" (Jn 4:19-20). There is more going on in Jn 4 than Jesus chatting with an immoral bimbo. Shame on us for stereotyping her.

Joseph's (planned) divorce of Mary. We have seen that in the New Testament world marriage was a collective decision and involved family
throughout the process. First, the families agreed on the marriage, and
then the man and woman were engaged with much celebration. While the
woman was now legally considered the man's wife, she remained in her
own household. Later, her husband returned and took her to his own
home, where the marriage was consummated. This is more understandable
when we remember that many marriages were arranged while they were
children. This marriage process goes without being said in Matthew's
story of Joseph pondering whether to divorce Mary.[7]

Nazareth was a small village, with a population of likely no more than
four hundred people. There was likely a celebration at Mary's family home.[8]
The town would know they were engaged. Joseph was considered Mary's
betrothed, her husband (Mt 1:16). But before Joseph takes Mary home and
consummates the marriage, he hears she is pregnant. Matthew tells us, "Because Joseph her husband was faithful to the law, and yet did not want to
expose her to public disgrace, he had in mind to divorce her quietly" (Mt
1:19). What did Joseph mean by quietly divorcing her? You couldn't hide
it. Eventually, people would see the marriage was off, meaning he had divorced her. If they wondered the reason for the divorce, it would appear
obvious to all that Joseph had divorced Mary because she was pregnant by
someone else. She could tell the story of the angel and of still being a virgin,
but that story would be as believable then as it would be if you heard it from
your neighbor's daughter. (Mary's vindication likely didn't come until the
resurrection. She paid a dear price for being the Lord's handmaiden.)

So, what does Joseph hope to do by divorcing her *quietly*? The term "to
expose her to public disgrace" means more than it might to individualists,

---

[7]Raymond E. Brown, *The Birth of the Messiah: A Commentary on the Infancy Narratives in the Gospels
of Matthew and Luke* (New York: Doubleday, 1993), 123-24. It also goes without being said in other
biblical stories, most notably Mt 25:1-13; Jn 3:29; and possibly even rhetorically in Jn 14:1-3.

[8]Craig A. Evans, *Jesus and His World: The Archaeological Evidence* (Louisville, KY: Westminster John
Knox, 2012), 13. The evidence we have of Jewish betrothal customs at the time is somewhat scant
but suggests some form of meal or celebration was held at the bride's home around the time of
engagement. See Michael L. Satlow, *Jewish Marriage in Antiquity* (Princeton, NJ: Princeton University Press, 2001), 163-64.

where it is personal embarrassment. It is used for Jesus mocking the powers (Col 2:15) and for apostates mocking Jesus (Heb 6:6). It's a shaming term to make a public example of someone. Joseph decides to divorce Mary because he is "righteous" and will follow Jewish law on such matters. At the same time, he decides not to do it in a way that would make a public spectacle of Mary. In the first century, Jewish divorce could be conducted as long as there were two witnesses present, and as we have seen, Jewish men did not need to give a reason. Joseph could take two trusted friends to Mary's household and declared he divorced her without giving the reason why.[9] Surely questions would later be raised as the bump appeared, but Mary would not be exposed to public shaming.

Then the angel tells Joseph: "Joseph son of David, do not be afraid to take Mary home as your wife, because what is conceived in her is from the Holy Spirit. She will give birth to a son, and you are to give him the name Jesus, because he will save his people from their sins" (Mt 1:20-21). We should not assume, though, that the matter was swept under the rug or that some honorable solution was reached. Mary (and Joseph!) endured a lifetime of shaming comments. Even as an adult, Jesus was still hearing snide comments about his parentage. When Jesus talks about his father (meaning his heavenly Father), the leaders retort: "We are not illegitimate children" (Jn 8:41). Then (and still today) marriages, unwed pregnancies, and divorces could be public knowledge and people treated badly as a result. The Rome Daily News (the *Acta*) reported both official news and local gossip; marriages, divorces, and unwed pregnancies fell into both categories.[10]

What an amazing, but unexpected and difficult, beginning Jesus had. Regardless of one's parentage and the circumstances involved in one's parents' lives, it is never the child's fault. Yet, children are often shamed for it.[11] Jesus understands the challenges of many who are part of complex family situations.

---

[9]L. Cantwell, "The Parentage of Jesus: Mt 1:18-21," *Novum Testamentum* 24, no. 4 (1982): 305.

[10]For a recent discussion of the *Acta*, see Brian Wright, *Communal Reading in the Time of Jesus: A Window into Early Christian Reading Practices* (Minneapolis: Fortress, 2017).

[11]This would be a classic example of the *mis*use of shame, which we will discuss in chap. 12.

RUTH AND REDEFINING KINSHIP

Kinship plays an obvious role in many biblical stories. In fact, we could argue that the kinship story of Abraham, and the promises God gave him, is a featured narrative throughout the Bible. It is, after all, the story of God's family. What went without being said is how deep these kinship lines ran in the ancient world. They governed who you were, what your position in society was, and how you viewed and treated others.

The book of Ruth is not only the story of two individuals, a woman named Ruth and a man named Boaz. A key purpose of the book is to talk about collective identity, rather than being a sweet love story. When there is a famine in Judah, Elimelek takes his household—his wife, Naomi, and their two sons—to live in Moab. There, Elimelek dies. Naomi's sons marry women from the Moabites, named Orpah and Ruth. However, both Naomi's sons also die, so Naomi is left with no father of her household to care for her. This places Naomi in a precarious situation, which is greatly compounded since she is among the Moabites, with whom she has no kinship connections. Naomi thinks she is too old to marry into a new household and gain the protection of that "father," so when she hears the famine in Judah has ended, she decides to return to Bethlehem. She hopes that her kinship group will care for her; after all, she is from "us" in Bethlehem. Perhaps Naomi also thought that even if they didn't, she could rely on provisions in the law that reflected God's concern for those without a household: "When you are harvesting in your field and you overlook a sheaf, do not go back to get it. Leave it for the foreigner, the fatherless and the widow" (Deut 24:19; see Deut 10:18).[12]

Orpah and Ruth, on the other hand, are young enough to remarry. Neither widow could be taken in by her late husband's brother through levirate marriage (explained earlier; Deut 25:5-6), because both Naomi's sons have died. No brothers-in-law remain, so Naomi declares that her family has no way to provide for Orpah and Ruth and no legal claim on

---

[12]We shouldn't just imagine young children when the Bible speaks of the fatherless; Naomi and Ruth are fatherless.

them.[13] She tells them to go back to their mother's household. There they could hopefully remarry into households and find protection from new fathers. Naomi reasons this makes a much more secure future for them than going with her and having to rely on Naomi's (looser) kinship connection with more distant clansmen. It is a reasonable conclusion, since neither Orpah nor Ruth has any blood connections of their own with the clan.

To make matters worse, there were reasons Israelites might not feel obliged to care for Moabite women.[14] When the Israelites came out of Egypt and were going through Moabite land, the Moabites refused to give them bread and water. For this reason, Moabites were barred from entering the assembly of the Lord (Deut 23:3-4). Worse still, they had hired Balaam to curse Israel (Num 22:1-8). Furthermore, while Israel was staying in Shittim, some of the Hebrew men began to indulge in sexual immorality with Moabite women, who led them to sacrifice to their gods (Num 25:1-5). Moabites were seen as bad guys in Hebrew history. They harmed *us*. They led *our* fathers astray.

For us, "That's ancient history!" but not for collectivists. Remember the spray-painted slogans in Beirut, which remind their community today of the grave injustices inflicted on their great-grandfathers—"us"—during World War I by "them." We saw that Israelites remembered the story of the exodus and used it to remind themselves who *we* are. These stories of Moabite wrongdoing molded later Hebrew generations' sense of collective identity. Naturally, these stories shaped how *we* Israelites viewed *they* Moabites in Ruth's day.

Given this kinship backdrop, the narrator of Ruth keeps underscoring that Ruth is a Moabite woman (Ruth 1:22; 2:2, 6, 21; 4:5, 10). It is a powerful story in which the narrator is working to reshape the basis for Israelite kinship.[15] While Orpah heeds Naomi's advice and returns to her former

---

[13]Tikva Frymer-Kensky, *Reading the Women of the Bible: A New Interpretation of Their Stories* (New York: Schocken Books, 2002), 248.

[14]Agnethe Siquans, "Foreignness and Poverty in the Book of Ruth: A Legal Way for a Poor Foreign Woman to Be Integrated into Israel," *Journal of Biblical Literature* 128, no. 3 (2009): 447.

[15]Siquans, "Foreignness and Poverty," 447; Peter H. W. Lau, *Identity and Ethics in the Book of Ruth: A Social Identity Approach* (Berlin: de Gruyter, 2011), 117.

household, Ruth refuses. She says, "Where you go I will go, and where you stay I will stay. Your people will be my people and your God my God" (Ruth 1:16). Ruth commits to remain with Naomi and her people despite having no obligation to do so and no household as a safety net. She also commits to take on Naomi's God, the God of the Israelites, as her own. Ruth becomes a prototype of God reorganizing kinship lines.

Next, the narrator introduces Boaz. We are told he is a wealthy landowner in Bethlehem, with a connection of sorts to Naomi—he is in the same clan as her late husband, Elimelek. We are no doubt supposed to immediately compare his status to Naomi's, see the relationship, and so begin to wonder whether Boaz will be faithful and just and will choose to help them.

Boaz hears about Ruth's faithful commitment to her mother-in-law since the death of her husband, and how she chose to leave her father's household to live among the Israelites. This story doesn't fit the usual stereotype of Moabites. Boaz thinks she deserves reciprocal faithfulness and expresses the hope the Lord will repay her too, "under whose wings" Boaz says she has taken refuge (Ruth 2:12). As chicks are safe under their mother's wings, so God's wings are a common metaphor for the protection God provides (e.g., Ps 17:8; 91:4). That evening Ruth tells Naomi she gleaned in the field of a man called Boaz. Naomi blesses him for showing kindness to the living and the dead (including the living Naomi and the dead Elimelek). The word for kindness here is *khesed*, which is hard to translate. *Khesed* is often used to speak of someone showing commitment to a partner that goes above and beyond what they are contractually obligated to show.[16] Naomi explains, "That man is our close relative; he is one of our guardian-redeemers" (Ruth 2:20).

Guardian-redeemer is not a kinship term we banter about today. The law stipulates that if poverty forces someone to sell their land, other males among their kinsfolk are required to buy it back (Lev 25:25-34) to keep

---

[16]Daniel J. Elazar, "Covenant as the Basis of the Jewish Political Tradition," in *Kinship and Consent: The Jewish Political Tradition and Its Contemporary Uses*, ed. Daniel J. Elazar (London: University Press of America, 1983), 46.

the land in the family. If one's debt was too deep, one would sell oneself into slavery to foreigners, and a male blood relative from one's clan could also buy one back (Lev 25:35-55). This process was called *redemption*. The male relative would *redeem* the person, bringing them back into the care of their kinfolk. There is currently a scholarly debate over whether the law obligated Boaz to act as Naomi and Ruth's guardian-redeemer. Whether or not Boaz was obligated, it is clear it was not expected. Naomi, certainly hopes Boaz might redeem them. Boaz announces he will buy the land and acquire Ruth the Moabite as his own wife. He retains the property and ensures the name of his dead kinsman lives on.

The narrator wants us to see links between Boaz/Ruth and God/Abraham. Boaz provides *khesed*, going above and beyond what he could be forced to do by duty, thereby showing great faithfulness to his kin and to a Moabite woman. Like Abraham, Ruth leaves her land and her father's household. Like Abraham, she follows the Lord. She is a model of faithful commitment to Elimelek's clan and to God. She is praised for showing *khesed* (Ruth 1:8). God shows faithfulness to Ruth, like he did to Abraham. He provides her with a son, through Boaz. This is a story of kinship, redemption, and faithful loyalty (*khesed*). Yet, we need to notice that it is also a story that redefines kinship. Naomi, Ruth, and Boaz all act in ways that twist their stories together and defy traditional blood identities. There is Hebrew versus Moabite history between them, but when they recall this history (and they often do in the story), God uses it to join them together rather than separate them. God's actions toward them overwrite old ethnic histories (think Ephesians). The story focuses on the faithfulness of foreigners, and the faithfulness of God, as expressed in kinship faithfulness. Kinship is still the key, but it is not kinship based in bloodlines but rather in faithfulness to God.

3

PATRONAGE
Gifts Had Strings Attached

"And how is work?" An Arab businessman, to whom I had recently taught some public speaking classes, called me on my phone. I wondered why he was calling, as we'd finished the classes a few weeks ago. We exchanged pleasantries, and yet the conversation seemed to keep going around. I wasn't sure what else to say. Did he want more lessons? Did he want his money back? I thought our relationship had been warming up. I couldn't figure out what he wanted, so after a while I just asked, "So, how can I help you?" He replied in a surprised tone of voice, "Oh, no, no, I just wanted to say hello and check you're doing okay." The conversation ended, a bit awkwardly, I felt.

We exchanged a few texts back and forth, and then perhaps a week or so later, he called to invite me for coffee. It went well. I still wasn't sure whether he wanted something, but I was glad we were becoming friends. Then, a week or so later, he called and asked for some help with something. It was a little thing, and I certainly didn't mind doing it. After I had lived in the Mediterranean a bit longer, I noticed that some other new relationships followed this pattern too. A former business client or trainee would call me or send me an email. They'd thank me for the help I had provided, say they appreciated my teaching skills, and tell me they thought of me often. Obviously, I thanked them—and stored the email for my future performance review at work.

I was sharing coffee with a close Arab friend when I received one of these calls. "What's going on?" I asked my friend, after the call. He said, "They are testing whether you want to be their friend." My first thought was, *Who is so insecure that they test newly acquired friends?* "Why not just ask?" I blurted. He stared across the table at me for a long minute. Clearly I did not understand what friendship means, he concluded. "Friendship is not about being friendly. We are friendly to everyone. Friendship is about being reliable. Friends can count on one another when they need help." These phone calls and texts were people's efforts to begin to build a friendship with me. People showed they appreciated and cared for me. They also tested whether I felt the same way toward them. Friendship was more than camaraderie or socialization. Collectives expect a friend to be someone they can rely on, and they wanted to see whether I viewed it the same way.

In my individualist world, I also have friends like that. Interestingly, we have to add an extra word to talk about them. We call them "good friends" or "close friends" or "old friends." In other words, in my world, *friend* refers to a broader group of acquaintances. Middle Easterners have just as many (probably more) acquaintances than me, but they don't consider them all to be friends. So, friendship in the Middle East generally carries a sense of far higher expectations than simply being on good terms with someone, or enjoying their company. Building a friendship takes a lot of time and investment and comes with many expectations.

In the ancient world too, people had high expectations of friends. While friends might be a concentric circle out from kinship, friendship still involved many ties. As with kin, ancient Mediterranean people expected to turn to their friends for all kinds of help. They also expected their friends would have high expectations of them. Society generally worked this way. When teaching about prayer, Jesus uses a parable about friendship: "Suppose you have a friend, and you go to him at midnight and say, 'Friend, lend me three loaves of bread; a friend of mine on a journey has come to me, and I have no food to offer him'" (Lk 11:5-6). For Jesus' listeners, asking a neighbor for help, even late at night, wasn't the surprising part of the parable. It is a glimpse into the everyday collective-group-depends-on-one-another way of life in Jesus' collective world. What do you do when you need bread? Of course, you ask neighbors whether they have some. What is surprising about Jesus' parable is the friend's response. It shocks (as Jesus' parables often do) because the neighbor turns down his friend in need.

Ancient Mediterranean people didn't view themselves as individuals who would get through life on their own. They were part of collective groups. As such, they thought in terms of the collective group getting through life together. When we understand this, we can better understand how communities in the biblical world worked. Communities got through life by everyone being mutually dependent on one another. Family, friends, neighbors, and even trade associates understood themselves to be part of collective groups who were to mutually support one another. Someone in need would turn to a friend for help. Later, they would reciprocate by helping their friend when he fell into some kind of need. Often they would be helping mutual friends simultaneously with different kinds of help.

This way of living in reciprocal dependency is preserved in texts, letters, and proverbs from the ancient world. Greek poet Hesiod wrote around 700 BC:

> Have the grain measured out properly when you borrow from a neighbor, and pay it back properly, in the same measure or even better, if you can. This way, when you are in need, you can find something to rely on.... Seek the company of those who seek yours. Give to the one who would give to you, and do not give to the one who would not. One gives to the giver, and gives not to the one who gives not.[1]

Reciprocal dependency runs through this text. People are to give to others and expect others to give to them. Jewish scribe Sirach, about two

---

[1]Hesiod, *Works and Days* 349-355, trans. Gregory Nagy, Center for Hellenic Studies, Harvard University, https://chs.harvard.edu/CHS/article/display/5290 (accessed November 28, 2018). We are grateful to John Barclay for pointing us to this quotation.

hundred years before Christ, wrote, "If you do good, know to whom you do it, and you will be thanked for your good deeds. Do good to the devout, and you will be repaid—if not by them, certainly by the Most High" (Sir 12:1-2 NRSV).[2] Sirach assumes reciprocity. He assumes people will reciprocate to the giver. Even if they don't, then obviously God will reciprocate. The Dicta Catonis, a collection of everyday folk sayings compiled in the third Christian century, says, "Be good to good people, lest you suffer loss," and, "Be grateful for services rendered, and so make yourself appreciated; you do not want to get a reputation for being a bottomless pit." These examples from people at different times and in different places show that these attitudes toward mutual dependency were pervasive in the Mediterranean world.[3]

It is likely that over half of the urban population of the first century Mediterranean world was "poor." Some of these people lived just around the minimum subsistence level and perhaps 10 to 20 percent of people lived desperately below the minimum subsistence level.[4] We can imagine neighbors, friends, and family members mutually supporting one another by exchanging food, goods, and services to ensure their collective community survived. That is, collective groups survived by all the members depending on one another. "We support we." When someone gives bread to their neighbor, their neighbor prospers (or survives). Later, when the giver falls into need, the neighbor is able to care for them. Mutual support was fundamental to the way collective groups worked. This is the picture of Acts 4 ("there was no needy person among them"), which was the church fulfilling the vision of generosity in Deut 15 ("there will be no poor among you").

---

[2] See John Barclay, unpublished handout, The Firth Post Graduate Seminar 2018, Department of Theology and Religious Studies, University of Nottingham, UK.

[3] John M. G. Barclay, *Paul and the Gift* (Grand Rapids, MI: Eerdmans, 2015), 25n59.

[4] These are based on scholars' best broad estimates. The overarching thing to note is that it was the norm for people in first-century society to struggle to make basic ends meet. For a recent overview of the discussion, see Timothy A. Brookins, "Economic Profiling of Early Christian Communities," in *Paul and Economics: A Handbook*, ed. Thomas R. Blanton IV and Raymond Pickett (Minneapolis: Fortress, 2017), 57-88.

We misunderstand this dynamic when we think it is about one person caring for another: "I" give to "you" and "you" give to "me." This understanding comes from and leads us back to an individualist way of thinking about identity. Collectives think of reciprocal dependency more in terms of "we give to we." We are a group, and the support flows constantly between people who are *we*. This reciprocal giving reinforces and solidifies the sense of *we*. It was the glue of the ancient collective world. That's why, while collectives may be very generous and hold high expectations for members of their group, they are less likely to give to those outside their group. If collective groups with very limited resources give to outsiders, they may struggle to survive themselves. It makes some sense to only give to those who will reciprocate and not throw your resources away on just anyone in need.

The Gospels reveal that people in the world around Jesus thought in this way also. Jesus says, "And if you do good to those who are good to you, what credit is that to you? Even sinners do that" (Lk 6:33). Jesus is saying that doing good to those who do it to you is totally *normal*. He is saying everybody lives like that, even sinners. We could summarize this sentiment in the ancient way of thinking as, reciprocity is everything, so do good to others so they will reciprocate when you are in need. If they don't help you, don't help them back.

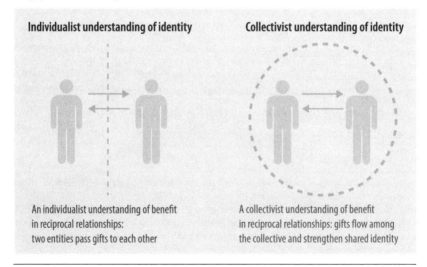

Individualist understanding of identity   **Collectivist understanding of identity**

An individualist understanding of benefit   A collectivist understanding of benefit
in reciprocal relationships: in reciprocal relationships: gifts flow among
two entities pass gifts to each other   the collective and strengthen shared identity

Figure 3.1. Visualizing understandings of benefit in reciprocal relationships

LOPSIDED FRIENDSHIPS

So far, we have focused on reciprocity between people who could reciprocate in like ways. Each party might not provide exactly the same benefits, but generally they would be benefits of similar worth. We might call this kind of reciprocity *symmetrical*, when people of similar social status and with similar means and needs helped one another in similar ways. Poor people cared for one another in their collective group of similarly poor neighbors. Wealthy people invited one another to dinners and expected reciprocation, to be invited to special events in a similar way (Lk 14:12).[5] But it wasn't always like this. Sometimes relationships existed between people who had different means and were not socially equal.

Implicit in this arrangement is an important truth: inequality among people permeated the Greco-Roman world.[6] It is part of the modern Western world also, but we like to pretend it isn't. That's because as individualists (at least theoretically) we value treating everyone equally and ensuring everyone has equal opportunities in life. In America, our founding documents assert, "We hold this truth to be self-evident, that all men are created equal." It goes without being said (it is self-evident) that equality is something to aim for, to uphold, to honor. While this may feel self-evident to us individualists, it is actually just a cultural value.

In the ancient Mediterranean world, treating people equally was not a cultural value. They believed that people should be treated differently. It was self-evident to them that the collective groups to which they belonged determined their opportunities and the way they should be treated. Many collective cultures see it this way today.

Now, one collective community, like members of a kinship group, could include a number of people who had different status, power, and finances.

---

[5]Jesus is challenging a practice around him wherein wealthier people were inviting one another but not those who were poorer than them. Jesus was critiquing reciprocity that was happening only between equals. See the discussion of the use of symmetrical and asymmetrical terms to conceptualize forms of reciprocity in Zeba A. Crook, "Reciprocity: Covenantal Exchange as a Test Case," in *Ancient Israel: The Old Testament in Its Social Context*, ed. Philip F. Esler (Minneapolis: Fortress, 2006), 81.
[6]See Steven J. Friesen, Sarah A. James, and Daniel N. Schowalter, "Inequality in Corinth," in *Corinth in Contrast: Studies in Inequality*, ed. Steven J. Friesen, Sarah A. James, and Daniel N. Schowalter (Leiden, Netherlands: Brill, 2014), 2.

They were reciprocally bound to care for one another, and yet they had different means and were not socially equal. If reciprocal generosity was the glue of ancient communities, the question arises, How did mutually dependent reciprocal friendships work when the people in the relationship had very different means and social statuses? The answer is patronage.

Scholars use the term *patronage* or *patron-client relationships* to talk about reciprocal relationships between unequal parties. They term the greater party in the relationship the patron and the weaker party the client. Patron-client relationships are just that, relationships. They are joined by the glue of reciprocity, just like all other relationships. But the relationship is socially or economically lopsided.[7] We might call this *asymmetrical* reciprocity.

Perhaps an illustration will clarify. Let's suppose there is a wealthy man in Philippi named Diocles. His family made its fortune a few generations earlier in the gold mines near the city. He owns a number of estates in Macedonia. A few insulae (city blocks) away, a man named Belen owns a family bakery. His father and his grandfather before him baked barley loaves and sacrificial cakes to sell. Bakers worshiped Fornax, the goddess of ovens. One day, Belen must have angered the goddess—or so he reasons—because his bakery catches fire and is destroyed. Although there are a few banks in Philippi, no bank will loan monies to a cursed baker. And how would he repay the loan anyway? Like many in the ancient world, he barely provides for his family as it is. His only hope is a relationship.

So Belen goes to visit Diocles. That morning, as every morning, Diocles's "friends" line up at their patron's door. Each meets to see whether Diocles needs anything done that day, to make any requests for help, and to receive any benefits he wishes to give. These "friends" all have an established relationship with Diocles as their patron. Belen joins the end of the line. He explains his problem and asks for help rebuilding his bakery. Diocles is not required, either socially or morally, to help Belen. But he is able and decides to help. Patronage (benefaction) is a virtue stressed for the wealthy. So Diocles gives the baker the resources to rebuild the bakery. He might provide funds. He might ask another of his "friends" who is a builder

---

[7]Julian Pitt-Rivers, *The People of the Sierra* (London: Weidenfield and Nicholson, 1954), 140.

to assist Belen, and another "friend" to provide new wood and thatch. Likely, Diocles will offer a mix of help drawn from his social network.

Belen obviously did not earn this gift and will not be able to pay it back. But he will be expected to reciprocate. Diocles has invested in Belen's life, and so Belen will want to invest in Diocles's life. He will do this by showing gratitude to Diocles. Belen's gratitude is more than words. Belen will be loyal to Diocles. From now on, he bakes bread for Diocles's family and all the people who work in Diocles's extended circle.[8] He does it because he wants to participate in Diocles's life. He is grateful. Likewise, Diocles will ensure that Belen receives a fair price for his bread and all the customers Belen can handle. From now on Belen will show up every morning at Diocles's house with all Diocles's other "friends" to ask whether Diocles needs anything and to ask for help.

The community would have seen the fire and know Belen's plight. They all know Diocles helped the baker, and many will give Diocles honor for it. Belen in particular will boast of Diocles's goodness to all who will listen. Likely his customers will hear all about how grateful he is to Diocles. This is not just transactional. They are in relationship.

While patron-client relationships were reciprocal, they were not always close and affectionate. See how a satirist from the first century, Juvenal, paints this morning scene of people coming to their patron's house: "Look now at the meagre dole set down upon the threshold for a toga-clad mob to scramble for! Yet the patron first peers into your face, fearing that you may be claiming under someone else's name: once recognized, you will get your share."[9]

The relationship is asymmetrical; it is a patron-client relationship. When my friend at the start of the chapter said people were calling me to see whether I wanted to be their friend, he didn't necessarily mean we would have an equal-status friendship. Some may have been trying to place me into their patronage networks, or try to become part of mine.

---

[8] In ch. 2, we noted that some of these clients who did business with Diocles would be spoken of as being part of his household.

[9] Juvenal, *Satires* 1.95-107, in *Juvenal and Persius*, trans. G. G. Ramsay, Loeb Classical Library (Cambridge, MA: Harvard University Press, 1940). I am grateful to Samuel Dill for pointing out this citation in *Roman Society from Nero to Marcus Aurelius* (London: Macmillan, 1919), 72.

Patrons and clients. While we use the terms *patron* and *client* to describe the different statuses of Diocles and Belen in their relationship,
these are scholarly terms to describe the dynamics of this reciprocal relationship.[10] Ancients sometimes used these terms, but most often they
used the language of friendship.[11] Oftentimes they simply did not need to
point out the relational expectations at all; ancients understood what went
without being said.[12] When Pliny wrote to someone he was giving help to
and said, "The length of our friendship pledges you not to forget this gift,"
the recipient knew what he meant. He didn't need to be told this was patronage. He lived in a world glued together by reciprocity, gratitude, and
services. We, however, don't live in this collective system, and so scholars
develop etic terms such as *patron-client relationships* to help us see it from
the outside looking in.[13]

---

[10]Social historians use the term *patron-client relationship* in a general way to refer to relationships
that are reciprocal, asymmetrical, and based in personal loyalty. This shorthand is used to refer to
a range of relationships in a range of cultural contexts that embody these characteristics. These
relationships often work differently in different cultures. This terminology, however, can lead to
confusion when we discuss the first-century Roman world. Romans used the Latin terms *patronus*
and *cliens* to refer to one very specific form of asymmetrical relationship in Roman society called
patrocinium. See Jonathan Marshall, *Jesus, Patrons and Benefactors: Roman Palestine and the Gospel
of Luke,* WUNT 259 (Tübingen: Mohr Siebeck, 2009), 6. When we speak about patrons and clients and patronage in the Greco-Roman world, we are using it in the more general sociohistorical
way as a shorthand to speak of all kinds of asymmetrical, reciprocal relationships, as we explain in
the chapter. We are not limiting our discussion just to the system of *patrocinium.* In order to avoid
confusion, we thought about using *benefactor-beneficiary,* but again, in English this language seems
to convey too much emphasis on finance, leading to another form of confusion where we think of
it in mainly financial terms. Talking about patronage is hard. Modern English terms don't fit well.
[11]Carolyn Osiek and David L. Balch, *Families in the New Testament World: Households and House
Churches* (Louisville, KY: Westminster John Knox, 1997), 49-50.
[12]Most of the texts we have that talk about patronage networks are written by members of the elite
in the ancient Mediterranean world. This is the case for most texts on most subjects. It seems likely
that the rest of the population also used such networks. The New Testament writings are an example of texts written by nonelites, and we see the language of patronage and networks of relationships and personal recommendations in Paul's letters. See Osiek and Balch, *Families in the New
Testament World,* 53.
[13]An *etic* word is used by outsiders trying to describe another culture, while *emic* words come from
inside a culture. Often an etic word is a singular, rather artificial, conceptual term. Etic words are
helpful, but they do obscure, by suggesting that a complex idea, or even a whole range of complex
aspects, is really this simple one-word thing. Etic words are great to get started, but quickly one
discovers they obscure as much as they clarify. While we do not see terms such as patron-client
relationship in the biblical texts, we see the dynamics at work. The Bible doesn't name this dynamic
because it went without being said.

Luke portrays Jesus as a patron.[14] He does good and benefits those in need of help in a number of ways, very generously. When recounting the story of the Last Supper, Luke tells us,

> After taking the cup, he gave thanks and said, "Take this and divide it among you. For I tell you I will not drink again from the fruit of the vine until the kingdom of God comes."
>
> And he took bread, gave thanks and broke it, and gave it to them, saying, "This is my body given for you; do this in remembrance of me."
>
> In the same way, after the supper he took the cup, saying, "This cup is the new covenant in my blood, which is poured out for you. But the hand of him who is going to betray me is with mine on the table. The Son of Man will go as it has been decreed. But woe to that man who betrays him!" They began to question among themselves which of them it might be who would do this. (Lk 22:17-23)

Among many things, Jesus is portrayed as a wonderfully generous patron in this passage. Jesus will choose to give his very life, his body and blood, for his disciples. Yet at that very table eating with Jesus was one who will not show gratitude or loyalty. He will in fact betray Jesus. We can sense how the themes of benefits, reciprocity, and gratitude behind this caused the disciples to begin to question who might do such a thing. Luke doesn't need to say this explicitly. We feel it. Collectives would have felt it even more strongly. The dynamics of patronage and gratitude were woven into the foundational values of collective society.

Gifts have strings attached (and that's good). Ancient Roman philosopher Seneca discusses benefaction in one of the great writings of antiquity, which one modern scholar describes as "a brilliant example of a philosopher at work on the actual mechanisms of society."[15] In other words, Seneca is philosophizing about a value that usually went without being said. Seneca explains it by allegorizing the common image of the three graces as three young maidens dancing:

---

[14]Marshall, *Jesus, Patrons and Benefactors*, 331-32.

[15]Troels Engberg-Pedersen, "Gift-Giving and Friendship: Seneca and Paul in Romans 1–8 on the Logic of God's χαρις and Its Human Response," *Harvard Theological Review* 101 (2008): 18.

Why the Graces are three in number and why they are sisters, why they have their hands interlocked ... and [why they] are clad in loose and transparent garb. Some would have it appear that there is one for bestowing a benefit, another for receiving it, and a third for returning it. ... Why do the sisters hand in hand dance in a ring which returns upon itself? For the reason that a benefit passing in its course from hand to hand returns nevertheless to the giver ... and it is fitting that there should be nothing to bind or restrict them, and so the maidens wear flowing robes, and these, too, are transparent because benefits desire to be seen.[16]

Seneca points out that the eldest sister starts the process. Patronage starts with one side giving a gift or benefit, but there must be reciprocity for it to work. It is a circle, a relationship. We describe the way gifts worked here in a way that we individualists normally use negatively: gifts have *strings attached*. Ancients would agree but mean it in a positive way: they hold hands. Either way, the gifts bound the more powerful patron and the weaker client together. Clients were always weaker. For example, Jesus tells a parable about a servant who is a client of his master (Lk 16:1-13). When the servant hears he will be dismissed, he is in a weaker place and so shrewdly acts to create ties of obligation with others. This will mean he has reciprocal relationships to fall back on when he is dismissed by his current patron. We can be quick to judge the servant, and possibly rightly so, but in his world, he was largely disempowered. Jesus does not call him righteous, but he does point out he is shrewd at giving gifts with strings attached (at his former master's expense).

Patrons give various kinds of gifts. Seneca writes to potential patrons, "Help one person with money, another with credit, another with influence, another with advice, another with sound precepts" (*On Benefits* 1.2.4).[17] Gifts could be material support such as money, land, or materials. They could be other kinds of support such as protection and connections. Patronage often flourishes in cultures with higher levels of inequality and

---

[16]Seneca, *On Benefits* 1.3, in *Moral Essays*, vol. 3, *De Beneficiis*, trans. John W. Basore, Loeb Classical Library (Cambridge, MA: Harvard University Press, 1934), 13-15.

[17]See discussion in David A. deSilva, *Honor, Patronage, Kinship and Purity: Unlocking New Testament Culture* (Downers Grove, IL: IVP Academic, 2000), 97.

lower levels of governance, where power and resources become concentrated around those who are elites, such as royalty, politicians, civil servants, landowners, and businesspeople. They often control access to resources and function as doorways to them.

I have Arab friends with good qualifications who cannot find a job. Their problem is they don't know people who can provide them access to these jobs. It is easy for modern Westerners to sit in judgment, allowing our assumption that everyone should have equal access to determine our evaluation of how things should work in a culture that is very different. In reality, sometimes our belief that our culture is based in equal opportunities is not always accurate. While we may like to feel we are above connections and middlemen, resources and opportunities in our own culture sometimes depend on whom you know.[18]

So before we judge patrons, we might ask a different question. Why do these busy elite leaders take the time to do this at all? Why not simply get on with their lives and forget those around them? Because they are not individualists. They live in collective cultures, which expect people to care for their community. Being a gracious and generous patron is a sign of dignity and respect. Seneca encourages fellow elite patrons to "give for the sake of giving" (*On Benefits* 1.2).

As in antiquity, many modern collective cultures view giving gifts and services as a virtue. Society thought that a "good person" (*agathos*) was the kind of person who used their wealth and skills to give to those who depended on them for success and protection. Those who had wealth and connections had more opportunities to act in this way. They would be esteemed and called good by society. Paul says, "Very rarely will anyone die for a righteous person, though for a good person someone might possibly dare to die" (Rom 5:7). By "good person" Paul probably has a sort of wealthy patron in mind.[19] Someone might dare to die for such a good

---

[18]For example, in Will Smith's movie *The Pursuit of Happyness*, the overt message is that Chris Gardner succeeds because he works hard. In the movie, though, an executive (a patron) notices Chris working hard and helps him; otherwise, he would not have succeeded.

[19]Andrew D. Clarke, *Secular and Christian Leadership in Corinth: A Socio-historical & Exegetical Study of 1 Corinthians 1–6* (Leiden, Netherlands: Brill, 1993), 23.

person because society considered them important and esteemed them (seemingly more than a righteous person).

Today, Middle Eastern society expects wealthy people to use their wealth to benefit others in society and praises them for it. Many elite leaders in the Middle East recognize this expectation. Some regularly hold something called a *diwan*, usually held in a big reception room. Let's say you are a baker today in Damascus. Your shop didn't have a fire, but you need medical care for an accident that happened at work, and you can't afford it. You belong to Bassam's community. Bassam is a wealthy, powerful man in your area of town and not coincidentally a member of your (very) extended clan and religious sect. Bassam holds his *diwan* on Fridays. Anyone who is a member of his community can go to the *diwan* and stand in line. Hosts might serve coffee while you wait and distribute numbered tickets so you knew your place in line. When Bassam, the patron, arrives, he moves down the line and hears everyone's requests. An aide may stand nearby and take notes. If Bassam can (and is so inclined), he will help. Doesn't this sound a lot like Belen waiting for Diocles? One friend of mine complains that because her father was a local patron, their home was always full of people waiting to speak to her dad.

While this may all sound very altruistic, we should recognize the power dynamic in patron-client relationships. While either a patron or a client can initiate the relationship, it remains lopsided (asymmetrical). Clients are dependent on a patron's good will. Sometimes patrons help; other times they do not. In today's fallen world, I have heard stories where clients had to jump through a number of hoops before they win the favor of a potential patron. Patrons use these unspoken hoops as a way of testing clients and finding those they feel will indeed benefit them. Seneca says, "Give for the sake of giving." That he wrote it suggests that some patrons did not.

Clients give gratitude. Clients reciprocated to their patron, not with like gifts, because they could not do so, but with gifts of a different kind, including gratitude. By gratitude, ancients didn't just mean a warm, fuzzy feeling inside. They meant expressions of gratitude, things such as honoring the patron, obeying them, and giving them loyalty. A generation before Jesus, a client named Plancus wrote to Cicero,

> I cannot refrain from thanking you in view of the course of events and of your services. But, by heaven! I blush to do it. For an intimacy as close as that which you have wished me to have with you seems not to require any formal thanks, nor do I willingly pay the poor recompense of words in return for your supreme kindness, and I would rather, when we meet, prove my gratitude by my respect, my obedience to your wishes, and my constant attentions. But if to live on is my fate, in this same respect, obedience to your wishes, and constant attentions, I will surpass all your beloved friends and even your devoted relatives.[20]

Given the importance ancients placed on recipients having gratitude for gifts and services, it follows therefore that the greatest wrong clients could commit was to be ungrateful to their patrons. In a list of the worst kinds of people, Seneca notes, "homicides, tyrants, thieves, adulterers, robbers, sacrilegious men, and traitors there always will be; but worse than all these is the crime of ingratitude" (*On Benefits* 1.10.4). Again, just a generation before Jesus, Virgil writes that the worst section of hell (Tartarus) is reserved for the Titans who rebelled against the gods and for the particularly despicable, such as brothers who disown another or expel their parents, clients who defraud their patrons, and those who won't give to their kinsmen or a friend in need (*Aeneid* 6.609). In a letter from the Christian period, a patron complains to his clients that they are being ungrateful: "You have received many favors . . . from us, and I am exceedingly amazed that you remember none of them but speak badly of us. That is characteristic of a person with an ungrateful disposition. . . . For the ungrateful . . . forget noble men . . . and in addition ill treat their [patrons] . . . as though they were enemies."[21] There is evidence that some patrons threatened to withdraw their patronage if they considered their clients to be ungrateful.[22]

---

[20]Cicero, Letters to Friends 10.24, ed. and trans. D. R. Shackleton Bailey, Loeb Classical Library (Cambridge, MA: Harvard University Press, 2001).

[21]Pseudo-Libanius, *Epistolary Styles*, 64. See James R. Harrison, *Paul's Language of Grace in Its Greco-Roman Context*, WUNT 172 (Tübingen: Mohr Siebeck, 2013), 71.

[22]Harrison, *Paul's Language of Grace in Its Greco-Roman Context*, 72.

Quintus Cicero advised his older brother Marcus on how to campaign for a political office. He reminds Marcus of people he in some way helped or had a connection with and says: "See that you hold on by admonitions, requests, or any other means of making it clear that there will never be another chance for those who owe you a debt to thank you [*gratiae*], or for the well-disposed to put you under an obligation to themselves" (*Handbook of Electioneering* 4).[23]

Ironically, a parallel example recently surfaced in Uganda. According to the CNN news report:

> A disgruntled politician who suffered a defeat in Uganda's parliamentary elections has reacted by removing boreholes [well pumps] he commissioned while in office. . . . Patrick Okumu-Ringa was reported to have dismantled around 10 boreholes earlier in the week and told locals to find another source of water. The politician told Uganda's New Vision he believed locals abused "his generosity" and refused to support his bid for a re-election. "Our people are not appreciative. All I wanted from them was votes. I have educated so many children, but all they tell me is I have done nothing," Okumu-Ringa was reported as saying in the newspaper.[24]

The CNN reporter is amazed and aghast (and a bit judgmental) about what the politician did. It is reported as if incredible, but in a collectivist world, it makes sense. "How should this injustice be rectified?" we might ask. First, people might not view it as an injustice. The people chose to elect a different patron. Second, while we might expect the ousted politician to put the boreholes back, likely the newly elected politician will replace them and thereby establish his own relationship with the people. His gift will have strings attached; it will bind them together. He will expect their loyalty (votes), and they will expect his benefaction (water wells).

---

[23]Cicero, *Letters to Quintus and Brutus, Letter Fragments, Letter to Octavian, Invectives, Handbook of Electioneering*, ed. and trans. D. R. Shackleton Bailey, Loeb Classical Library 462 (Cambridge, MA: Harvard University Press, 2002), 407. Scholars debate whether Quintus Cicero actually wrote this document. What concerns us here is not specifically who wrote the text but the advice the text carries and how this sheds light on reciprocity and obligation.

[24]Segun Akande, "Ugandan Lawmaker Dismantles Community Boreholes After Losing Election," CNN, August 10, 2018, www.cnn.com/2018/08/10/africa/uganda-lawmaker-removes-borehole/index.html.

It will be clear by now that gratitude, obligation, and loyalty under-girded the system of patronage. There were no contracts or legal documents, and the relationship was not enforceable by law. Asymmetrical, mutual giving usually didn't work in a tit-for-tat, turn-taking way. It was frowned on (and very difficult in any case) to keep some kind of account of who did what. Without contracts, both patrons and clients recognized there was a social obligation to continue the relationship. They shared in mutual benefits together and so were obliged to continue the exchange.[25] They trusted the other party would give when they were in need. Gifts and gratitude was the air they breathed, the grease of society.

Both the ancient example from Rome and the modern one from Uganda contain language of patronage. Cicero speaks of friends as a way of talking about people under *obligation* who feel a duty to show *gratitude*. They are then expected to reciprocate by voting for Marcus Cicero. Likewise, the Ugandan speaks about how his people failed to appreciate his generosity when all he asked for were votes (reciprocation). This is precisely what Quintus Cicero advises: utilize this sense of obligation and gratitude to get elected. While ancients sometimes used terms for patrons and clients, they more often spoke about gifts, obligation, gratitude, and friendship. Everybody knew the ways these things tied people together: it went without being said.

Western ideas about gift giving can lead us off course. In Western culture, we regularly give gifts to our friends. We give birthday gifts, graduation gifts, gifts at weddings and baby showers. We also give bigger gifts, such as money or even a car at times. But we like to think that these gifts are given with no strings attached. In fact, the notion that the ideal gift is the one given with no strings attached permeates our Western approach to giving. We can think that if a gift carries strings, it is somehow tainted. Jesus himself seems to argue this: "But when you give to the needy, do not let your left hand know what your right hand is doing, so that your giving may be in secret. Then your Father, who sees what is done in secret, will

---

[25]That we have ancient letters in which patrons and/or clients complain about the other not reciprocating shows that the process didn't always work like the ideal.

reward you" (Mt 6:3-4). We need to be careful not to misread Jesus. Jesus is arguing for the heart (motives) of the giver. In the passage, Jesus takes the three acts of piety (giving, praying, and fasting) and argues that it matters *why* it is done. The heart is the key. So in giving, Jesus wants people to give from generosity to please God, who will then reciprocate ("your Father . . . will reward you"). Another teaching of Jesus is sometimes used to reject reciprocity:

> Then Jesus said to his host, "When you give a luncheon or dinner, do not invite your friends, your brothers or sisters, your relatives, or your rich neighbors; if you do, they may invite you back and so you will be repaid. But when you give a banquet, invite the poor, the crippled, the lame, the blind, and you will be blessed. Although they cannot repay you, you will be repaid at the resurrection of the righteous." (Lk 14:12-14)

It should be noted that Jesus rejects the shallow motive of inviting only those who can invite you back to a similar dinner. Rather, we are to invite the disempowered. By doing this, we have given a gift to God, who will reciprocate to us. Granted, Jesus' teachings here are radical as they are elsewhere, but Jesus' teachings about guarding our motives are not a wholesale rejection of reciprocity. He just wants to make sure we are seeking reciprocation from God for our giving, praying, and fasting, rather than from people.

Westerners like it when gifts have no strings attached. We feel that if a friendship is predicated on gift giving, then our relationship isn't *true* friendship. Our Eastern friends frown. They simply didn't (and don't) view gift giving in a disinterested way. No strings means no bonds. Gifts with no strings don't establish lasting relationships—no patrons or protectors. First-century people (and those in modern collective cultures) understood gifts to be relationship forming. Giving gifts is an expression of care and interest for another person. Among collectives, gifts are given to create a bond between people (Seneca, *On Benefits* 6.41.2).[26]

---

[26]See David A. deSilva, "'We Are Debtors': Grace and Obligation in Paul and Seneca," in *Paul and Seneca in Dialogue*, ed. Joey Dodson and David Briones, New Testament and Ancient Philosophy Series (Leiden, Netherlands: Brill, 2017), 153.

Often what Westerners want to avoid in gift giving is a sense of obligation, which usually has a negative sense. We hate feeling obligated to do something. Arabs speak about the sense of obligation and gratitude that someone feels after they receive a gift or service from someone very differently. They call it "acknowledging the beauty." Seneca likewise argues gifts are to be transparent so that all can admire the beauty.

So for collectives, gifts are good, and it is good that they lead to a sense of gratitude and obligation to respond, because this binds people together in relationship. It is in this context Proverbs says, "Everyone is the friend of one who gives gifts" (Prov 19:6). I had always misunderstood that verse to be condemning gift giving because it creates false friends. I never noticed that Proverbs doesn't call them false friends. That is not what Proverbs means. Gifts build friendships in a patronage world. Yet in my Western world, when I see gifts at work in relationships, I am quick to condemn them as bribes. The Bible is clear that gifts can be used for good or for ill. We must be careful not to see all reciprocal gift giving, and the obligation it produces on recipients to act to benefit the giver, as corrupt. It wasn't (but it could be).

We will look at this more in the next chapter. Here we are outlining the dynamics of reciprocity and patronage so we can better understand what went without being said in the way relationships worked in the ancient world.

BE PERFECT LIKE YOUR HEAVENLY FATHER

When each of your authors moved to a collective culture, we were keen to build friendships. I turned to many Arab friends for advice for building friendships. One common thing I heard was, "Treat others as they treat you." They meant that if someone shows you care, reciprocate care. If someone gives you money, reciprocate with money. If someone tries to pull you down, pull them down. This is not a sentiment of Arab culture only. Indonesian has a term, *membalas*, that means "to reciprocate." Over the years, I realized I used *membalas* a lot more in conversations there than I ever used *reciprocate* (or equivalents) back here in America. It was just part of life in a collective society. It was also common in Jesus' day:

> You have heard that it was said, "Eye for eye, and tooth for tooth." But I tell
> you, do not resist an evil person. If anyone slaps you on the right cheek,
> turn to them the other cheek also. And if anyone wants to sue you and take
> your shirt, hand over your coat as well. If anyone forces you to go one mile,
> go with them two miles. Give to the one who asks you, and do not turn
> away from the one who wants to borrow from you. (Mt 5:38-42)

Jesus is radically redefining things here, as he often does, but we should
note two things. First, reciprocity is assumed and permeates the passage.
Second, Jesus is redefining reciprocity but not eliminating it. Those who
are harmed feel they should reciprocate harm. Part of reciprocity was that
you reciprocated with love to your friend and harm to your enemy. We
already saw that Jesus taught people to give and lend to anyone in need,
not just those whom you expect will reciprocate. Jesus redefines reciprocity. "And if anyone wants to sue you and take your shirt, hand over
your coat as well" (Mt 5:40). How is this reciprocity? A person is seeking
to sue you for your shirt. Jesus says give it to them. Don't defend. But then
he adds, "Hand over your coat as well." Clearly the adversary does not
think they have a right to this. After all, they are not suing for the coat as
well. Giving the coat is a gift—a gift to an adversary. This is not a disinterested gift. Gifts in his reciprocal world sought to establish friendships.
Giving the coat would be a gesture of magnanimity, goodwill, even a
desire for relationship. It seeks to turn the adversary into a friend.

Jesus goes on to teach:

> You have heard that it was said, "Love your neighbor and hate your enemy."
> But I tell you, love your enemies and pray for those who persecute you, that
> you may be children of your Father in heaven. He causes his sun to rise on
> the evil and the good, and sends rain on the righteous and the unrighteous.
> If you love those who love you, what reward will you get? Are not even the
> tax collectors doing that? And if you greet only your own people, what are
> you doing more than others? Do not even pagans do that? Be perfect,
> therefore, as your heavenly Father is perfect. (Mt 5:43-48)

Jesus portrays God as a tremendously generous patron. In the reciprocal
world of antiquity, many patrons would look for clients who would

reciprocate their benefits. Jesus points out that God benefits us with rain. But God does not send rain only on those who are good. He sends rain on the righteous (which could be expected) and the unrighteous (which is very different). Jesus calls us to imitate our heavenly Father. We are not to love only those who love us, like the world does. We are to welcome all, not only those who welcome us. In doing so, we live out the ethic that underlies God's patronage. He acts to bless because he can, not because he thinks someone deserves it. When we benefit others on this basis, we are perfect, as our heavenly Father is perfect. We seek to use gifts to make enemies into friends in the same way God used a gift, Jesus, to turn us into friends "while we were yet sinners" (Rom 5:8).

CONCLUSION

We have seen that blood (kinship) was part of the glue of the ancient world. Now we have added patronage with its gifts and reciprocity. It is unsurprising to find that themes, issues, and opportunities relating to patronage underlie many stories and relationships throughout the Bible. Yet, because it usually went without being said, I had rarely noticed it as a modern individualist reader.

Let me offer a personal story. Many Western crosscultural workers come from wealthy countries and have many valuable connections. As a result, Westerners can be wary of using these things in case they build dependency among local people. As a result, Westerners tend to hold back from giving financial or other material benefits to people. There are some good elements to this, such as not controlling less wealthy people through our gifts. But most of our aversion to dependency is that Western cultures value independence, and so creating dependency seems to us like a self-evidently unhelpful thing. We like our independence, and we don't like relying on others. We quote, "God helps those who help themselves," as if it were in the Bible. It was English political theorist Algernon Sidney, not God, who originated the phrase. We can thank Benjamin Franklin (*Poor Richard's Almanac*, 1736) for ingraining it into American society. It isn't biblical. In fact, one can argue it is antibiblical. God helps those who depend on him—and each other. The correct answer to Cain's question, "Am I my brother's keeper?" (Gen 4:9) is supposed to be "Yes!"

We saw that Proverbs says, "Everyone is the friend of one who gives gifts" (Prov 19:6). A former student of mine once took me and my wife out for a meal. He picked us up in his car, took us to an expensive restaurant, and bought us a really nice meal. When we were talking over food, I mentioned we were going to use a taxi company to pick someone up from the airport because we didn't own a car. He offered me one of his cars. Until this day, I have warm feelings of friendship toward him. His gestures showed me he wanted to be involved in my life; he wanted to invest in a friendship. Yet, for a long time, I had not wanted to give to local people for fear of building dependency. By avoiding dependency, I avoided "ties that bind," the kind of ties that should mark a Christian family. Friends (like family) depend on one another. A Lebanese pastor explains,

> I take a lot of people to dinner. I have a special budget just to take people to dinner. I don't bribe anyone—they know that. I say it up front. I don't break the law for anyone's sake, but I treat people nice. I become their friend. That sometimes translates into becoming the keeper of their secrets and the counsellor for their problems. Of course, I give them all these services for nothing. But against that, when I need something, I can pick up the phone and say, "Look, I have an issue with thus-and-so. What should I do?"[27]

Perhaps we Western Christians need to worry a bit less about creating one-sided dependency and more on creating friendships that hold hands (have strings attached). This of course, mean both parties relying on the other.

---

[27]Karen L. H. Shaw has similar advice, along with lots more, in *Wealth and Piety: Middle Eastern Perspectives for Expat Workers* (Littleton, CO: William Carey, 2018), 175-76.

4

PATRONAGE

The System and the Players

I WANTED TO TAKE A COURSE ON ARAB POETRY. I heard that a university would let people apply to audit courses for free. I went to the president's office, which was quite daunting, and I filled out the paperwork. A while later I still hadn't heard anything, so I went back to the president's office to ask whether my request had been granted. His secretary looked embarrassed and said I should come back a week later. This happened a few times. One day I was with my friend Hassan and mentioned that I was going to the university later that day to check on the request. As I was explaining the story, Hassan said, "Oh, let me make a call for you." He phoned someone at the president's office. After a few pleasantries, he mentioned my name, that I was a friend, and that I had submitted a request to audit. He asked the person to help me with the request. He hung up and said, "There you go; don't worry about it." I thanked him for his kind gesture, but I still planned to visit the secretary that afternoon to try to move things along. I didn't need to. A short while later my phone rang. The president's secretary told me that she had good news. The president had granted my request.

PATRONAGE STRIKES ME THE WRONG WAY

As a modern individualist, what Hassan did strikes me as wrong. I shouldn't have gotten my application advanced just because Hassan had connections. It cuts against some of my deeply held individualist values. "Everyone is supposed to be treated the same," I insist. In fact, we are confident our preference that everyone be treated the same is in the Bible somewhere. We are confident James was prohibiting favoritism and not just favoritism for evil purposes (Jas 2:1-9). Actually, we find all kinds of examples in the Bible of God treating someone as special because of connections. Rahab is spared the fate of everyone else in Jericho because a spy calls up Joshua on the phone (so to speak). "*Ideally*, though, shouldn't everyone be treated like everyone else?" I might still whine. Well, actually, we don't want God to treat us like everyone else on Judgment Day. I want special treatment precisely because I know someone. I believe my connection with Jesus will get me preferential treatment on Judgment Day. More than just a future hope, I don't want God to stick my prayers today in the same stack with the rest of the world's. When I say, "I am a child of the King," am I not saying that I am special, that I have an inside angle on heaven? When I ask that sweet old saint at church to pray for me, am I not asking her to do what my friend Hassan did? I need to be careful not to import my individualist dislike of patronage into the biblical world. Patronage runs so much against the values of individualist culture that it might surprise us how important patron-client relationships are in Scripture.

THE ROOTS OF PATRONAGE IN THE OLD TESTAMENT

There are many reciprocal relationships in the Old Testament. Some of these are unequal relationships based in formal covenants between stronger and weaker groups of people. For example, the weaker people of Jabesh-Gilead say to the stronger Nahash the Ammonite, "Make a treaty with us, and we will be subject to you" (1 Sam 11:1). In these treaties, both parties had obligations to one another. The stronger party was obligated to provide a form of protection to the weaker party. The weaker party was obligated to give exclusive loyalty to the stronger party, whom they were to honor and obey (and pay taxes to). These asymmetrical relationships were formalized in treaties with blessings and curses attached.[1] When the

---

[1] Zeba Crook, "Reciprocity: Covenant Exchange as a Test Case," in *Ancient Israel: The Old Testament in Its Social Context*, ed. Philip F. Esler (Minneapolis: Fortress, 2006), 85. Scholars note such treaties usually comprised a preamble, history of the relationship, treaty clauses, invocation of gods,

Gibeonites rush to make a treaty with Joshua because they recognize he is a stronger party, they pretend to be peoples from a distant kingdom (Josh 9:3-14). They speak of themselves as his "servants" (Josh 9:8). By entering into the treaty, Joshua will be obligated to protect them. Their deception works. Joshua does not attack them, because "the leaders of the assembly had sworn an oath to them by the LORD, the God of Israel" (Josh 9:18).

When we read about treaties, we should ask about the power dynamic in the relationship. Which is the stronger party? Why is a treaty necessary? Often protection can be offered with a veiled threat; the protector is actually the aggressor. Assyria had an aggressive policy, binding weaker kingdoms to themselves through such covenants.[2] Israelite king Hoshea enters into a treaty with Assyria. God objects because Hoshea is seeking protection from Assyria rather than from him (2 Kings 17:3-4). More significantly, the treaty means being bound to Assyria, rather than to Yahweh (God).[3] Israel has found a new patron.

These *suzerain-vassal* relationships were asymmetrical. The stronger party (suzerain) protected the weaker (vassal) party, who gave them obedience and gifts. Scholars call these special suzerain-vassal relationships "covenant relationships." Are they patron-client relationships? Perhaps, yes, but such treaties are a very specific subset of a much larger concept. When we are talking about patronage in general, we are not referring to these asymmetrical relationships based in treaties. Patronage relationships were generally unwritten.

There were also many less formal reciprocal relationships between stronger and weaker peoples in the Old Testament. Although not formal treaties, they were still binding. There were expectations on both parties that bound them together. These expectations were based in dependence, reciprocity, and gratitude—patronage. Patron-client relationships were not about two individuals relating together. Patrons cared for groups of

---

and curses and blessings. See Noel Weeks, *Admonition and Curse: The Ancient Near Eastern Treaty/ Covenant Form as a Problem in Inter-cultural Relationships* (London: T&T Clark, 2004), 68.

[2] James Maxwell Miller and John H. Hayes, *A History of Ancient Israel and Judah* (Louisville, KY: Westminster John Knox, 1986), 320.

[3] J. Andrew Dearman, *The Book of Hosea*, NICOT (Grand Rapids, MI: Eerdmans, 2010), 298.

people. Abraham was the father and thus the patron of his whole family.
Abimelek allowed Abraham (and his family) to live among his people.[4]
Abraham was the weaker partner and was expected to reciprocate to the
stronger party in the relationship. Abraham had initiated the relationship
by offering a gift, the ideal gift in some ways, because this gift made Abi-
melek not just a patron but a kinsman. The trouble was, Abraham's gift is
Sarah. God does not approve and warns Abimelek in a dream not to touch
Sarah. Abimelek heeds the divine warning. It seems to Abimelek that
Abraham, far from offering the ideal gift, is in fact reciprocating evil when
Abimelek has only offered good: "Then Abimelek called Abraham in and
said, 'What have you done to us? How have I wronged you that you have
brought such great guilt upon me and my kingdom? You have done things
to me that should never be done'" (Gen 20:9), by offering a gift that would
bring divine curses on Abimelek.

While reciprocal relationships between unequal partners are common
in the Old Testament, both among kin and between nonkinship groups,
most examples that make it into the Bible are either kinship or formal
covenantal relationships. The much more informal system of patronage
per se does not seem to be widespread (or, more likely, is just not
mentioned).[5] Nonetheless, we do see some examples of these relationships. Recognizing they were patron-client relationships with strings attached can help us better understand what is going on.

Gideon and the Israelites. During the time of the conquest, Gideon
rescued Israel (Judg 6:1-12). Actually, God rescued Israel using Gideon
as his mediator, as we will see in later chapters. In response, the people of
Israel should have viewed God as their patron and remained loyal to him
(Judg 6:1-10). They should have reciprocated loyalty to Gideon's family,
too. However, when Gideon died, the Israelites turned back to Baal-Berith
as their god. The text laments, "They also failed to show any loyalty to the
family of Jerub-Baal (that is, Gideon) in spite of all the good things he had

---

[4]We should notice the status difference between Abimelek and Abraham, who sojourned on Abimelek's land. Even Abimelek's name carries status. It means "my father is king." Status mattered
greatly in such cultures.

[5]Crook, "Reciprocity," 86-87.

done for them" (Judg 8:35). Ideally, they should have been loyal to God, and they weren't. They weren't even loyal to God's servant, Gideon. Loyalty should have been reciprocated in return for benefits. Lots of stories in the book of Judges scandalize us, but this one is also supposed to offend us: "Can you imagine such ingratitude!"

Elisha and the Shunammite woman. We have seen some failed patronage relationships. Let's see one that works. The way both sides of an asymmetrical relationship were loyal to each other is beautifully illustrated in the story of Elisha and the wealthy Shunammite woman (2 Kings 4:8-36; 8:1-6).[6] There are no kinship ties here. She is a Shunammite, that is, not an Israelite. When Elisha passes through Shunem, a wealthy non-Israelite woman urges him to stay for a meal. Elisha has no kinfolk in the town and so is dependent on others to provide for his needs. The woman is acting as a patroness to Elisha. She seems to be motivated to care for Elisha because she deems him a worthy client. She tells her husband, "I know that this man who often comes our way is a holy man of God" (2 Kings 4:9). From then on, whenever Elisha passes through town, he stops at their home to eat. She even suggests that they build a room for Elisha to stay in when he visits.

Ancient readers expected what happens next. Elisha wants to reciprocate these gifts and services. This impulse reinforced to the early biblical audience that Elisha is an honorable man: he knows how to reciprocate. Gratitude was the original reciprocation. She then reciprocated with the guest room. Now Elisha needs to reciprocate. (Remember the three dancing graces, who keep passing gifts among themselves.) Elisha tells his servant Gehazi to tell the Shunammite woman, "You have gone to all this trouble for us. Now what can be done for you? Can we speak on your behalf to the king or the commander of the army?" (2 Kings 4:13).[7] The

---

[6]So argue Raymond Westbrook, "Patronage in the Ancient Near East," *Journal of the Economic and Social History of the Orient* 48, no. 2 (2005): 210-33; Dorothea H. Bertschmann, "Hosting Jesus: Revisiting Luke's 'Sinful Woman' (Luke 7.36-50) as a Tale of Two Hosts," *Journal for the Study of the New Testament* 40, no. 1 (2017): 33.

[7]Asking a servant to do this seems odd to us. Why doesn't he just ask her himself? Gehazi is the mediator, as we will see in chap. 6.

woman replies, "I have a home among my own people." She is talking about more than real estate. She means her family already has a place in the power structure. She already has a support network, her kinship group, and so has no need for Elisha to mediate for her with those in authority. But Elisha still wants to reciprocate and so asks Gehazi whether he knows of anything Elisha could do for her. Gehazi tells Elisha that the woman has no son and her husband is old. Elisha tells her that she will have a child. This prophecy is offered as a reciprocal response to her gifts of hospitality and care. Presumably the Shunammite woman initially interpreted this prophecy as a well wish. When she has a child, it transforms the relationship. To that point, she had assumed that in their unequal relationship *she* was the patron. Suddenly, she realizes Elisha is the empowered one. She is the client![8] Sometime later, her son dies. The woman rushes to Elisha to ask for help. She approaches him as a client and reminds Elisha that she was not the one who asked originally for a son. Elisha chose to give the gift and now is failing to provide what he promised.[9] Elisha goes with her and restores the boy to life.

This story illustrates some of the beauty of patronage. It is essential to note, though, that the most important thing is not the gift but the relationship that is formed by the gift and, later, is symbolized with gifts. Elisha and this woman have a bond—the strings-attached kind of bond that we in the West sometimes avoid. This bond ties them together so that years later, Elisha protects her again. First, Elisha tells her to leave the land for seven years because a famine is coming. Second, in her absence, others seize her house and lands. When she returns to the land, she appeals to the king (2 Kings 8:3). Elisha steps in to intercede on behalf of his client; he provides a service as her patron.[10] His servant Gehazi tells the king that she is the woman for whom Elisha worked miracles. The king sees she is Elisha's client and tells his officials to return everything that belonged to her.

---

[8]Westbrook, "Patronage in the Ancient Near East," 229.

[9]As we will see later, this is a mild form of shaming to encourage Elisha to act.

[10]Seneca notes influence was one of the gifts patrons offered. See Seneca, *On Benefits* 1.2.4.

At the start of this story, the woman relied on her own wealth and kinship, but in the end, patronage, with its security network, protects her. Proverbs warns not to trust in riches. The biblical message from the Shunammite woman is that God will protect. In this case, he uses the societal system of patronage.

PATRONAGE IN THE NEW TESTAMENT

By the time of the first century, patronage had grown into a foundational social structure across the Mediterranean world. Thus we should not be surprised to find many kinds of patron-client relationships in the New Testament. In fact, the system was so widespread in the first-century Greco-Roman world that when the writers of the New Testament mention these relationships, they assume that everyone will know what was going on. It is helpful to draw out a few examples to illustrate how patronage is in the background of some New Testament stories.

Phoebe. Corinth was a major city of the Greco-Roman world. It was built on a strategic, narrow stretch of land separating two bodies of water in the Mediterranean. For geographic reasons, it was extremely advantageous for shipping companies to pass their freight through Corinth, which made Corinth wealthy and a strategic passage point for travelers crisscrossing the empire by ship. In the first century, Corinth was bustling, a bit like San Francisco during the Gold Rush, a town of opportunity and migrants. An inscription in Corinth from about the time Paul was in the city praises a patroness called Junia Theadora who migrated to Corinth. She was a newcomer, originally from Lycia (modern Turkey). The inscription calls her a benefactress and praises her for the way she gave patronage (*prostasian*) to Lycian travelers.[11] Part of the inscription reads:

> Junia Theadora ... who is a friend of the Lycians and had dedicated her life to earning the gratitude of all the Lycians, has bestowed numerous benefits also on many of our citizens; and, revealing the generosity of her nature,

---

[11]Jerome Murphy-O'Connor, *St. Paul's Corinth: Texts and Archaeology*, 3rd ed. (Collegeville, MN: Liturgical Press, 2002), 82; Efrain Agosto, "Paul and Commendation," in *Paul in the Greco-Roman World: A Handbook*, ed. J. Paul Sampley (Harrisburg, PA: Trinity Press International, 2003), 123.

she does not cease, because of her goodwill, from offering hospitality to all the Lycians and receiving them in her own house and she continues particularly to act on behalf of our citizens in regard to any favor asked.

Patronage honors are woven throughout the inscription. Her clients express their gratitude by praising her character "so that Junia herself, and the city of Corinth at the same time, may be aware of the loyalty of our city to her."[12] Junia is praised for being a generous patron who benefits many citizens and does so because of her goodwill; she acts on any favor asked of her. Her benefaction is reciprocated by the gratitude and loyalty of all the Lycians, those who are part of her "we."

Paul mentions another worthy patroness from the region of Corinth. In his letter to the Romans (written from Corinth) around the same time as the Junia inscription, Paul writes: "I commend to you our sister Phoebe, a deacon of the church in Cenchreae. I ask you to receive her in the Lord in a way worthy of his people and to give her any help she may need from you, for she has been the benefactor of many people, including me" (Rom 16:1-2). Paul's commendation of Phoebe as a "deacon" sparks a lot of debate in some circles, but we shouldn't overlook that Paul also commends her for being the benefactor of many. Paul calls her a *prostatis* (benefactor), a cognate of the term *prostasian* (patronage) used in the inscription about Junia.[13] We get the picture from Romans that Phoebe was an important patroness in the early church in Corinth. She opened her home to host gatherings of believers in the port of Cenchreae and probably also received and helped take care of the needs of traveling Christians (likely including Paul) as they arrived at the port.

Felix. Patronage dynamics are at work in Paul's interaction with Felix the Roman governor. When the Jewish leadership brings their charges against Paul before Felix, they use a lawyer named Tertullus, probably because the trial was in Latin. Tertullus uses a common approach. Typically, clients praised their patron's prowess and knowledge, rehearsing all the ways the patron had benefited them in the past. This litany culminated in

---

[12]Murphy-O'Connor, *St. Paul's Corinth*, 83.
[13]Murphy-O'Connor, *St. Paul's Corinth*, 84.

the client expressing their profound gratitude to the patron.[14] Repeating the patronage history helped to reinforce the strings attached between them. Obligations and reciprocity would hang in the air. Then, the client would make a request. Tertullus does this with Felix: "We have enjoyed a long period of peace under you, and your foresight has brought about reforms in this nation. Everywhere and in every way, most excellent Felix, we acknowledge this with profound gratitude. But in order not to weary you further, I would request that you be kind enough to hear us briefly" (Acts 24:2-4).

Tertullus's approach was typical, if uninspired. The delegation praises Felix as a ruler (patron) who provided peace, noting they are grateful to him in every way. Tertullus's case should have been a slam dunk. They are asking for Paul to be released for a Jewish trial (which should only have flogging as a punishment). But Luke helps us understand that the leaders had no intention of giving Paul a fair trial. Possibly, Paul was going to "have an accident" along the way. Whether Felix knew this is immaterial. I doubt he would have cared. The Jewish leaders were right to expect Felix to reciprocate, like a good patron, by handing over Paul. Felix doesn't comply.

A bit of background may help understand why Felix doesn't turn Paul over. Felix had been a disastrous governor. He had stirred up more ill will and problems than any other governor. A historian of the time says that Felix thought "he could do any evil act with impunity" because he had an influential brother in Rome who would protect him (Tacitus, *Annals* 12.54).[15] Tertullus's praise of Felix for being a good patron is just political fluff, and everyone knows it.

Nonetheless, Felix should have reciprocated by granting their request against Paul. In the end, Felix was motivated by greed. Felix is a poor patron (as well as a poor administrator). Paul mentioned he was in Jerusalem to deliver an offering (Acts 24:17). When Felix hears "offering," he sees dollar signs. Luke tells us Felix holds Paul because "he was hoping

---

[14]James R. Harrison, *Paul's Language of Grace in Its Greco-Roman Context* (Eugene, OR: Wipf & Stock, 2017), 68.

[15]See Ben Witherington III, *The Acts of the Apostles: A Socio-Rhetorical Commentary* (Grand Rapids, MI: Eerdmans, 1998), 705.

that Paul would offer him a bribe" (Acts 24:26). Paul doesn't. Felix keeps him in jail for two years and then Felix is recalled to Rome. He should have cleared out his court backlog, including a ruling on (i.e., released) Paul. Yet, he didn't. Instead, he purposefully left Paul locked up in prison. Luke says he did so "because Felix wanted to grant a favor to the Jews" (Acts 24:27), thinking he might need their reciprocation later.

Patrons as protectors. We see the dynamics of patronage used (and abused) throughout the story of Felix and Paul. The Jewish delegation *praises* Felix as their patron for providing them with peace. They appeal to this patronage when making a request for him to act in their interests against Paul. Felix sees himself as a patron. He is looking for ways to do *favors* for the Jews in order to co-opt them as his loyal clients. Felix does not act in the interests of Paul. Neither, though, does he act in the genuine interests of the Jews. Ultimately, Felix acts solely in *his own* interests—the worst behavior of a patron. He does not use his imbalanced power to serve the communities who were dependent on him, neither Paul nor the Jewish delegation.[16] He uses his resources and power to benefit himself and maintain his position by seeking a bribe. Seneca would be appalled, as Luke likely expects us to be.

CONCLUSION: BECOMING ATTACHED TO THE RIGHT PEOPLE

One of our friends wanted to get married. Her fiancé worked a low-paying job, and they struggled to save any money toward the wedding costs. It was going to take years to be able to afford even the simplest of weddings. One day, as we were talking, she told us her grandmother had offered to pay for the wedding. "That's great news," we said. She explained that she had turned the offer down. She said, "We hope to live abroad.

---

[16]Like politics today, ancient politics were complicated. Other factors were likely in play. Felix was replaced by (Porcius) Festus, who was a descendent of the Porcius clan. The right of appeal to Caesar (*provocatio*) was technically part of the *Lex Iulia de vi Publica* (17 BC) but had its roots in the actions of P. Porcius Laeca (195 BC). It is easy to understand how Festus might respect the Porcian law. See Michael J. G. Gray-Fow, "Why Festus, Not Felix? Paul's *Caesarem Appello*," *Journal of the Evangelical Theological Society* 59, no. 3 (2016): 473-85, esp. 475-76.

My grandmother doesn't want us to, and I'm afraid that if we accept this gift, she will use it to obligate us to stay. We want to be grateful, and we know that if we accept her paying for our wedding, we won't be able to go against her wishes in the future. That would show her ingratitude." They politely turned the gift down.

Arabs call this "loading someone down with beauty." The gift is beautiful, and the giver looks like a generous benefactor. But it is given to control others by placing them into the debt of the giver. The beautiful gift or service is not given to bless but to obligate.

Paul had patrons. In Paul's world, staying in the home of an influential person often meant receiving their patronage. Wealthy benefactors often hosted guests, clients, and other friends passing through. The inscription for Junia Theadora notes how her benefaction involved hosting people in her home. In Philippi, Paul and his companions go to a place of prayer. A woman there named Lydia is a dealer in purple cloth and likely wealthy.[17] Lydia and her household were baptized. She invites Paul and his companions to stay in her home: "'If you consider me a believer in the Lord,' she said, 'come and stay at my house.' And she persuaded us" (Acts 16:15). Likely Lydia acted as a patron for Paul. Paul later mentions that he was financially supported by the Philippian church at times, probably meaning Lydia and/or the jailer (2 Cor 11:8; Phil 4:18-19).

This makes it more striking that Paul refuses to accept gifts from members of the Corinthian church. Paul's refusal seems to have angered some members (1 Cor 9). Some slander Paul by suggesting his refusal to accept their support indicates he isn't an actual apostle. Paul has to defend his apostleship as a result. The reason Paul refused to accept their financial support is that gifts have strings attached.

---

[17]There are a number of reasons to conclude that Lydia was wealthy. First, purple cloth was sought by the wealthy and was expensive. Second, as a trader, Lydia likely had economic means to buy bulk purchases. Third, she seems to be the head of her household. These factors point to Lydia being wealthy. Even if we take these to be low level, we get a picture of Lydia being wealthy in her world. We should remember the economic makeup of society in the Greco-Roman world, which we described in chap. 3. Having any form of means to place Lydia above subsistence-level life would have made her wealthy, somewhere in the top 30 percent in her society. See Richard S. Ascough, *Lydia: Paul's Cosmopolitan Hostess* (Collegeville, MN: Liturgical Press, 2009), 50-51.

We have argued the positive aspect of strings. Gifts bind the parties together. We have also seen the negative aspect of strings: the bond can be exploited. Recently, Sheikh Mohammed Hussein, a judge in a Lebanese family court, told us, "I will not let someone buy my lunch, because one day it will cost me three times. One day he will be in my court. I will need to look my eye into his eye. I will feel something. No. I must be able to judge fairly."[18] The church in Corinth was torn by factions. In collective cultures, factions usually need a patron. The patron gives the group honor, unites them, and represents them. These factions can speak of themselves as follows of [the patron]. These factions in the church in Corinth have (or claim to have) a patron. Some factions are claiming their own apostle: Cephas, Paul, or Apollos (1 Cor 1:12).[19] If Paul accepted financial support from any of the patrons in these factions, he would become indebted—tied—to that faction of the church; he would become we. It seems some of the patrons in these factions were angered that Paul would not accept their patronage. Paul wisely doesn't allow them to gain control of him through their patronage.

Paul adds, "I robbed other churches by receiving support from them so as to serve you [plural]" (2 Cor 11:8). The plural *you* is particularly significant and probably means all the factions. So is it hypocrisy for Paul to accept the patronage of Lydia in Philippi and of other churches and not of someone in Corinth? No. Paul understood that the value of a gift depended on the motives of the patron. All gifts have strings attached, so it was crucial that he discern what *kind* of strings were attached.[20] Tentmaking was not Paul's universal missionary strategy. He was more often supported by a patron. Paul's universal missionary strategy was to make sure that nothing interfered with following Jesus. When a patron's support

---

[18]Sheikh Mohammed, "Panel Discussion," International Patronage Conference, Beirut, October 4, 2018. Honest (or corrupt) judges are no more (or less) common in collectivist as individualist cultures.

[19]That Cephas, Peter's Aramaic name, is used might suggest some of these factions also fell around kinship. Perhaps a Palestinian Jewish faction claimed to follow Cephas and Alexandrian Hellenistic Jews claimed the great Greek speaker Apollos. Oftentimes patronage and kinship overlap, as we shall see in chap. 5.

[20]We noted earlier that those passages often used to suggest that Jesus argues for patrons to give without strings attached probably are about patrons giving with the right motives.

enabled him to do that, he accepted the gifts with thanksgiving—as God's provision. When the patron's gift had strings that would hinder, Paul chose to refuse the gift and to work with his hands.

Paul understood the patronage system very well. He knew its strengths and potential weaknesses, and avoided being bound or limited by patronage when it hindered him in what God had called him to. Other times, he drew on patronage to build what God had called him to. In fact, he leveraged the patronage system as a beautiful image of the greatest of all relationships: the gospel.

5

PATRONAGE

Grace, Faith, and the Language of Patronage

"I'd describe it as weeping," the judge said, leaning back in his chair. He was satisfied he had come up with a term to describe patronage. It had been a long quest, and I didn't much like the ending. For years, I had been trying to find the Arabic term for patronage. It began a decade ago when I was talking with a friend who was an academic in Arabic literature. He asked me what I was researching at the time, and I said the Arabic word for *patronage*. He scratched his head thoughtfully and said, "I'm sorry, I didn't understand you. Can you explain what you mean?" I assumed I had mispronounced the word so I said it more carefully. "No, no, I understand the word," he said. "I just don't know what you mean by it." I took a pen and diagrammed a patron-client relationship with the gifts flowing between the parties. I told a couple of stories. My friend said, "Oh yes, this is a very big part of our culture. You should definitely teach people about this aspect of Arab culture." When I asked him to provide me with the correct term, he leaned back in his chair and closed his eyes. After a few seconds, he said, "We don't really have this term." He continued to give me many examples of what Arabs would say to talk about it. They were all metaphors and euphemisms, but he couldn't think of an abstract term.

This happened a number of times with students, trainees, friends, and pastors. Eventually, I began to realize that Arabs just don't really use a single term to describe patronage. It is so vast, so much a part of Arab culture, that they had never needed to describe it from the outside. Everyone knows what goes without being said. Everyone got the metaphors. So, when my judge friend, who is very highly educated in the Arabic language, smiled and told me he knew the term, I was excited. Until he said, "Weeping."

I was confused. "You mean crying?" He said, "Yes." "How so?" I asked. "Well," he replied, "people come to me and weep crocodile tears. We expect someone to care for us, so we go to them and weep." He didn't mean literally. He meant that clients show they are in need and ask a patron to provide for them. As a would-be patron, this was his take on the system from his point of view. Language and culture are usually two sides of the same coin. It is very important to learn the ways insiders in a culture speak about their culture. While it can be confusing—because they assume you know what is going without being said—it is usually the best way to understand how culture really works. So, how does the Bible talk about patronage?

THE LANGUAGE OF PATRONAGE IN THE BIBLE

When God describes himself as a shepherd, he isn't discussing animal husbandry. He isn't arguing that raising sheep is the most divine of all professions. We know that, but what may have gone without being said is that shepherding was actually a very common metaphor that ancients used to speak about patronage.[1] The patron is the shepherd. He or she uses their power to lead and care for their flock. The flock are the clients. Shepherds protect the flock from harm. They provide the flock with food and ensure their material needs are guaranteed. A flock knows who their shepherd (their patron) is. They are expected to listen to their patron's voice. They are to loyally follow him. A flock with a good shepherd is a well-fed, well-protected, and well-led group of people. Ensuring this is the shepherd's job.

Arabs still use this metaphor today. One day I was going through a poor area of town in a taxi. The driver was notably upset with what we could

---

[1]Rachana Kamtekar, "The Politics of Plato's Socrates," in *A Companion to Socrates*, ed. Sara Ahbel-Rappe and Rachana Kamtekar (Malden, MA: Wiley-Blackwell, 2009), 222.

see all around us. I asked him whether he was okay. He jabbed his finger at all the run-down houses. "Our shepherds are slaughtering us, while they grow fat." He didn't explain any more than that. He expected me to understand. It's a common metaphor; it went without being said. Both the taxi driver and Ezekiel understood the responsibility shepherds hold toward their flock. Through his prophet Ezekiel, God rebukes the leaders of Israel. He calls them bad shepherds: "The word of the LORD came to me: 'Son of man, prophesy against the shepherds of Israel; prophesy and say to them: "This is what the Sovereign Lord says: Woe to you shepherds of Israel who only take care of yourselves! Should not shepherds take care of the flock?"'" (Ezek 34:1-2). Like the people in the taxi driver's city, these leaders had forsaken the health of their flock for their own gain.

Ezekiel 34:1-6 continues the metaphor. They have slaughtered the choice sheep and clothed themselves with their wool. They have allowed the sheep to be scattered and lost. They have forsaken those who were weak and injured. The people are sheep without a true shepherd.[2] How does God propose to solve this problem? Through Ezekiel, God promises: "For this is what the Sovereign LORD says: I myself will search for my sheep and look after them. As a shepherd looks after his scattered flock when he is with them, so will I look after my sheep. I will rescue them" (Ezek 34:11-12).

Jesus is referring to Ezekiel when he tells the Jewish leaders of his day, "I am the good shepherd" (Jn 10:11-17). Jesus is condemning the leaders as bad shepherds. More importantly, by saying that he is the good shepherd, he is claiming to be God. Although there is some amazing theology here, we don't want to overlook the obvious. The good shepherd image is a collective image. Jesus doesn't just walk around with one sheep. The good shepherd rescues the lost sheep by restoring it to its flock (Lk 15:1-7).

The New Testament uses the metaphor of shepherding to speak about the responsibility of leaders to care for their people. Peter tells the elders, "Be shepherds of God's flock that is under your care, watching over them" (1 Pet 5:2). Jude calls the false leaders "shepherds who feed

---

[2]Jesus uses the metaphor of sheep without a shepherd. "When he saw the crowds, he had compassion on them, because they were harassed and helpless, like sheep without a shepherd" (Mt 9:36).

only themselves" (Jude 12). In other words, like Felix, who detained Paul in hopes of a bribe, Jude's false leaders use their status and resources only for themselves. The New Testament writers expect readers to understand what they mean, just like the taxi driver expected me to.

FATHERS, SHEPHERDS, KINGS, AND OTHER COMMON PATRONAGE TERMS

Often the players of the biblical world blended its cultural structures (just like we do today). We don't mean they were confused. We mean they could use more than one system at a time. Patronage and kinship often overlap in collective cultures, for two reasons. First, a kinsman was often the first choice for a patron. Recall our example of the Philippian baker Belen, whose bakery burned down. If Belen's family had included some kinsman who was financially able to rescue him, he would have gone there first. Relatives often act as patrons to their kin, such as an uncle who provides work for a niece, or a grandfather who guides the decisions of all those in his family.[3] In those situations, the overlap between patronage and kinship is not just figurative but literal. The uncle is still kin, of course, but is using his greater status to benefit those in his family. The family will reciprocate with respect and loyalty. When this happened, ancients didn't switch from the language of kinship to the language of patronage. They would just keep calling their uncle "uncle." There was no need to change terms; everyone understood what was going on. Often, though, as in our story of Belen, patronage relationships happened between people who shared no blood connection.

Patronage was a complementary system to kinship in the ancient world, sometimes intertwined, other times working parallel. When people in antiquity used kinship language to talk about patronage, it was not an attempt to mask what was going on. They thought kinship language worked well as a metaphor for talking about patronage. Kinfolk were loyal to one another and relied on one another. They trusted one another to provide

---

[3]Patricia Brown, *Spirit in the Writings of John: Johannine Pneumatology in Social-Scientific Perspective,* Journal for the Study of the New Testament Supplement Series 253 (London: T&T Clark, 2003), 32.

reciprocal, mutual care. The bounds between patrons and clients worked in similar ways, so people often picked up kinship language to describe these patronage relationships.[4]

Kings often use kinship language because it describes their patron-client relationship with their kingdom. In his autobiography, King Abdullah II of Jordan writes, "On the night before [my father's] funeral I went to bed with a family of four, and I woke up the next morning with a family of five million."[5] King Abdullah II describes his role as being like a father to his people. This isn't just flowery language. He understands the relationship to include dynamics of responsibility, dependency, protection, and care. The metaphor of parenting expresses these well. David says, "Come, my children, listen to me; I will teach you the fear of the LORD" (Ps 34:11). He is not addressing his physical children but all his hearers. He wishes to guide and counsel them. He has a heart toward them like a father has to his children.

Ancient kings did this as well. In a letter from the time of Moses, a client king complains that his people are under pressure from an enemy. Note the kinship language: "Tell the king of Alashiya, my father; the king of Ugarit your son says: I fall at my father's feet. . . . Father, the enemy ships have come. They have burned down my villages and have done evil things to the land. Does my father not know . . . ?"[6] The client king calls the more powerful king "father." He calls himself "your son." He's expressing the dynamics of their relationship. Fathers should protect their sons. Sons respect their fathers.

It's not just kings who used kinship language to talk about their patron-client relationships. When Naaman's servants come to him, they call him "father" (2 Kings 5:13). Likewise, the king of Israel is recognizing the

---

[4]Klaas Dijkstra, *Life and Loyalty: A Study in the Socio-religious Culture of Syria and Mesopotamia in the Greco-Roman Period Based on Epigraphical Evidence* (Leiden, Netherlands: Brill, 1995), 26.

[5]King Abdullah II, *Our Last Best Chance: The Pursuit of Peace in a Time of Peril* (London: Penguin Books, 2012), 70. While these relationships may be based in treaties, we are using *patron-client* to describe the asymmetrical, mutual support relationship that exists. We find limiting the patron-client terminology only ever to describing relationships with no treaty can be a little too theoretical.

[6]Marc Van de Mieroop, *The Eastern Mediterranean in the Age of Ramesses II* (Oxford: Wiley-Blackwell, 2009), 244.

stronger party (Elisha) has just given him a gift (enemy soldiers) and calls him "father" (2 Kings 6:21). Both Naaman's servants and King Jehoram are using kinship language to show reverence and respect to the greater party.

New Testament writers used shepherding and kinship language to talk about the patronage dynamics that existed between church leaders and their flock. For example, when Paul writes to the Corinthian church, he calls himself their "father" (1 Cor 4:15).[7] When he speaks about Timothy, Paul says, "But you know that Timothy has proved himself, because as a son with his father he has served with me in the work of the gospel" (Phil 2:22). Paul sees the relationship as being the same as a kinship relationship.

Patronage was widespread and often went without being said in the ancient world, and like modern Arabs, New Testament writers also left it unsaid. Like modern collectivists, they used metaphors (father-children and shepherd-flock) to describe dynamics that are to be at work in the church. Also like modern collectivists, the Greco-Roman world used such a wide range of terms to talk about patronage because patronage extended into so many areas of the culture. Pastors are not simply to call themselves shepherds. They are to shepherd the flock (Acts 20:28, Jn 21:16; 1 Pet 5:2-4). The metaphor explains the way they are to act. Leaders are not to call themselves fathers. They are to father the family of believers. Patronage is the structure, but they use metaphors to speak about it. Those earthly metaphors came with their own vocabulary, which New Testament writers commandeered to describe heavenly concepts.

GRACE, FAITH, AND PATRONAGE

One of the most common terms Greeks used to speak about the reciprocal patronage system was *charis*. They used *charis* to refer to the way patrons gave benefits to their clients. They also used *charis* to refer to the gifts themselves, the benefaction, such as aid, protection, funds, assistance, or whatever. They also used *charis* to refer to the way clients reciprocated

---

[7]What about Jesus' command to call no one father (Mt 23:9)? He is condemning the current shepherds of Israel, the patrons (fathers) and teachers. He says they should only have one patron and teacher. As with other teachings of Jesus, this is likely hyperbole to make his point.

with gratitude. *Charis* could be used to speak of the giver, the gift, and the recipients' gift in response. When an ancient Greek person heard the word *charis*, they would naturally think of the flow of patronage all around them.[8] *Charis* was what was constantly being passed between the three graces as they danced. It was what held them in the circle of dance.

Greek speakers also used *pistis* to talk about patron-client relationships. *Pistis* can mean "trust," "loyalty," "faith," or "faithfulness" in English, depending on the context. *Pistis* described the way a patron was faithful or loyal in acting to benefit their clients.[9] *Pistis* referred to the way clients trusted that their patron would indeed care for them and provide them with benefits. When a client expressed *pistis* to/in/for a patron, it meant the client trusted that the patron could (and would) provide what they had promised.[10] When clients trusted their patron, they were loyal to them and didn't look for others to provide. In this way, *pistis* could also carry a sense of a client's loyalty to their patron, driven by trusting in the patron to provide.

Charis and *pistis* frequently occur in Paul's writings, where they are translated "grace" (*charis*) and "faith" (*pistis*). Paul commandeers the everyday terms Mediterranean people used to talk about patronage to help explain the new relationship believers have with God, through Jesus Christ. To explain the mysterious salvation of God, Paul portrays it as a relationship they understood. When Paul wants to describe the way God showed kindness and faithfulness to us by giving us his Son, he used *charis*, the way a patron generously chose to have favor on clients and bestow gifts on them. For example, Paul writes, "For if the many died by the trespass of the one man, how much more did God's grace

---

[8]David A. deSilva, *Honor, Patronage, Kinship and Purity: Unlocking New Testament Culture* (Downers Grove, IL: IVP Academic, 2000), 104-5; James. D. G. Dunn, *The Theology of Paul the Apostle* (Grand Rapids, MI: Eerdmans, 2006), 321.

[9]Erik Heen, "Pistis," in *Routledge Encyclopedia of Ancient Religions*, ed. Eric Orlin (New York: Routledge, 2016), 728. Engberg-Pedersen notes that Seneca did use *fides* (the Latin parallel to *pistis*) to refer to the client's response, but not nearly as often as Paul did. See Troels Engberg-Pedersen, "Gift-Giving and Friendship: Seneca and Paul in Romans 1–8 on the Logic of God's Χάρις and Its Human Response," *Harvard Theological Review* 101, no. 1 (2008): 39n44.

[10]David A. deSilva, *4 Maccabees*, Guides to Apocrypha and Pseudepigrapha (Sheffield: Sheffield Academic Press, 1998), 128.

[*charis*] and the gift that came by the grace [*chariti*] of the one man, Jesus Christ, overflow to the many!" (Rom 5:15). When Paul thinks about the way God is faithful to his people and continues to care for and protect them, he picks up the word *pistis* to speak about "God's faithfulness" (Rom 3:3; 1 Cor 1:9; 10:13).

When Paul wants to describe the way Christians trust in God alone, in the light of having received his favor and gifts, he speaks of their *pistis*. For example, Paul writes, "to the one who does not work but trusts [*pisteuonti*] God who justifies the ungodly, their faith [*pistis*] is credited as righteousness" (Rom 4:5). Everyone understood. Christians trust in the faithfulness of God, like clients trust in the faithfulness of their patron. This was normal language. Yet, when we strip these words from their original patronage context, we can lose some of Paul's meaning.

As a modern Western Christian, I understand *charis* (grace) fairly well. My pastors and teachers drilled into me that *charis*, grace, is the unmerited favor, undeserved kindness, which God bestows on me. Just as Diocles, our imaginary patron in Philippi, wasn't obligated to rescue Belen but chose to, so God was not required to rescue me. He chose to benefit me. It really is grace, and God has lavished his grace on us (Eph 1:7-8). That part of the image I understand.

For a first-century Mediterranean, the appropriate response to God lavishing *charis* on us is naturally *pistis*, faith. My understanding of faith needed a better understanding of the context of first-century patronage. A client's faith (*pistis*) wasn't believing a list of concepts about the patron but trusting in the patron. Paul expects us to "trust" or "have faith" in what God has indeed done. A natural result of this trust in what God has done for us is that we stop searching around for other patrons or ways of gaining protection. We stop trying to somehow earn favor in God's sight. We have no need for these things because we have *already* received *charis* from God. We are therefore loyal (*pistis*) to God. We give him our allegiance, as opposed to other patrons.

While more recently people are becoming aware of the role of *pistis* in patron-client relationships, it's becoming more common to hear people talking about faith as allegiance.[11] This can be overplayed. First, in ancient patronage, a client would not have understood a question such as, "Do you trust your patron or are you loyal to them?" It wasn't either trust or allegiance. As part of receiving the gift, a client didn't decide between trusting the patron or being loyal to them. They might have insisted these were the same thing! Are we saved by assenting to ideas about Jesus or by loyalty to Jesus? The answer is yes. A client *believed* certain things about the patron. Belen believed Diocles was trustworthy and able to rescue him. But the client was also expected to be *loyal*. Belen now baked his bread for Diocles. So also, as followers of Christ, we believe certain things, "that Christ died for our sins according to the Scriptures, that he was buried, that he was raised on the third day according to the Scriptures, and that he appeared to Cephas, and then to the Twelve" (1 Cor 15:3-5). Trusting in this leads us to allegiance to God. Now our lives revolve around our new lord, king, shepherd, and benefactor. We stop searching for others, because we have trusted in what Christ has done for us. Like Belen, we don't bake bread for any other god. Like Belen, every morning we should line up at our patron's door to receive his benefaction and to ask what he might require of us this day. We do not do this to try to earn favor. We do this because we trust we have already been given favor in Christ. We are part of his household. *Pistis*, our trust in what God has done, naturally means we put all our dependence and trust in him. Rather than running around trying to please God, we put all our trust and allegiance in the confidence that he has already bestowed favor on us in Christ.

WE NEED TO READ PAUL IN HIS
FIRST-CENTURY CONTEXT

You have probably heard that the key to biblical interpretation is context, context, context. Well, it is. Paul uses patronage to explain salvation. God provides us *charis*, which we translate "grace." Paul says we are to respond with *pistis*, which we translate "faith." These are great translations, but to

---

[11]See, e.g., Matthew Bates, *Salvation by Allegiance Alone: Rethinking Faith, Works, and the Gospel of Jesus the King* (Grand Rapids, MI: Baker Academic, 2017).

understand better what Paul meant, we need to remember the context: patronage. When put together (grace + faith), those signify a patronage relationship. God provides us the gift of salvation, and we respond by trusting in it: "For it is by grace [*charis*] you have been saved, through faith [*pistis*]," Paul writes, "and this is not from yourselves, it is the gift of God" (Eph 2:8-9). The New Testament took everyday ideas that everyone understood to explain the spiritual truths of God. Even though we didn't deserve it (Rom 5:8), God is the most generous of all patrons and lavished undeserved gifts on us (Eph 1:7-8). If we choose to accept his benefaction by joining his household (Eph 2:19), showing it by trust and loyalty, then we can face every day with confidence, knowing our Patron is ready give (Heb 4:16).

Yet, Paul's patronage language can cause a problem for us individualists in the West. First, most of the time we don't even recognize he's talking about patronage. After all, *grace* and *faith* in English have nothing to do with patronage. We think of them as purely theological terms. Understandings of patronage in Paul's world are slowly catching on in the West (this book is one example). Yet, while we need to be aware of the context in which Paul wrote, we still need to be careful to read what Paul himself said, in that context. When people learn that Paul used the language of patronage to talk about grace and faith, they can then simply take the way patronage worked among people in the first century and read it into what Paul is saying about God. This can lead to a significant misreading of Paul. In order to understand Paul in his context, it is important for us to recognize two things. First, that Paul drew on the context of patronage as one metaphor to explain the gospel. Second, Paul had something very different to say about the way God acted as a patron.

Seneca criticized some first-century patrons because they were not giving benefits to those they could, and they would stop if people were not grateful and deserving clients. That was not the behavior of an ideal patron. Paul would have agreed. When Paul talks about grace and faith, he does not mean God acts like a fallen first-century patron who only gives grace to those he feels deserve it because they are loyal to him. The better we understand first-century patronage, the better we can see where what Paul says about God also breaks with the patronage mold around him in his world. First, Paul says we have all *already* fallen short of being deserving clients. God chose to give us the gift while we were still sinners. This shows the basis of his love for us. "But God demonstrates his own love for us in this: While we were still sinners, Christ died for us" (Rom 5:8). So Paul has shown that Abraham was credited righteousness, not because he was perfectly loyal in the ensuing relationship, but because he trusted in God's promise (Rom 4:18-22). The key to understanding Paul is not to focus on the characteristics of the clients but the patron. As clients we are no better (and sometimes worse) than a typical client. God, however, is not like the typical patron. God generously gives patronage to all, including undeserving and treacherous clients, because he can and wants to.

We have seen that either party could initiate the patron-client relationship. When someone approached a human patron, they weren't sure he or she would choose to give them benefaction. Our imaginary Philippian baker Belen hoped Diocles would. When someone wrote a letter to ask for a favor, they would assure the reader that they would be grateful. They were hoping their promise to be a good client would persuade the patron to benefit them. We have already fallen short of deserving God's patronage. The good news (of the New Testament) is that it's the other way around with God. We are not hoping God will decide we are worthy clients. Paul has explained, "But God *demonstrates his own love for us* in this: While we were still sinners, Christ died for us" (Rom 5:8). The cross shows us God has acted in history to benefit and save us and start a relationship with us as our protector. God initiated the relationship. We simply choose whether *we want* to accept his gift and join his household.

Second, those who trust in God's offer of patronage to them—whoever accepts the *charis*—enter into a relationship with him. Grace and faith are the language of *relationship*. This is not a case of one day trusting in a patron and then spending the rest of our lives absent of the relationship and the patron's presence in our lives. That would not be patronage at all.

Like patronage, trusting in grace is not a one-off transaction but the beginning of an ongoing relationship. The gift had strings attached, to tie us together. Just as the relationship began in trust in an unmerited gift of benefaction, it continues on this basis too. Paul envisions—and established—communities of people who trust in God's ongoing patronage to them. *Patronage created new households.* It creates kinship bonds. Paul expects this new network to grow in strength and transform all other alliances. We will see later that households have boundaries, and boundaries define values. Paul insists on this as well.

Finally, *pistis* is slowly being understood as not meaning "believing in a list of doctrines" but "loyalty to God as our patron and Jesus as King." The mistake that remains is that this new understanding is still being squeezed into an individualist framework. I (as an individual) am being loyal to and trusting in Jesus. But grace and faith are not about me having an individual, isolated relationship with God. Faith means swearing allegiance to Jesus and his household. It isn't "me and Jesus." By God's grace, I am made part of God's household. I have not earned it by being a deserving client, nor am I part of it because I share Abraham's blood (kinship). I have been brought into it through trusting in God's grace to me, even when I was an undeserving sinner. I don't invite Jesus into my heart. I join his flock. I become part of his we.

The good news is that in Christ's life and death and resurrection, God has demonstrated to us—all of us—that despite our sin and lostness, our lack of faithfulness to him, God is more generous than we could ever have imagined. Understanding patronage tones down a common evangelical emphasis on needing to underscore our unworthiness.[12] For Paul, conversion didn't require an existential crisis. It is as this-worldly as it is otherworldly.

Rather than reject us, God has acted to benefit us. He sent his one and only son to save us. The shepherd took the responsibility to restore his flock. He calls out to them. The cross calls out to us of God's action to

---

[12]"You are more sinful and flawed than you ever dared believe, but more accepted and loved than you ever dared hope." See Tim Keller, https://timothykeller.com/intro, accessed February 29, 2020. I like the expression, but it puts a strong emphasis on our lack of deserving.

restore us. It tells us the relationship he wants to have with us. It is the same message to every single person in the world. We see it, and we choose whether we want to put our trust in this patron and join his flock. If we don't trust in him, we aren't his. If we do, we are. We can make this decision based on the character of God we see revealed to us through his actions toward us in sending his son.

6

BROKERAGE IN THE BIBLICAL WORLD

I Get By with a ~~Little~~ Lot of Help from My Friends

CAR CRASHES IN THE MIDDLE EAST CAN BE quite the spectacle. When I first moved there, I wondered about the crowds that gathered quickly following a crash. Everyone seemed to be standing around, talking excitedly, pointing this way and that. Some were on the phone. More were rushing to get there. Cars pulled over, and others got out. It is quite the scene.

I later learned what was happening was brokerage or mediation. The people gathering were trying to solve the problem in the interests of everyone. If my car bumped into yours and we can figure out that someone from your extended family knows someone who knows someone from mine, then we can often find a better resolution than waiting for the police to arrive. This will save everybody money. (This is good for both sides.) If we can't do that, then we each will try to gather the oldest or most honorable or best-connected person (at least to the police) to the scene. This person is there to help represent and mediate on behalf of his friend of a friend (whom they often call "someone close to me") to ensure that his friend is treated fairly. Someone else will be doing the same for the other side. In my experience, folks generally just want to make sure what happens is fair.[1]

Mediators were an essential part of the biblical world. When a problem arose, often one side would seek a mediator to represent their interests to

---

[1]Of course, rascals and manipulators exist there, just as they do in my Florida neighborhood.

the other side. The best mediators had a connection to both sides. Take this familiar story, for example. At one point in their history, the Jews were an oppressed member of the Persian Empire. While in Persia, they run afoul of some influential people, who persuade the Persian king: "There is a certain people dispersed among the peoples in all the provinces of your kingdom who keep themselves separate. . . . It is not in the king's best interests to tolerate them. If it pleases the king, let a decree be issued to destroy them" (Esther 3:8-9). The "certain people" are the Jews. So when the king agrees, the Jews are in peril. Their response is not to lodge a formal complaint with the king. That would make things worse. They would seem to be a complaining people and clearly worthy of everything they were going to get. Instead, they seek a mediator. Esther was raised a Jew and has now joined the harem of the Persian king—not necessarily the usual career path for a Jewish girl. She is, though, the best option the Jews have for mediating with the king. Now, the Jews need someone who can influence Esther to mediate for them. They choose Mordecai, who raised her. Mordecai sends a copy of the edict and an explanation of their peril in order to urge her "to go into the king's presence to beg for mercy and to plead with him for her people" (Esther 4:8). Of their available options, she is the best mediator (if she is willing) because she is close to both parties. She belongs to the Jews *and* to the Persian king.

This story illustrates a vital element of ancient collectivist society that differs from most individualist cultures, where people are (allegedly) viewed equally. When everyone is equal, if I use someone to try to gain influence in my favor, that stinks of unfairness. In fact, we can argue it is unjust. Yet, in a world where equality doesn't exist, one side usually is exerting pressure on those under them. Finding someone to advocate upward was usually a good idea. A mediator was seeking justice for those who could not gain it otherwise.

When Job has a complaint against God, he has a problem. He and God are not equals (obviously). Job needed a mediator because of the massive power gap between himself and God. This problem doesn't just apply to someone complaining against God. It was the common plight of the ancient world. One side usually had the power advantage. Unfortunately for Job, the usual solution, a mediator, wasn't available to sort out his problem. He laments:

> How can mere mortals prove their innocence before God?
> Though they wished to dispute with him, . . .
> If only there were someone to mediate between us,
>   someone to bring us together. (Job 9:2-3, 33)

This passage in Job shows that the *normal* solution was to find someone to mediate.

DESCRIBING THE INDESCRIBABLE

In biblical texts, the role of this mediating person is almost never spelled out. That's because the dynamic went without being said. In scholarly discussions, this person is often termed a broker. We will use both terms, *mediator* and *broker*, interchangeably to describe this role. This mediating or brokering role was such a foundational way the world worked that people rarely explained it. We see the mediator at work in stories such as the book of Esther, even though the writer never explains explicitly that Esther is a broker between the king and Mordecai. The author didn't feel the need to point it out. It is obvious. It goes without being said. The king doesn't demand that the accused party come forward, and Mordecai never asks to meet the king. He doesn't need to. Each side works through a mediator. The broker travels between the two parties. In fact, brokers were the bridge between the two parties.

Mediation or brokerage was used not just to solve disputes or to relieve persecution. The English word *mediation* could suggest it focuses on problems, while *brokerage* sounds financial. Mediation or brokerage in collectivist cultures is used in just about every sphere of life. When I as an individualist want to purchase something, I go directly to the seller and negotiate myself. It is an impersonal transaction: "It's just business." In fact, I like to keep business separate from friends. I don't want a personal relationship with the cashier at the department store. Abroad, by contrast, sellers give a better deal to people they know than to some stranger in the street. This is why foreigners pay more than a local. To an individualist, that seems unfair. We should all be treated the same. But my Eastern friends say it with pride: "We look out for our own, as we should." So when I am in a collective culture and I want to make an important purchase, I seek out someone who knows me *and* who also knows the seller. Books about mediation will usually describe a movement from buyer to mediator to seller. It's useful for explaining the basic idea, but such a straight line rarely happens. It depends whom you know and whom they know. It is more common for me to know someone who knows someone who knows the seller.

So it is with Esther and Mordecai. The Jewish people use Mordecai as their mediator. Esther uses Hathak, one of the king's eunuchs who attended her, as a mediator with Mordecai (Esther 4:9-17). We might miss Hathak in the story. Mordecai speaks via Hathak to Esther, who mediates with the king. Several layers of mediators are involved. Some have small roles (such as Hathak), while some have very big roles with a lot of influence on others involved (such as Mordecai and Esther). In this way, complex networks of mediators and brokers linked people in the ancient world together in a way that is hard for us individualists to imagine. We said brokers were bridges over which communications passed; we could also say brokers were the strings that created a spider's web of connections among collectivists.

The middleman. When I wanted to rent an apartment in Jordan, I didn't go to the owner. I found a friend who knew someone who knew the owner, who spoke to the owner for me. He helped us work out some of the negotiation, preparing both sides and passing on how the other felt about things. The result of his work was a successful deal. I haven't spoken with the landlord since. All my communication with the landlord passes across the mediating bridge of the person who set up the deal.

When Randy and I met in Beirut to start this book, I used Airbnb to rent him an apartment for a week. Nothing seems more individualist than Airbnb. Yet when Randy contacted the owner for arrival details, he found himself emailing with "the owner's friend." He had not offended the owner. It is just ingrained in their culture to use a mediator, even for Airbnb. To most individualists, this seems too complicated and too much bother. "Just sell the dumb thing!" I insist. Or, "Just rent the flat!" To my Middle Eastern friends, this isn't bother; it's instinct. It occurs without thought. In Indonesia, most of the business I conducted used a *pengantar*. The word means someone who accompanies you or leads you to someone else. It was hard to translate but even harder to conduct business without one. The *pengantar* was a broker. I wish I had understood that sooner.

While individualists may complain about the middleman, collectivists complain about a different problem: finding a good mediator. A number of years ago a cartoon aired on Arab TV. In the cartoon, a man discovers a genie in a lamp. The genie is lazy. He offers the man only one wish. So, the man asks the genie to grant him a very well-connected mediator. The genie scratches his head and offers him millions of dollars, an easier task than finding him such a powerful mediator. Eventually, the genie does bring him a powerful mediator. The man proceeds to ask this mediator for favors, which he is able to provide far better than the genie. In fact, the mediator even intervenes with the genie to persuade him to grant the man more wishes. As in the West, cartoons often comment on cultural values. Here the story illustrates that having a powerful mediator can get things done and provide you with advantages, but it can be difficult to find one.[2]

We see brokerage happening in the ancient world as well. Pliny the Younger lived a generation after Jesus. He was contacted by someone (of lower status) he knew. This "friend" of Pliny wants to buy some property. This friend is probably a client of Pliny (the dynamic of patronage at work). Pliny attempts to provide this benefit to his client. Pliny doesn't personally own what the client needs, so as his patron, Pliny finds another way to help. Pliny mediates for him with someone who does own it. To do this, Pliny writes to yet another friend of his who knows the owner of the property.

---

[2] This cartoon is also critiquing the role of mediators. Those who have a very well-connected mediator can be above the system and have privileged access, against what is fair. See the critique by Ekkardt A. Sonntag, "Jesus, the Good Wasta? Reading the Epistle to the Hebrews in Light of a Middle-Eastern Social Phenomenon" (PhD diss., Vrije Universiteit Amsterdam, 2015), 60-61.

So we have a buyer asking his patron (Pliny) to mediate; then Pliny reaches out to his friend, who mediates on Pliny's behalf with the seller. Often, as in this situation, one gift a patron provides is the connection to someone else. Just as kinship and patronage overlap, so also do patronage and brokerage. Sometimes all three can overlap. It's possible some of those in Pliny's story were kinfolk.

When Pliny brokers for his client, he becomes the bridge over which the transaction occurs. He is therefore a patron and a broker. He brokers for his client with his friend (who is likely a patron of the seller) via a letter: "My friend Tranquillus has an inclination to purchase a small farm, of which, as I am informed, an acquaintance of yours intends to dispose. I beg you would endeavor he may have it upon reasonable terms. . . . I mention these particulars to let you see how much he will be obliged to me as I shall to you if you help me."[3] Pliny points out that each person will be appropriately grateful and will be tied, "obliged," by the appropriate strings, including, of course, even Pliny, who will be "obliged" by his sense of gratitude to his friend. Gratitude and the resulting sense of obligation joined people together and oils the gears of brokerage.

We see the structures of patronage and brokerage are muddled together. Pliny is a patron to the buyer. He provides him with a valuable gift: connection to others. Meanwhile, Pliny becomes a client of the one he asks for help, although they may well be peers, or Pliny may even be superior in rank. Is this patronage or brokerage? Both. Patronage is one relationship, but it often falls into a network of relationships where patrons and clients act as brokers. The ancient world comprised many different patron-client relationships, which usually connected into a network. Furthermore, there were multiple networks. Brokers were the bridges. They linked relationships and even networks together. Pliny's letter offers a glimpse into one of these networks and how he navigates it to gain benefits. Reciprocity, services, and gratitude flow all through the multiple relationships in the network, with brokers as the connections.

---

[3]Pliny, *Epistle* 1.24. We are indebted to Tricia Brown for pointing out this text in *Spirit in the Writings of John: Johannine Pneumatology in Social-Scientific Perspective*, Journal for the Study of the New Testament Supplement Series 253 (London: T&T Clark, 2003), 29-30.

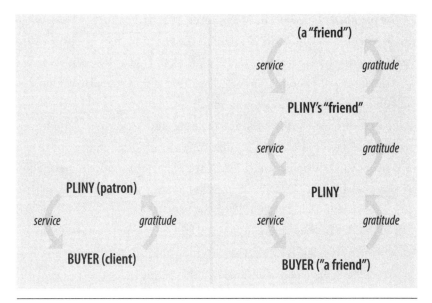

Figure 6.1. The patron-client relationship within the wider network of reciprocal relationships

A friend or an older brother (whether or not they really are). There were many ways of referring to broker-mediators in the ancient Mediterranean world. One technical Greek term came from the word *middle*, but people very often referred to brokers using other more relational and euphemistic terms such as *friend, older brother,* or *a relative*, such as Pliny's "friend" Tranquillus or the "acquaintance" of his letter recipient.[4] The point is to indicate relationship, since brokerage is a deeply relational matter. The result, though, is that the patron, the client, and the broker could all be referred to as a "friend." In the New Testament, the word *friend* rarely (if ever) means what we modern individualists mean by the term.

Collective cultures deeply honor people who broker. Individualists don't often use brokers in everyday life. In fact, we tend to be suspicious of them, often using derogatory terms to refer to them, such as *middleman*. We feel accomplished when we can cut out the middleman. That's the last thing most Mediterranean or Asian folks (or biblical characters) would want to do (1 Tim 2:6). In fact, the work of brokers plays a primary role in many biblical stories.

---

[4]*Mesitēs* derives from the word *mesos* ("in the middle"). There were other terms as well.

The purpose of mediation. We will see in biblical stories of brokerage the following key elements of mediation. First, the best mediators are strongly connected to both parties. People would rarely seek out someone who did not have a connection with the other side. After all, a bridge that isn't connected to both sides isn't much of a bridge. On the other hand, someone who does fit the bill often feels cultural pressure to play the mediating role. He or she will recognize they are a logical choice. They will recognize, too, an opportunity to help their friends and to grow even stronger relational bonds. As with patronage and kinship relations, obligation and gratitude play key roles in brokerage.

A second key ingredient is that an effective mediator needs to be trusted by both sides. It's their trusted status that allows them to mediate. As Westerners, we can misunderstand this to mean neutrality or objectivity. A British friend of mine was once placed in a difficult discussion, mediating between one of his local friends and some other locals. My British friend was trying to be impartial and moderate the discussion. Afterward his local friend was really angry with him: "If you were my friend you would have been defending me." Objectivity is a myth common to the modern West but not expected in most of the world. After all, Esther wasn't expected to be neutral on the subject. She is a Jew, and her people are in grave peril. Nonetheless, both Mordecai and the Persian king trust Esther. Because both parties trust her, Queen Esther is able to broker. She is a trusted bridge.

Third, the mediator works hard to clarify the exchange, the mutual benefit to both parties of the proposed resolution, or sale, or whatever is the goal of their mediation. Individualists can misunderstand this as merely negotiating an exchange, whereupon the bridge disappears. No, the mediator creates a relationship between the two parties. It is never just an impersonal transaction. Brokerage produces a bridge that lasts. If the relationship between the two parties becomes strained, the mediator will maintain or repair it. Brokers are the relational link from the beginning and ongoing. Effective brokerage results not only in the immediate goal, but also in a new or restored longer-term relationship.

EXAMPLES OF MEDIATION/BROKERAGE
IN THE OLD TESTAMENT

Although a specific term for a mediator isn't used, brokerage permeates the stories of the Old Testament.[5] When Sarah dies, Abraham needs a place to bury her. He wants to buy a plot of land from Ephron, son of Zohar. Abraham does not ask Ephron directly. Instead, he asks a group of leaders (Hittites) to mediate (Gen 23). Although Abraham is recognized as a "mighty prince" among them (Gen 23:6), he still uses a broker to arrange the purchase of the land. Everyone involved assumes things will work better if a mediator is found. The mediator(s) travels back and forth until the purchase was settled and later works to maintain the relationship between Abraham and Ephron if issues arose (as is often the case).

Abraham himself also serves as a mediator on occasion. Abraham and Lot are both wealthy men with large flocks and herds. "Their possessions were so great that they were not able to stay together. And quarrelling arose between Abram's herders and Lot's" (Gen 13:6-7).

This story is ripe for modern misunderstanding. We might assume Abraham "owned" all those things and the herders were employees, or perhaps that all the herders are relatives working in the family business. We see immediately that this is not the case. Lot isn't working for Abraham. He wouldn't be the only relative who wasn't. Their relationship is much more akin to patronage (with distant kinship ties). Many if not most of the herders were relatives in some way of *both* Abraham *and* Lot. Abraham was the "father" (patron) so everything "belonged" to Abraham, but a herder would likely have insisted his particular flock was his. While Lot was a relative and dependent on Abraham, it is clear that Lot's herders did not feel connected to Abraham's. Abraham and Lot were both patrons (fathers) over large groups. Now conflict has erupted between these groups. How will this be solved?

Abraham goes to Lot. They work out a solution. We might be tempted to read this story as if Abraham and Lot hung out together; after all, they

---

[5]Albrecht Oepke, "μεσίτης," in *Theological Dictionary of the New Testament*, ed. Gerhard Kittel and Gerhard Friedrich, trans. Geoffrey W. Bromiley (Grand Rapids, MI: Eerdmans, 1964–1976), 4:614.

are relatives. We should not imagine that Abraham overheard Lot's herders arguing with his and brought the matter up over dinner. Rather, the herders had a problem. They sought a mediator. Abraham is perfect because he is high-ranking, he is their patron, and he is close to Lot, who has similar influence over the other side. Abraham is received by Lot, who listens to his proposal and agrees to follow it. If the conflict were with other herders (such as the Canaanites or Perizzites, Gen 13:7), then Abraham would have negotiated with their patron. As we noted, in the ancient world, mediation was often mixed with patronage and in this case, kinship. It is very unlikely this was the only time there was an issue between Abraham's herders and others. It's likely the Bible tells us about this particular one only in order to explain how and why Lot ended up in Sodom, a long way from Abraham, and why Abraham later felt obligated to rescue him.

MEDIATION/BROKERAGE IN THE NEW TESTAMENT

We find brokerage often in the New Testament writings, including the Gospels, Acts, and the Epistles. Sometimes the writers explicitly point out brokerage-mediation to explain a person's role. Other times they don't. One of the ways the New Testament writers speak about Jesus is as a broker-mediator. Paul writes, "For there is one God and one mediator between God and mankind, the man Christ Jesus" (1 Tim 2:5).

A centurion needs help, so he finds a "friend." When a centurion's slave is desperately ill, he wants Jesus' help. He doesn't go to Jesus directly. We should not be surprised that he sends mediators:

> There a centurion's servant, whom his master valued highly, was sick and about to die. The centurion heard of Jesus and sent some elders of the Jews to him, asking him to come and heal his servant. When they came to Jesus, they pleaded earnestly with him, "This man deserves to have you do this, because he loves our nation and has built our synagogue." So Jesus went with them. (Lk 7:2-6)

The centurion considers the Jewish elders to be good mediators because (1) they have a connection to him—in fact, they are indebted to him, for he has helped them by building their synagogue; (2) they are of good status—they are elders in their community; and (3) they are connected to Jesus—they are Jews. What we are supposed to notice—what went without being said but that Luke *expects* us as readers to notice—is that these elders actually do a bad job of mediating. Although they "pleaded earnestly," their argument is flawed in several ways.

First, they are assuming that the centurion is of higher status than Jesus and that the centurion's good deeds must compel Jesus to act: "this man deserves to have you do this because he loves our nation and has built our synagogue" (Lk 7:4-5). Second, these elders are clients of the centurion (praising him as good clients do). But Luke expects us to notice they are treating Jesus as their peer and thus asking him to become a fellow client of the centurion. If Jesus is willing to help, then they naturally *expect* Jesus to go to the centurion's house. As we saw, clients show up when summoned. As Luke's readers, though, we know Jesus will not consider himself a client indebted to the centurion. Thus, as readers, we should not expect Jesus to go. After all, who is this man to summon Jesus? Nor should Jesus care that this Gentile paid for a synagogue. Moreover, Jesus will not feel obligated to obey some local elders. Luke sets us up to expect Jesus to refuse.

Luke's story continues to unfold in unexpected ways. First, Jesus goes with the elders after all. Second, the centurion, unlike the elders, does not treat Jesus as his client. He addresses Jesus as *kyrie* (lord, sir), a term that is never used to address inferior parties such as clients. Rather, *kyrie* is how a client would address a patron. Nothing in the story unfolds as the culture might expect. The normal plot is reversed—a common device of Luke. Though the Jewish elders view the Centurion as their patron, the centurion acts like a potential client of Jesus. When the centurion hears that Jesus is on the way to his house, he sends another group of "friends" with a message that Jesus ought not to enter his house, because he himself argues he is *not* deserving. Rather, he sees himself as a potential client, asking mediators to go to a potential patron to seek his help. The Jewish elders had misunderstood the relationship between the parties (Lk 7:6).

The centurion recognizes Jesus is of higher status. He also knows Jesus has the authority to heal from afar—something else the elders failed to see. In the midst of the elders' misunderstandings, which we are expected to notice, Luke makes his point about the centurion's exceptional faith (Lk 7:9-10). He accepts Jesus' gift (*charis*) and, as a good client, shows *pistis* (trust) in Jesus.

A wedding needs help, so they find a "friend," who asks her son. Weddings are a big deal in the modern Middle East. They are paid for by the groom's family and so are often (mis)considered as a sign of how much the groom's family loves and values their son and his new wife. Given this common view, people remember a bad or cheap wedding for a long time. In my travels in the Mediterranean, I have heard lots of neighbors gossiping about how little someone's wedding cost, such as how the wedding venue was not a five-star hotel. If the groom's own family doesn't respect the couple, so the reasoning goes, then there must be some valid reason. Perhaps there is some hidden vice or flaw in the groom or bride. I have heard stories of someone missing out on a good job or an important promotion because of a cheap wedding. The employer assumes the inexpensive wedding was a visible sign of some hidden issue. All to say, a wedding is about more than just the nuptials of two people; it is a community event that usually results in a community's verdict on the marriage and the importance of the families in the community.

Jesus' mother has some role in a wedding in Cana, less than ten miles from Nazareth. Likely she is related in a significant way to the family. Jesus is invited and brings along his disciples, perhaps as unexpected guests. It may be for this reason that the family runs out of wine and Mary involves Jesus. We don't know. But whatever the reason, this is more than a catering mishap. The social standing of the family is at risk. It may be thought the family is stingy (remember the importance of generosity) or that they don't really value the bride and groom. Mary acts as a broker and comes to Jesus to ask him to help.

Jesus responds, "Woman, why do you involve me?" (Jn 2:4). The phrase is literally "What to me and to you?" It is an odd comment that

English translations try to smooth out. Much ink has been spilled in commentaries to make sense of Jesus' response. It may be linked back to another time God miraculously provided drink (2 Kings 3), where the same phrase is used by the prophet Elisha. In any case, Jesus does miraculously intervene. Mary successfully brokers between the family and Jesus. Mary brokers not to resolve a catering snafu but to rescue the reputation of the families in the eyes of the community (and perhaps for any fault from her family, Jesus, bringing a dozen extra guests).

CONCLUSION: KINSMEN, PATRONS, AND BROKERS

Brokerage was so fundamental to New Testament society that it didn't have to be talked about; it went without being said. Remembering this helps us avoid misreading, such as seeing apparent contradictions between different accounts of the same story. For example in Mark, James and John ask to sit on the right and left hand of Jesus in his coming kingdom (Mk 10:35-39). In Matthew it is their mother who asks (Mt 20:20-22). That is, Matthew mentions a mediator and Mark doesn't. The mother is asking on *behalf* of her sons, so in the end the sons are the ones making the request. Matthew mentions the mediator; Mark lets it go without being said. Mark and Matthew are both recounting the story accurately.

Likewise, the way Matthew tells the story of the centurion with the sick servant (Lk 7) gives the impression the centurion went directly to Jesus without a mediator (Mt 8). Matthew has simplified the story. For Matthew, the role of a mediator went *entirely* without being said. His Eastern readers wouldn't have been surprised to learn from Luke's account that there was a mediator, nor surprised that Matthew left out such a minor detail. The authors likely included or excluded these details to support the themes they were trying to communicate. Luke likely includes it in his account of the centurion to reinforce the reversal theme. Perhaps Matthew includes the mediator in his story about James and John as a way of offering commentary on the brothers' motives: they wanted the seats of honor. Nonetheless, they could find no better mediator than their own mom.

Let's return to our story of Belen the imaginary Philippian baker from chapter three. As authors, we must confess to oversimplifying the illustration in the earlier chapter. In his original plight, Belen would not have just gotten in the back of the line at Diocles's house. He would have found a client of Diocles to mediate for him and to tell Diocles his plight. Once the relationship was formed, then Belen would line up with the other clients. So now let's return to Belen and his barley loaves, which he now bakes for Diocles and his household in gratitude for his patronage. Barley sellers all belonged to their (barley) trade guild, just as Belen belonged to the bakers' trade guild. The bakers may have referred to their group as "the worshipers of Fornax," but they were a functional trade guild, just as the barley sellers may have been "followers of the goddess Alphito."[6] Ancients could not simply move to a town and open a business. The necessary relationships with all the correct guilds were required. Thus, Paul is able to work as a tentmaker only where he is able to get access to the local guild, mediating a connection. Luke implies such mediation by explicitly mentioning Aquila and Priscilla (Acts 18:2-3). Let us suppose Belen is told one day by Cyprian, his barley seller, that all the barley sellers are doubling the price of barley. Belen is devastated. What can he do? The only thing he *can* do is seek the help of his patron.[7] The following morning, after waiting in line, he tells Diocles the news. Diocles asks some questions, and then assures Belen he will help him. Diocles must now mediate on behalf of his client. At his next dinner party, Diocles invites his peer, Septimus, to dinner. Septimus happens to be the friend (a.k.a. patron) of Cyprian, the barley seller. After a fine dinner and chit-chat, Diocles mentions to Septimus that he has a friend who has a problem. His friend is going to face true hardship because the price of barley has doubled. Septimus expresses his deep sorrow and notes that he also has a friend who is experiencing true difficulty because he cannot sell his barley for enough profit.

---

[6]Alphito was often portrayed as an old woman with white hair (the color of flour) and was often associated with barley (*alphiton*).

[7]Likewise, Paul tells the Philippians when they have need to turn to their patron, God (Phil 4:6).

What ensues as a dinner conversation is also a trade negotiation. Eventually, Diocles and Septimus broker a fair price for barley. The patrons mediate for their clients. A few days later, Cyprian the barley seller tells Belen that he has heard Belen's woes and will sell his barley for a reduced price, and Belen accepts the arrangement (as Diocles has told him to do). Good patrons (then and now) assist their clients in navigating the inequities of life, providing access, removing barriers, and mediating challenges. Brokers went back and forth negotiating.

It is for this reason Jesus describes himself as coming and going: "You heard me say, 'I am going away and I am coming back to you'" (Jn 14:28), and "I came from the Father and entered the world; now I am leaving the world and going back to the Father" (Jn 16:28). There is incarnational theology here. Clearly, John is signaling Jesus' divine origin. But John is also using an image his readers would know well, describing the work of a mediator.[8] They travel back and forth mediating between the parties, usually at the initiative of one. In John 16:28, Jesus notes that it was the Father who initiated the mediation, not us.

Mediators were an important part of the biblical world. Brokerage is all about relationships and connecting people together (the way services flow along those relationships is built on the relationship being secure). When our salvation is described in brokerage terms, for example, "For there is one God and one mediator between God and mankind, the man Christ Jesus, who gave himself as a ransom for all people. This has now been witnessed to at the proper time" (1 Tim 2:5-6), the result is not just that we receive forgiveness through Jesus. We do of course, and the text is clear about that. But the result is even more encompassing: an enduring relationship is established. John writes, "My dear children, I write this to you so that you will not sin. But if anybody does sin, we have an advocate with the Father—Jesus Christ, the Righteous One. He is the atoning sacrifice for our sins, and not only for ours but also for the sins of the whole

---

[8]For more on this, see Jerome H. Neyrey, "'I Am the Door' (John 10:7, 9): Jesus the Broker in the Fourth Gospel," *Catholic Biblical Quarterly* 69, no. 2 (2007): 271-91.

world" (1 Jn 2:1-2). We don't want to sin, but when we do, we can rest assured that we have a perfect broker, Jesus, who continues to maintain our relationship. We can trust our broker, Jesus Christ, the mediator between God and people.

PART 2

SOCIAL TOOLS

Enforcing and Reinforcing Our Values

"THERE THEY ARE," HE SAID. There were a few brown tents in the distance. My friend was taking me to visit a Bedouin family. As we walked over the crunchy desert ground toward the tents, we heard a long loud shout. I was alarmed, but my friend said they were welcoming us. A teenage boy came running as fast as he could. He welcomed us and guided us into a tent that had an open side. A number of men, who were reclining on cushions, quickly stood and gestured for us to sit beside them. A younger son served us coffee in small cups. When we finished he refilled them again and again. The sheikh kept welcoming us.

After an hour or so, I said to my friend, "Well, maybe we should be going." My friend looked back at me, surprised. "No. There is no way we can leave. The sheikh is preparing food for us. His sons have already killed some chickens. They are waiting for a cousin to return from collecting sticks for the fire. It will take at least a couple of hours. He will not let us leave before then." I said, "Oh, they don't need to do that. We don't need to eat." He said, "We must. We're his guests." We sat and waited. After an hour or so, a huge meal was spread for us. We ate, and when I had finished, the sheikh tossed another piece of chicken to me. "Eat," he said. I did. Then he did it again. Eventually, my friend explained we had to leave because it was getting dark. We stood up, and the sheikh walked us back to the car. As we walked back, I jokingly pointed at our small car in the road and then at his pickup truck and said, "Nice." It was great to pay him a compliment and be relational.

A few minutes later, a large argument broke out between my friend on the one hand, and the sheikh and his sons on the other. Arms flew, voices were raised, and the sons were grabbing my friend by the arm to take him away. I almost panicked, but I could tell my friend was at ease. After a long, heated discussion, everyone shook hands and kissed one another on the cheeks, and we got into our car. My friend was quiet and content to drive, but I wasn't about to leave it alone. "What was that all about?" My friend shrugged and said, "The sheikh wanted to give you his truck. It was a small gift to a guest in need. I argued we didn't need it. Fortunately, I convinced them. It wasn't just the cost. That truck is their only means of transport." When I asked why it happened, he said it was my fault. I had complimented the truck. "You are their guest. It is a matter of honor to them, to honor you." They never mentioned honor during all the hours of our visit. It was only mentioned when I asked my friend to explain what was going on. Otherwise, it would have gone without being said.

Here's another story where honor isn't mentioned: that of Abraham and his three visitors (Gen 18:1-16). Abraham has run from his tent to greet them. He impresses on them to eat and then offers help. It is a matter of honor for Abraham, even though the word *honor* is not mentioned in the Genesis story. It went without being said.

TOOLS, BUCKETS, LENSES, AND OTHER INADEQUATE METAPHORS

Values have to be constantly enforced and reinforced in a culture or they will eventually be lost. In America there is a lot of moaning by older Americans that the younger generation has lost this or that traditional American value. The fault lies not with the younger generation but with the older one that failed to adequately teach it, enforce it, and constantly reinforce it.

The ways a culture maintains its values are specific to a culture, but there are a few general methods. Individualist cultures will use, for example, stories, goals, and guilt. "The early bird gets the worm." "If you want to be successful, you need to learn the value of hard work." Children's stories such as "The Little Red Hen" and "Cinderella" create values that are deeply rooted in the American worldview. The guy is supposed to relentlessly pursue the girl, like the prince pursued Cinderella. (At least the right guy is supposed to; otherwise it is stalking.) Anyone who has had a mother put a guilt trip on them knows its power. Those are common individualist tools. Collectivist cultures have other ways. We will discuss three major ones in this section: honor, shame, and boundaries.

Just as key cultural values go without being said, so too the means for teaching, enforcing, and reinforcing those values also function below the surface. Because these means of enforcing a value are always connected to the value they are enforcing, the means are sometimes misidentified as values. For example, honor and shame are commonly discussed as values in collectivist cultures. In actuality, honor is not a value but a means of enforcing and reinforcing a value.

I was speaking to some Chinese friends recently about this chapter and described honor as a culture tool for enforcing values. I thought an angry mob was about to form. I had clearly offended them. "Honor is *not* a tool!" they sputtered. "It is absolutely not a tool." "What is it?" I asked. "Help me understand. What role does it play in helping children learn how to act?" They thought for a moment, then added, "Well, it is the means . . ." And then they stopped, clearly recognizing the conversation was about to go in a direction they didn't like. They fumbled around a bit, just as I do when trying to explain some deep American tool, such as guilt. Recently, an American grad student whined to me about his workload. I said, "Toughen up, cupcake!" (I was in a warm, compassionate mood at the time.) I was guilting him into toughening up. When I later tried to explain what that meant to an Asian student, I fumbled around a while. The American value of being tough is harder to explain than you might first think. Deep values are hard to describe because they usually go without being said.

Although my Chinese friends immediately and completely agreed honor was not a tool, they debated for several minutes about what it was. Finally, they looked at me and announced, "Honor is like a bucket." They further explained, "You put an important value in it, like one you wish to teach children, and it helps them to understand it." They all nodded their heads, having clearly explicated the cultural role of honor to me. They were now satisfied, but I was confused. Another friend, Jackson Wu, who was listening in (and laughing) at the time and who is an expert on honor in the Asian world, suggested I use the image of eyeglasses: "Honor is the lens that collective people use." I suspect he was teasing me, since I had used that image in another book, *Misreading Scripture with Western Eyes*. I like the image of lenses, but it still doesn't quite capture the role honor (and shame and boundaries) plays in collective cultures. They have an active role, and lenses—and buckets—don't.

I am comfortable admitting that we don't have a good metaphor for this. Honor, shame, and boundaries are the means or the method or the manner by which, or the bucket in which, collective cultures pass along their key values, such as kinship, patronage, and brokerage. Individualist cultures have their own tools, such as guilt (and innocence) and an introspective conscience.[9] The Holy Spirit clearly uses those tools in the hearts of Westerners to bring about repentance, just as he uses honor and shame to bring Easterners to repentance and saving grace. Ironically, each culture tends to think the Spirit *only* uses its particular tools, or that other tools are inadequate, so people want to import their tools into other cultures. Thus, Westerners can't imagine how the Spirit can convict anyone without using guilt; yet many Asian cultures don't even have a word for guilt. They likewise can't imagine how the Spirit can accomplish anything in a culture without honor. God understands and uses both. We are not yet ready to

---

[9]We are not yet ready to say definitively what are the cultural tools for individualist cultures (since that is not the topic of this book), although we suspect guilt is one of them. Krister Stendahl, in a landmark essay, shows how Paul did not have an introspective conscience. See Stendahl, "The Apostle Paul and the Introspective Conscience of the West," *Harvard Theological Review* 56 (1963): 199-215. This essay was the invited address at the Annual Meeting of the American Psychological Association, September 3, 1961.

say that honor, shame, and boundaries are the sole or most definitive means for collectivist cultures, but we are ready to say they are some key means (or methods or manners or buckets).

WHAT'S IN A WORD (OR TWO)?

Part of our challenge is that the English language lacks sufficiently nuanced terms to describe the things we're discussing. On the other hand, English has plenty of nuanced terminology for things that are important to us. Here's an example: It rains a lot in Britain. When we look out of the window, we might say that it's "pouring," "spitting," "sleeting," "teeming," "hammering it down," or even "raining cats and dogs." There might be "drizzle," "mizzle," "showers," "spots," "sunshowers," "cloudbursts," a "deluge," or a "downpour." British English has lots of words for rain. This is because Britain experiences lots of kinds of rain. We need to know whether to expect spots or a deluge to know whether to wear our wellies. The nuance matters. Arabs, by contrast, only use one colloquial word for rain—*shita*—which is the same word for winter! They don't need to develop a rich colloquial way of speaking about rain, because it's not a big part of their life.

Honor, shame, and boundaries *are* a big part of life in collective cultures, so they have a wide vocabulary to talk about them. In English we tend to use just a few words.[10] As a result, we are trying to look at a high-definition photo on a low-resolution setting. The problem is not the photo but the setting. We might say, for example, that the Old Testament (Hebrew) has at least ten words for shame. A better way to say it is that English has one word for ten different (Hebrew) things. Our language lacks the resolution needed to understand the topic clearly. The simple reason is that we don't need it. Our culture uses other tools (or buckets). Even the terminology can be misleading. Discussions in the West usually talk about honor and shame, which seems to imply they are opposites. We are going to show they are not.

---

[10]Michael Herzfeld, "Honour and Shame: Problems in the Comparative Analysis of Moral Systems," *Man* 15, no. 2 (1980): 339.

Our low-resolution understanding of honor and shame poses several problems for us when we read the Bible. First, we struggle to understand the different kinds of honor and shame at work in the biblical world because we don't have sufficient words to describe them. Second, honor, shame, and boundaries have popular definitions in the West. *Honor* often feels romantic. "He's a man of honor" reminds us of chivalrous times. "That's a shame" suggests something inconvenient or unfortunate, but not disastrous. *Boundaries* usually denote "limitations," which we instinctively want to challenge. Third, in modern Western usage, all three concepts— honor, shame, and boundaries—often refer to an individual. In the biblical world, as well as in collectivist cultures today, honor, shame, and boundaries are collective tools (methods, buckets) used by communities, not individuals. They require a people, not a person, for them even to work. A man is considered honorable because he belongs to an honorable family or community. Likewise, many collectivists *want* boundaries, while my culture resists them. This is because honor, shame, and boundaries tie communities together. When the sheikh offered me his car, he assumed it would bind us together in relationship. He didn't need to say that; it went without being said.

You likely feel pretty confused. English words fail us. But the problem isn't just an issue of finding the right translation. Honor, shame, and boundaries in this way are not part of our world, but they were part of the biblical world. This next part will explore how the world of the Bible used honor, shame and boundaries, often without being said, to enforce and reinforce community values.

7

HAVING HONOR

Everybody Has Some

"YOU SPEAK GOOD ARABIC . . . FOR A FOREIGNER." I was in a cafe when Dr. Amer spoke to me. He was an Arabic language professor at a college down the street. I was curious. "How did you become a professor?" He said he used to be a military officer. He loved his job, and when he retired, he found it hard. He no longer had his status, no personal driver, no soldiers to respect him. "I didn't know my place anymore, so I decided to become a doctor." He spent five years, and much of his pension, to earn a PhD. He didn't explain why he did it. It didn't need explaining, since it went without being said (in his world). He would be honored by the community with a title that could not be lost. I might counter that he already had a pension that would not be lost. Biblical writers would have understood: "A good name is more desirable than great riches; to be esteemed is better than silver or gold" (Prov 22:1).

Ancient Hebrew society sought to enforce one of its values by teaching, "A gracious woman attains honor, and ruthless men attain riches" (Prov 11:16 NASB). Old Testament scholars call this way of speaking antithetical parallelism. The same idea is taught by saying opposites. It uses the pattern "a wise man does A, but a foolish man does B." It is a very common device in Proverbs, where contrasts are made between the righteous and the wicked, the rich and the poor, the diligent and the lazy.[1] In this proverb,

---

[1]Dianne Bergant, *Israel's Wisdom Literature: A Liberation-Critical Reading* (Minneapolis: Fortress, 1997), 86.

though, the comparison is more subtle. It compares a kindhearted woman and ruthless men and between gaining honor and wealth. We all know people who think that gaining wealth is a sign of honor. This proverb carefully nuances the difference. Gaining wealth is different from gaining honor in this passage. Ruthless men gain wealth but not honor.[2] Scripture is encouraging us not to equate the two.

Collectivists, ancient and modern, understand that honor is a greater treasure than gold. But there's more to the concept of honor than that. Proverbs and Dr. Amer agree about the significance of honor. But each of them was using honor to reinforce a different value. Dr. Amer sought honor to reinforce the values of prestige, respect, and social standing. His community would provide him better parking spots, invitations to events and meetings, respectful greetings in the market. The values Proverbs intended to reinforce were righteous living (making right decisions) and earning the praise of God. This is an important distinction. Many societies use honor to reinforce their values. We have to be careful not to confuse honor (the tool) with the value. We can say things such as, "In the ancient world, wealth was considered honorable." That is not true in this proverb. But this proverb doesn't do away with honor. Rather, it enforces another value. In this chapter, we'll look at the importance of honor in the biblical world. We'll also look at the importance of sorting out the difference between honor and the values honor is being used to reinforce.

SAME HONOR, DIFFERENT VALUES

When we were writing this, Randy celebrated his sixtieth birthday. His American friends sang, "Happy birthday!" His Indonesian friends sang, "Long life with honor!" Both Randy and his Asian friends want him to have a life full of honor, but they would likely disagree over the values required to be considered honorable. Randy's American friends would want him to be independent, tough, a self-starter, a leader (not a follower). His Indonesian friends would want him to value harmony, face (whatever that

---

[2]The NIV translation slightly paraphrases in order to make this clearer: "A kindhearted woman gains honor, but ruthless men gain only wealth."

means), hospitality, and being considered upright. (Whose list looks more like Paul's qualifications for an elder in Titus 1:6-8?) Both groups certainly want Randy to be honorable, but they have different values.

Seneca was a polished Roman aristocrat who lived about the time of Jesus. James and John were young and brash fishermen in the backwaters of the Roman Empire. These men couldn't really be less similar. Yet, they shared something in common. They wanted honor. James and John ask Jesus, "Let one of us sit at your right and the other at your left in your glory" (Mk 10:37). Mark's story assumes several things that went without being said. First, sitting close to Jesus means holding an honorable position. Second, when they say "in your glory," they mean when he will get his earthly kingdom. Third, they don't yet know how the story will end, how Jesus will get his kingdom. But they know they want to share in Jesus' glory. Elsewhere, the disciples rejoice at the honor of having authority over evil spirits (Lk 10:17). Jesus responds they should rather rejoice in the honor of having their name recorded in heaven (Lk 10:20). Jesus agrees that honor is good; the disciples just want honor for the wrong value. Seneca also wanted honor, but neither of the values Jesus mentioned would have been honored particularly by Seneca.

Scholars commonly talk about the ancient Near East or the Greco-Roman world. These are helpful taglines, but we should remember that they are referring to some very large areas. The Greco-Roman world spanned from modern-day England to Egypt. It included diverse languages, cultures, and peoples. It was not any less diverse than Europe today. The Aramaic-speaking village of Capernaum in Galilee was very different from multicultural Corinth, but both are lumped under the title "Greco-Roman world."

Ancient people were talking and writing about honorable values in Hebrew, Greek, Latin, and Aramaic, in villages, cities, philosophical schools, and palaces. Everyone agreed honor was important; yet they differed over what values produced honor.[3] By way of example, Michael

---

[3] The Cynics probably weren't an exception in terms of valuing honor. They argued people should be unmoved by considerations of honor, but what they meant were actually the typical values that

Herzfeld, a modern anthropologist, studied honor in three villages in modern Greece. While he found they all valued honor, they had somewhat different views on *what* they considered honorable. This was in three nearby villages. He noted that while Westerners struggle to understand how Mediterranean honor works, it is *not* because the indigenous communities themselves are confused.[4] Each village knew what was honorable. We Westerners look at different values and call them honor. It helps to remember that although collective cultures have different values, all think the way to enforce and reinforce these values is by honor, by considering the possession of a particular value to be honorable.

THE MOST IMPORTANT THINGS ARE HARD TO DEFINE

Honor is not easy to define. Since a person can earn honor by honorable deeds and/or traits, a poor farmer can have more ethical honor than a rich ruler. Yet a ruler has a more honorable title and status than a poor farmer. So which is honor—a title, wealth, or ethics? Actually, all are sources of honor, and yet they are not identical. All of them are at the core of honor, and the answer to which one is *most* central depends on which community you ask. Despite the best efforts of scholars, honor can't be distilled into a neat philosophical statement.[5] It does not surrender to a simple definition. Let's use an illustration. Paul, in trying to describe the effects of the Spirit on the life of a believer, calls them the fruit (singular) of the Spirit. It is the one fruit the Spirit produces in the life of a believer. This singular fruit is a love-joy-peace-patience-kindness-goodness-gentleness-faithfulness-self-control-kind of fruit. The Spirit doesn't produce nine fruits. It produces one hard-to-describe thing.

---

honor reinforced. They still honored the best Cynics among them, selecting them as teachers and prizing those who best forsook traditional values.

[4]Michael Herzfeld, "Honor and Shame: Problems in the Comparative Analysis of Moral Systems," *Man* 15 (1980): 348.

[5]Peter Oakes studied the order which the names of witnesses to auctions are listed in a document in Pompeii. The higher up the list a name came would seem to indicate higher status and honor of the person. Interestingly, the place of a name does not correlate to the wealth of that person. Other factors influenced their status. This indicates that economic status was related to but cannot be directly equated with social status. See Oakes, *Reading Romans in Pompeii: Paul's Letter at Ground Level* (Minneapolis: Fortress, 2009), 56.

We have mentioned that Hebrew and Greek speakers used a range of terms to talk about honor, such as *glory, praise, respect, weight, reverence, reputation,* and *esteem.*[6] These terms orbit the ancient concept of honor. Often in a story none of these terms appeared. People described someone doing something and expected others to recognize that what the person did was honorable or dishonorable. Sometimes we individualist readers suspect honor is at work, such as when James and John ask to be seated beside Jesus, but other times we might miss it entirely, such as when the temple authorities ask Jesus, "Who gave you this authority?" (Mt 21:23). Asking a public question in Mediterranean cultures could indicate honor was in play, as we will see later. In any case, Matthew expects his audience to recognize Jesus is in an honor contest, while we might just see a harmless request for information.

Let's consider another story. "At that time the disciples came to Jesus and asked, 'Who, then, is the greatest in the kingdom of heaven?' He called a little child to him, and placed the child among them. And he said, 'Truly I tell you, unless you change and become like little children, you will never enter the kingdom of heaven'" (Mt 18:1-3). The connection between James and John's question about glory (honor) and Jesus' command to become like a child may not be immediately clear. What does Jesus mean by "become like little children"? Matthew doesn't say. In our culture, we value a child's simple faith, believing without facts. Aside from the questionable value of believing without facts, the passage isn't about faith.[7] It is about seeking status and honor. The disciples were arguing about who is greatest, and Jesus urges them to become like children, who are not concerned with worldly status. A child sees no difference between a company's president and its janitor. "Whoever takes the lowly position of this child is the greatest in the kingdom of heaven" (Mt 18:4). Jesus doesn't mean to "have simple faith" but to show a lack of concern about seeking status. Paul praises Timothy for serving him like a child serves a

---

[6]David A. deSilva, *Honor, Patronage, Kinship and Purity: Unlocking New Testament Culture* (Downers Grove, IL: InterVarsity Press, 2000), 27-28.

[7]Scripture emphasizes believing because of facts. *Because* the Lord delivered you out of Egypt, you are to. . . .

father (Phil 2:22). Paul doesn't mean serving with simple faith (or serving poorly, as children sometimes do) but serving without thought of one's own status. Often Jesus is in conflict with the Pharisees because he has different values and thus honors different things.

This is an odd analogy, but stay with us. Honor is like a black hole. Black holes cannot be seen. They are noticed because of the distortion they create around them. Physicists figure out there is an invisible gravitational hole by the way things around it are affected. In a similar way, honor is often not seen easily in a biblical story, but like a gravity well, something unseen seems to be affecting the way people were acting.

Honor is complex. Biblical commentators often talk about someone having more honor than someone else. It can seem like honor is similar to one's bank account. If we stay with the financial analogy, then honor is more of a portfolio than a single stock. There are multiple sources that all add honor. When someone in the modern Mediterranean world (and likely in first-century Bethany or Thessalonica) considered their honor, they considered a group of values. A man might be an important religious teacher, so his community would bump up his honor score. But he might not be wealthy or have political power, so they would bump it down a bit (whether a lot or a little depends on how much his group valued religious teachers versus wealth). When he visits his home village, he is still his mother's son and his elder brother's younger sibling. How do those factors impact his honor score? It depends how his family is viewed by his community. I once said to a wealthy businessman friend, "In this culture, wealth is honored, so people always give millionaires honor." (I may have been a bit smug when I said it.) "Maybe," my friend hedged. "If his parents were poorer, then he has honor because he has gained wealth/status. The poorer his parents, the more honor he has acquired. But, if his parents were billionaires, then as a millionaire, he has actually lost status—lost honor."

Honor is collective. Individualist cultures, like most of the West, may bestow honor for titles, positions, and wealth, but on an individual basis—such as an honorary doctorate or a medal of honor. Collective cultures, like most of the East, by contrast, consider honor, well, collectively. For example, collective cultures consider bloodlines a very strong source of honor. A man is a member of a group with a history. A poor person could still have status today because of something an ancestor did hundreds of years ago. We may still be thinking too linearly and individually, thinking only in terms of honor descending down to *me*. Collective cultures think collectively. When one person gains honor, the rest of the collective group shares in that person's honor. Likewise, individual members share in the honor of the collective group. My Lebanese friend will boast about what his uncle did, because he shares in his uncle's honor as a whole family. When people come from an honored family, they will often mention their family name as if to say, "I'm part of our honor, and don't forget it."

So, when we see honor at play between two individual people in Scripture, we need to remember they are representatives of their people. The interaction between them often concerns the rest of their collective group. When Jesus and Simon the Pharisee talk (Lk 7:36-50), the contest over honor is not between Jesus and Simon alone. It concerns the rest of their groups: Jesus-and-his-followers and Simon-and-the-Pharisees. When Jesus allows a sinful woman to anoint him, the honor of his disciples is also in question. When Jesus wins the contest, the disciples also increase in honor (Mk 11:1-7). They are now disciples of a more honorable master. When the Samaritan woman meets Jesus, collective honor is at play (Jn 4:1-26). She is well aware the conversation between them is corporate: Jews and Samaritans. She notes Jacob gave *us* this well (Jn 4:12). It was a thousand years previous, but she still connects herself to Jacob (and thus to Abraham). She feels this honor is shared by all the Samaritan people. They honor Jacob because he is "our father" (Jn 4:12). The woman is standing up for her people and their honor to this Jewish man. Sure, Jews have Jerusalem, she reasons, but David gave them Jerusalem and the temple. She goes further back in history to Jacob and Abraham. She thinks she and Jesus are fencing over honorable bloodlines, the collective honor of their peoples.

ASCRIBED HONOR

One way people in collective cultures are given honor is that others *ascribe* (or assign) it to them. Bruce Malina writes that ascribed honor "is honor that you get simply for being you, not because of anything you do to acquire it. . . . Ascribed honor is the socially recognized claim to worth that befalls a person that happens passively."[8] Ascribed honor can come from the family you are born into, marry into, or are adopted into. Ascribed honor can come from a collective people's impressive history or the deeds performed by a member of one's group. The key is that ascribed honor is not earned. I have a friend in Beirut who often mentions her family name when she meets people. When people in her community learn she is from that family, they honor her. She can park her car wherever she likes. She gets preferential treatment in stores. She even gets better business opportunities. She is preferred over others because of her family. She didn't do anything to achieve or earn this honor; she was born into it. To Westerners, this seems unfair. Well, it is unfair. Before we rise up in arms to protest it, we must remember we are given certain rights and privileges as Christians because "We are children of God" (1 Jn 3:2). We didn't earn it. We were born (again) into it.

The honor of the firstborn. The most common way to be ascribed honor is from birth. The son of the emperor starts life with a large supply of ascribed honor. The son of a chief, a sheikh, has lots of honor. Most families have some measure of honor. In the ancient world, honor was ascribed to the firstborn son of a Galilean carpenter—just not much. In the ancient world, there was more ascribed honor in being the second-born son than the firstborn daughter. Sadly, that is still true in many collective cultures today. Recently at a conference we heard a brilliant young minister share her story. She was the eldest child of a Hong Kong minister. She spoke of her father's love for her, but she also added, "My father loved my brother more. It was obvious." It was still a painful memory for her. She told the story of family dinnertime, when her father cut and served the chicken. The son always got the first and best piece. She added that it would have

---

[8]Bruce J. Malina, *The New Testament World: Insights from Cultural Anthropology*, 3rd ed. (Louisville, KY: Westminster John Knox, 2001), 32.

stunned her had her father ever served it to her or her sister. He never did. Her culture ascribed more honor to her brother than her. Her father simply reflected that cultural value in his actions. The chicken was not important. It was just a drumstick. But the drumstick symbolized something very important, her worth in the family. The pain in her voice was fresh, even though twenty years had passed.

A nice coat didn't really matter much either, but what it symbolized did. Joseph's coat symbolized whom Jacob favored (Gen 37:3-4). It was Rachel's lineage, not Leah's, to whom Jacob ascribed the honor of inheritance. Joseph did not earn it; it was ascribed to him by Jacob.

When Paul defends his honor in front of the Sanhedrin, he lists his ascribed honor (Acts 23:1-10). This is a wise move on his part, since his achievements are in question (in the eyes of the Sanhedrin). Paul's ascribed honor, however, cannot be questioned. "Brothers, I am a Pharisee," Paul notes, "a son of Pharisees" (Acts 23:6 NASB). The Pharisees recognize the honor. They share in it too. That's why they come to his defense (at least temporarily).

The ascribed honor of anointing. Anointing someone with oil was a way of ascribing honor to them. God sends Samuel to anoint David. David hasn't done anything notable to deserve this honor at this point in his life. He defended his sheep. But shepherds routinely defended their sheep and weren't anointed for it. He was good with a sling. But many armies had sling throwers in them. It wasn't a mysterious skill. David killed Goliath. But Samuel anoints David before that deed. We are supposed to reach the obvious conclusion that this ascribed honor is a gracious gift from God. David hasn't done anything to deserve being anointed; the Bible makes it clear by saying God doesn't look on the outside (1 Sam 16:7). To make sure we don't miss just how gracious the gift is, the story elaborates how Samuel chooses him even though he is of low status *and* he isn't the firstborn of his father (1 Sam 16:11). God ascribes honor to someone others do not.

Saul is also given the gift of anointing, another ascribed honor. Saul later earns more honor in battle, but he also loses a lot of honor by his behavior. As an individualist, I could question whether Saul has any honor left based on his actions. But just as Paul didn't lose his ascribed honor in the eyes of the other Pharisees, so King Saul doesn't lose the honor *ascribed* to him by the prophet Samuel. When Saul is chasing David in order to kill him, David has multiple opportunities to kill Saul and refuses, because Saul has especially high honor: "Who can lay a hand on the LORD's anointed and be guiltless?" (1 Sam 26:9). Saul remains the Lord's anointed. While others might not value God's selection, David does. He honors whom God honors. Who Saul is (his ascribed honor) is more important than what he does, in David's eyes.

Jesus. We argued in the chapters on kinship that genealogies are important because they define someone's collective identity. Our Syrian friend mentions her genealogy because it says who she is. It also shows she is descended from Abraham (almost). That means she is due ascribed honor. It is part of her identity. Thus, genealogies ascribe honor. Descendants share in the honor of their ancestors. They didn't do anything besides being born into that family.

The genealogies of Jesus identify who Jesus is and counteract how Jesus' ascribed honor might otherwise be perceived. Jesus is from Nazareth. That's not much ascribed honor. In fact, Nathanael says, "Can anything good come from there?" (Jn 1:46).[9] More than that, there is no mention of the Messiah coming from Nazareth in the Old Testament. He was supposed to come from Judea (Mt 2:3-6). Jesus does in fact come from Judea, but Nathanael doesn't know that. Nathanael doesn't think Jesus the carpenter's son from Nazareth had the ascribed honor to be the Messiah. Others likely agree with him. So, Matthew uses genealogies to set the record straight that Jesus has the required honor. He is descended through honorable bloodlines, such as David and Abraham (Mt 1:1).

CONCLUSION

Jesus tells Nicodemus, "Very truly I tell you, no one can enter the kingdom of God unless they are born of water and the Spirit. Flesh gives birth to

---

[9]James H. Charlesworth, "Jesus Research and Archeology: A New Perspective," in *Jesus and Archaeology*, ed. James H. Charlesworth (Grand Rapids, MI: Eerdmans, 2006), 39.

flesh, but the Spirit gives birth to spirit" (Jn 3:5-6). Being a member of the kingdom of God is a very high-honor status, and it is ascribed. You have to be born (again) into it; it cannot be earned.[10] As we saw, David recognizes and honors Saul's ascribed honor. While honor can be ascribed, it can also be achieved. Dr. Amer represents achieved honor. Others probably look on at the way he is treated and think, *One day I want to gain a doctorate so I can be treated like Dr. Amer.* In this way honor functions as a tool (means, bucket or lens) for a collective group to maintain the group's identity by maintaining (enforcing and reinforcing) their collective values. When someone embodies or lives out the values the group honors, the group honors them. The values are thus reinforced for the entire group.

How much honor someone has depends on a constellation of factors and can be difficult for individualists to sort out. Actually, it isn't just a problem for modern individualists. In the Bible, we read stories, for example, where it is questioned whether someone has enough honor to do a certain thing (Mt 21:23). It was a collective issue. If we use the financial analogy again, maintaining one's honor balance sheet was everyone's business. Honor was everywhere, essential, and pursued, but it was based on different values. We can say *every collective group used honor* and *every collective group honored different things.*

---

[10]Tricia Gates Brown, *Spirit in the Writings of John: Johannine Pneumatology in Social-Scientific Perspective,* Journal for the Study of the New Testament Supplement Series 253 (New York: T&T Clark, 2003), 125.

8

GAINING HONOR

Everybody Wants More

PHARISEES WERE THE GOOD GUYS, the heroes of the average Jew. If scribes were the Bible professors of the first century, then Pharisees were the Sunday school teachers. Pharisees passionately believed God's law should be applied to every area of life. They gave of their time to teach others. They taught the general public how to live a God-pleasing life. For instance, the sudden appearance of ritual bathing pools all over Judea and Galilee a generation before Jesus is probably an indication of the growing influence of the Pharisees in everyday life.[1] Common people were becoming more concerned about purity.

But, if Pharisees were such good folks, why does Jesus seem to have more conflict with them than others? First, we should note that Jesus is pretty dismissive of the Sadducees: "You are in error because you do not know the Scriptures or the power of God" (Mt 22:29). That is a strong statement. Second, just about the nicest thing Jesus says to anyone is what he says to a teacher who is likely a Pharisee: "You are not far from the kingdom of God" (Mk 12:34). Third, Jesus actually recognizes that the *content* of the Pharisees' teaching is rather sound: "The teachers of the law and the Pharisees sit in Moses' seat. So you must be careful to do everything they tell you. But do not do what they do, for they do not practice what they preach" (Mt 23:2-3). So what exactly is Jesus' problem with

---

[1]Eckhard J. Schnabel, "Pharisees," in *The New Interpreters Dictionary of the Bible* (Nashville: Abingdon, 2009), 4:490.

Pharisees? It is not what they say but their hearts. Jesus points out: "Everything they do is done for people to see: They make their phylacteries wide and the tassels on their garments long; they love the place of honor at banquets and the most important seats in the synagogues; they love to be greeted with respect in the marketplaces and to be called 'Rabbi' by others" (Mt 23:5-7).

Jesus is pointing out that the problem is they want honor for the wrong reasons.

YOU CAN DO RIGHT WRONG

We have seen that honor is used to enforce and reinforce values; it is a good thing. But the Pharisees pursued honor based on the wrong values. They wanted to receive honor for doing the correct actions, not for having the correct motivations. Just as the disciples pursued honor for casting out demons rather than for having their names recorded in heaven (Lk 10:17-20), so also the Pharisees were correct to pursue honor, but were doing it to reinforce the wrong value. They were honoring the value of right actions, not right heart. As a result, the honor they received came from the wrong source. They pursued the recognition of *people* rather than *God* (Mt 23:1-11). And they got it. While these values produced honor among people around the Pharisees, they were not values God honored.

This isn't just a New Testament teaching. When searching for a king, the crowds honor the wrong values, appearance and height: "But the LORD said to Samuel, 'Do not consider his appearance or his height, for I have rejected him. The LORD does not look at the things people look at. People look at the outward appearance, but the LORD looks at the heart'" (1 Sam 16:7). Scripture doesn't criticize seeking honor or giving honor. Samuel is sent there for the purpose of giving honor. Scripture doesn't criticize honoring the right values.

ATTAINING AND INCREASING HONOR IN THE BIBLE

In the ancient Mediterranean world, honor was achieved in two common ways: by performing honorable deeds and through honor contests. These were the means to earn more honor, but what sometimes confuses individualists is that what was considered an honorable deed was different among Pharisees versus, say, Roman soldiers; yet both tried to achieve honor through deeds. This chapter will focus on exploring the ways biblical characters achieved honor by performing honorable deeds.

Jephthah. When we are introduced to Jephthah, the Bible tells us that "Jephthah the Gilead was a mighty warrior. His father was Gilead; his mother was a prostitute" (Judg 11:1). Gilead eventually has legitimate sons (it appears). These sons don't consider Jephthah to be part of their father's household.[2] They don't wish an illegitimate brother, the son of a prostitute, to inherit (Judg 11:7). Jephthah has no ascribed honor.

Later Jephthah arrives in the region near Tob.[3] He gathers a group of "worthless fellows" (Judg 11:3 NASB), or men without honor. We noted that groups establish their own lists of honorable deeds. In this case, these men honor Jephthah for his value as a mighty warrior and a leader (of scalawags). When the town of Gilead is threatened, the elders find themselves needing someone with warrior and leadership skills: "'Come,' they said, 'be our commander, so we can fight the Ammonites'" (Judg 11:6). So all is forgiven? Hardly. Jephthah reminds them of how he was dishonored and demands an even higher achieved honor than being a mighty warrior: he demands to be honored as their "head and commander" (Judg 11:9-11). Desperation leads the elders to agree.

David (and Goliath). David doesn't earn the anointing to become king. It is an ascribed honor. This ascribed honor, however, does not seem sufficient to rally the people to accept David as king. David needs to achieve additional honor in their eyes. Our biblical writer assures us that David achieved it by telling us the story of Goliath.

---

[2]Richard D. Nelson, *Judges: A Critical and Rhetorical Commentary* (New York: T&T Clark, 2017), 208n1. The other possibility is that "his father was Gilead" is referring to the town of Gilead, such as saying "his father was Chicago," a blunt way of noting his mother was a prostitute and no man claimed paternity. The other sons of Gilead were those of legitimate birth. This would be to make the contrast starker between his complete lack of ascribed honor and his later gain of achieved honor.

[3]The narrator is doing a play on words. *Tob* means "goodness." Whether it is an actual place name is disputed by scholars, but we are supposed to notice that he lives in the *vicinity* of goodness but not in the town.

It is easy for us to misread this story for two reasons. First, it is easy to fit the Goliath story into our modern Western value system, where we honor the little individual who takes on the big system. (Think of all the movies where this is the plot line.) *Of course*, we reason, *David should fight Goliath*. Second, we often misread this story because we can forget an important part of the backstory. When the people ask Samuel to select a king for them, they say, "Then we will be like all the other nations, with a king to lead us and to go out before us and fight our battles" (1 Sam 8:20). Saul fails to act like a king, "to go out before us and fight our battles," while David demonstrates *exactly* that behavior. David achieves the honor of being their king.

In the story of David's encounter with Goliath, what went without being said, what we are supposed to immediately notice, is that it is Saul's job to go fight Goliath. He is the king, and the king is to fight their battles for them. The text reminds us that Goliath is tall, but so is Saul (1 Sam 9:2). Goliath has great armor. Saul does too. We might say, well, Goliath is taller.[4] But that's not the difference the Bible highlights. Saul notes that Goliath "has been a warrior from his youth" (1 Sam 17:33). Saul is supposed to be confident that the Lord, Israel's God, will fight for him. Saul isn't confident. Here is the difference between Saul and David. David is the hero *not* because he's great with a sling. David is commended because he is confident that God will fight for him, "The Lord who rescued me from the paw of the lion and the paw of the bear will rescue me from the hand of this Philistine" (1 Sam 17:37). Growing up, I admired (honored) David for the *wrong* value. I honored him for being a good shot; Scripture honors him for trusting the Lord. That is the value that counts.

The biblical story was guiding me to honor David for the correct value, but I missed it because of what went without being said. Ancients knew

---

[4]Biblical manuscripts record two different heights for Goliath. Manuscripts from Qumran (4QSamª) and Greek translations from the time of Jesus (the Septuagint, or LXX) record Goliath at "four cubits and a span" (about 6'6"), while medieval Hebrew manuscripts (the Masoretic Text) record his height at "six cubits and a span" (about 9'9"). The actual story highlights Goliath's skills, not his height. See J. Daniel Hays, "Reconsidering the Height of Goliath," *Journal of the Evangelical Theological Society* 48, no. 4 (2005): 701-14.

well that armies used slingers.[5] An individual slinger, though, was much less of a threat against an equipped soldier. An opposing soldier facing an individual slinger was able to defend himself quite easily against the slinger. When the slinger starts to wind up, the soldier would duck behind his shield. Once the slinger was out of stones, he was defenseless. There was one minor risk, which any soldier would know. A slinger could begin a windup, and then when the soldier ducked behind his shield, the slinger could try to run up and get close enough to stab the soldier with a sword around the shield.

All of that background in ancient warfare we are *expected* to know. Now, it is important to note what the narrator does *explicitly* say. Not only does Goliath have a shield, but the narrator tells us the shield is so large Goliath has another man just to carry it. We are supposed to conclude immediately, "David has no real chance." The narrator also tells us that David picks up five stones. Again, we are supposed to think, "It's going to be a short battle." The winner seems clear to everyone. David can cast five rocks hard against Goliath's shield, but then David will be defenseless.

We are also supposed to notice two other things also. First, Saul wants David to wear his tunic and armor. This may be out of concern for David, but it is far more likely Saul wants the Israelites to think it is Saul going out to fight Goliath—as he is supposed to. Or Saul wants the army to see that even Saul wouldn't have stood a chance. Either way, David declines. Second, we are told specifically *where* Goliath is hit. Most likely, Goliath ducked behind his shield. When a stone didn't clank immediately against his shield, Goliath took a very, very fast peek over the top of the shield to make sure David wasn't running up. In the split second it took to peek, the stone arrived at precisely the place on the shield where Goliath chose to peek. David would have needed to launch the stone *before* Goliath started peeking. It wasn't a one-in-a-million shot. It wasn't a lucky break. It was a

---

[5]As early as 3000 BC, slingers were a devastating part of an army. Three hundred years after David, the Assyrians used slingers to help take the Israelite city of Lachish, throwing rocks over the city walls. Even in Roman times, slingers were still in use. Before Hannibal invaded Italy (about 200 BC), he left 500 slingers to help hold Spain, sent 870 slingers to Africa to defend Carthage, and then took about 1,000 with him to attack the Romans.

miracle. *Everybody* drew the conclusion: David's God fought for him, while Goliath's god did not. David was right to confidently trust in God. We are not supposed to say, "David killed Goliath." We are supposed to say, "God killed Goliath." Whatever conclusions we take from this story, the most important one is that we are to honor David not for being a great slinger but for trusting God. He is the kind of person who will make a good king.

I misread this story and often told it in a way that honored David for the wrong value. I ended up with an individualist (and American) moral of the story: little guys should self-confidently take on giants. No. It is a beautiful example of God's constant message. God assures Abram, "Do not be afraid, Abram. I am your shield" (Gen 15:1). God tells Isaac, "Do not be afraid, for I am with you" (Gen 26:24). He tells Jacob, "I am with you" (Gen 28:15). Fast-forward, and we see that God wants Joshua (and the people) to know "I am with you as I was with Moses" (Josh 3:7). God assures Isaiah, "So do not fear, for I am with you; do not be dismayed, for I am your God. I will strengthen you and help you" (Is 41:10; see also Is 43:5). Jeremiah hears the same message at least five times (Jer 1:8, 19; 15:20; 30:11; 42:11). Haggai is instructed to tell the people twice, "'I am with you,' declares the LORD" (Hag 1:13; 2:4). The biblical message doesn't change. What does Jesus tell us? Face Goliath if you are a good shot? No. "And surely I am with you always" (Mt 28:20). Honor David, but do it for the right value: for believing that God would be with him, as he promised.

Military prowess was certainly a major source of achieved honor in the ancient Mediterranean world, but it was not the only way. While honor can be achieved by noble deeds in every collective culture we personally know of, the things that constitute noble deeds often varies between one culture to another. In Mongolia, it can be skill with a horse. In Yemen, it can be jumping over camels. In Hong Kong, it can be advanced degrees. In Scotland, tossing around telephone poles seems to earn honor. In Lebanon, it can be impromptu poetry recitation. The same diversity was true of the ancient Mediterranean. For first-century Greeks, the ability to write and speak persuasively (whether speeches or poems) was highly valued, and those who excelled were honored. Winning a writing contest was a very honorable deed. Vitruvius tells that at the founding of the library at Alexandria, Ptolemy "consecrated games in honor of the Muses and Apollo" to give prizes to new writers. The major prize was *honor.*[6] Romans honored those who excelled athletically through games. Honoring the gods also brought one honor in pagan societies. We have already seen that being a generous patron brought honor as one's clients lavished honor on the patron's generosity.

For first-century Pharisees, honor could be gained by advancement in Torah, or by being zealous in teaching others (and enforcing) compliance, as seen in their traditions. Paul writes, "I was advancing in Judaism beyond many of my own age among my people and was extremely zealous for the traditions of my fathers" (Gal 1:14). Paul is indicating his achieved honor. In my individualist culture, boasting has negative overtones. "Don't boast," my grandmother warned. "Boasting is wrong." That's our values at work. So we quote Paul when he says love does not boast (1 Cor 13:4). We might even cite verses where Paul is condemning someone for boasting (Rom 1:30; 2:23; 4:2; 1 Cor 1:29; 5:6; 9:16; Eph 2:9). We fill in the gaps about why they are condemned: they are condemned for boasting, because boasting is wrong. Yet, if we look closely at these verses, Paul is not actually condemning boasting but boasting for the wrong reasons. Paul actually commends or engages in his own boasting (Rom 2:17; 3:27; 1 Cor 3:21; 2 Cor 1:12, 14; 5:12; 7:14; 8:24; 9:2, 3; 10:13, 15, 16, 17; 11:12, 17, 18, 21; 12:1, 5, 6; Gal 6:4, 14; 1 Thess 2:19; 2 Thess 1:4). Boasting in Paul's culture (and in many collective cultures) was to indicate achieved honor. Furthermore, since honor is collective, everyone else in Paul's group also benefited from his boasting. For individualists, boasting is a way to put

---

[6]Vitruvius, *On Architecture* 7, preface 4. This particular story takes an interesting turn, because all but one of the contestants is accused of and convicted of plagiarism. See *On Architecture* 7, preface 7. Their punishment included public rebuke. Because they had sought the prize of honor, their punishment included public shaming. See E. Randolph Richards, "Was Matthew a Plagiarist? Plagiarism in Greco-Roman Antiquity," in *Christian Origins and the Establishment of the Early Jesus Movement*, ed. Stanley Porter and Andrew W. Pitts, Texts and Editions for New Testament Study 12, Early Christianity in Its Hellenistic Context 4 (Leiden, Netherlands: Brill, 2018), 108-33.

yourself ahead of your peers. For collectivists, boasting is a way to put you and all your peers (group) ahead.

So far, we have been making a distinction between *ascribed* and *achieved* honor. This has been helpful to show the way honor works in both ways, but it could suggest someone had one or the other. As we saw with David, it took both ascribed (anointing) and achieved (Goliath) honor in order to add up to enough honor (in the eyes of the people) for David to be king. In fact, commonly someone's honor was evaluated by discussing both ascribed and achieved honor. Both were at work in the cases of David and Jephthah. Now, we will look at Paul.

The honor of Paul. Near the end of Acts, when Paul comes to Jerusalem, certain Jews from Asia see him in the temple and begin to stir up a crowd. They accuse Paul of preaching against the Jewish people and the law and of bringing a Gentile into the temple (Acts 21:27-30). Paul wants to defend himself before the crowd. He begins with kinship language: "Brothers and fathers" (Acts 22:1). Then he lists how he is honorable, not to brag but to tell the crowd, "Look, I'm worth listening to. I'm not just some thug you should ignore." In his speech, Paul lists both ascribed and achieved honors. He is a Jew, born in Tarsus of Cilicia (Acts 22:3), ascribed honors the crowd would value. Then Paul notes he excelled in his education, becoming a student of the leading teacher in Jerusalem, Gamaliel, an achieved honor they would esteem. He adds zeal: "I was just as zealous for God as any of you are today" (Acts 22:3), an honor achieved by only a few. Paul is successful. The crowd calms down and listens to him (Acts 22:22).

As in the examples of David and Paul, honor is more like a portfolio than a single source. A person is the sum of both achieved and ascribed honor. But rarely are they equal in weight. Someone is usually honored for royal blood (ascribed) far more than any of their deeds (achieved). David sees that Saul's ascribed honor as being the Lord's anointed far outweighs his behavior (with its little achieved honor). In the eyes of the crowds, Jesus has little ascribed honor: "Isn't this the carpenter's son?" (Mt 13:55). Yet, he has a lot of achieved honor: "Many people saw the signs he was performing and believed in his name" (Jn 2:23).

HONOR BETWEEN GROUPS

So far in this chapter, we have looked at cases of honor where those involved generally shared values. What happens when one collective group interacts with another and they don't share the same values? This sometimes happens in the New Testament when groups had different values and thus honored different things.

Jews and Gentiles were different collective groups. In general, they really didn't care about the value system of the other. Both absolutely cared about honor, but their *values* were different, so the traits and behaviors reinforced by honor (i.e., considered honorable) were different. Since they had different values, often there was no honor to be gained or lost in their interactions. Honor was used to enforce values, but one group could enforce a particular value not shared by the other. While Jews made up about 14 percent of the empire, they didn't integrate very well because they had some very different values from the rest of the pagan empire. Since their values didn't prevent them from paying taxes and obeying Roman laws, they were generally left alone. Keeping the Sabbath, observing food laws, and practicing circumcision were important to the Jews, so Jews honored those who did. They withheld honor from those who didn't (such as Gentiles). But Gentiles didn't care, so they felt they were losing no honor. They wrote it off as Jews being "a peculiar people."[7]

"While Gallio was proconsul of Achaia, the Jews of Corinth made a united attack on Paul and brought him to the place of judgment" (Acts 18:12). Paul's accusers strike to the heart of the matter. The charge they bring against Paul is a serious issue of honor to Jews. "'This man,' they charged, 'is persuading the people to worship God in ways contrary to the law'" (Acts 18:13). For Jews, keeping the law was a value they constantly reinforced. They accuse Paul of crossing a boundary. (We'll talk about boundaries later.) Before Paul can defend his honor, Gallio rules that Gentiles have no interest: "Just as Paul was about to speak, Gallio said to them, 'If you Jews were making a complaint about some misdemeanor or serious

---

[7]James D. G. Dunn, *The New Perspective on Paul*, rev. ed. (Grand Rapids, MI: Eerdmans, 2008), 109.

crime, it would be reasonable for me to listen to you. But since it involves questions about words and names and your own law—settle the matter yourselves. I will not be a judge of such things'" (Acts 18:14-15). It is not a matter of Roman law. Gallio and probably every other Roman in the Corinthian agora within earshot had no particular interest in the Jewish god or Jewish customs. As polytheists, they wouldn't have wanted to offend any god (or goddess), but they had no interest in the proper or improper ways to worship him. Gallio has no honor at stake in their debate. The Jews bring the wrong kind of charge against Paul—a point Gallio makes. This judicial mistake shames the Jews (which we'll talk about later). They beat the man who causes their shaming, but again Gallio has nothing at stake: "So he drove them off. Then the crowd there turned on Sosthenes the synagogue leader and beat him in front of the proconsul; and Gallio showed no concern whatever" (Acts 18:16-17).[8] There is no honor for Gallio to achieve (or lose) in their action, so he has "no concern."

Paul and Roman aristocrat Seneca had different values.[9] Seneca considered anger to always be a sin. Paul writes, "In your anger do not sin" (Eph 4:26). Likewise, Seneca would likely have disagreed in several ways with Paul's command, "Rather, in humility value others above yourselves" (Phil 2:3). What was a matter of honor to one group was insignificant to another. They saw no honor to be gained or lost.

It is not that Gentiles *never* cared what Jews and Christians did. When there was a value both groups shared, both groups saw that honor was involved. When Paul is in Thessalonica, Jews and Gentiles both feel Paul threatens the honor of their city. The authorities take action against Paul:

> When Paul and his companions had passed through Amphipolis and Apollonia, they came to Thessalonica, where there was a Jewish synagogue. As was his custom, Paul went into the synagogue. . . . Some of the Jews were

---

[8]It is not possible to know whether this is the same Sosthenes in 1 Cor 1:1, but as we will show in chap. 12, when shame is used too heavily (or unrelentingly) and thus inappropriately, it can drive a person out of the community to seek another one. It would be reasonable for their actions to encourage Sosthenes to find another community. God works through cultural systems.

[9]See, e.g., Joseph R. Dodson and David E. Briones, eds., *Paul and the Giants of Philosophy: Reading the Apostle in Greco-Roman Context* (Downers Grove, IL: InterVarsity Press, 2019).

persuaded and joined Paul and Silas, as did a large number of God-fearing Greeks and quite a few prominent women. But other Jews were jealous. (Acts 17:1-2, 4-5)

The Jews are angry. Luke is very clear why. Some patronesses have given Paul their support: "quite a few prominent women," Luke subtly notes. There is a potential loss of honor (and potential funding) for the Thessalonian Jews, if these prominent women stop acting as patronesses for the Jewish community. Thessalonian Gentiles, though, won't care because those patronesses will support some other Thessalonian cause. Some patronesses changing clients *within Thessalonica* will not upset city leaders. If the Jews want to incite the Gentiles against Paul, they will need to find another reason, a threat against a shared value. Luke continues the story:

> But other Jews were jealous; so they rounded up some bad characters from the marketplace, formed a mob and started a riot in the city. They rushed to Jason's house in search of Paul and Silas in order to bring them out to the crowd. But when they did not find them, they dragged Jason and some other believers before the city officials, shouting: "These men who have caused trouble all over the world have now come here, and Jason has welcomed them into his house. They are all defying Caesar's decrees, saying that there is another king, one called Jesus." When they heard this, the crowd and the city officials were thrown into turmoil. Then they made Jason and the others post bond and let them go. (Acts 17:5-9)

The Thessalonian Jews are smart enough to know they cannot charge Paul with gaining patronage from patronesses, however disruptive it could prove to be to them personally. Patrons supported whomever they wished. Instead they drum up another charge that will resonate with the racist attitudes of most Gentiles. The year before, Emperor Claudius had evicted Jews from Rome (Acts 18:2). It would seem reasonable to Thessalonian city officials that whatever contagion hit Rome has now spread to their city. This was a shared value: their city is in danger of unrest.

Protecting their city was a value shared by all Thessalonians, Jew and Gentile. Apparently, the Jews knew something of Paul's activities. They knew Paul was holding meetings in Jason's home and that Christians considered

Jesus to be king. Unlawful meetings and treason against Caesar (calling Jesus their king) were illegal. The Jews knew such charges would resonate with city leaders: these troublemakers (Paul and his friends) should be arrested or at least banished. Jason would be guilty of harboring troublemakers (something else Romans hated). If city officials permitted such activities, their honor (and thus their positions) would be at risk. Paul's opponents in Thessalonica knew to present a value that mattered to both Jews and Gentiles there. The honor involved would get a response.

CHANGING GROUP ALLEGIANCE

Gentiles valued respecting the gods. They honored those who did. Pythagoras was praised because he was an expert on the proper rituals to honor the gods.[10] The wealthy competed over who could give a greater gift to respect the gods, such as building or remodeling a temple or paying for a feast in honor of gods. When some Gentile Thessalonians joined the Christian community, what they honored changed. Honoring the gods was no longer esteemed. Rather, as Christians, they were to honor the one God. Paul reinforces that value by honoring them in a letter, noting how other churches honor them for doing so: "You became a model to all the believers in Macedonia and Achaia. . . . They tell how you turned to God from idols to serve the living and true God" (1 Thess 1:7, 9). Paul is using honor to reinforce the value. Their values changed, and so what was considered honorable changed too. Now they are honored for worshiping the one God, rather than worshiping idols. What was once a source of honor (respecting pagan gods) was no longer worthy of honor, but ridicule. Values changed because the Gentile Thessalonians changed communities. They now belonged to a new community with different values. This is part of the process of discipleship in honor-based cultures.[11]

---

[10]See, e.g., Carl Huffman, "Pythagoras," in *The Stanford Encyclopedia of Philosophy*, Winter 2018 ed., ed. Edward N. Zalta, https://plato.stanford.edu/archives/win2018/entries/pythagoras.

[11]It can be debated whether changing community leads to a change of values or whether a change of values leads to a change of community. Is it "believe, belong, behave" or "believe, behave, belong"? An interesting discipleship debate, but not essential for our point. Correlation is sufficient.

Paul changed what he honored, too, when he changed communities. As a Pharisee, he valued his *ascribed* honors: tribe of Benjamin, son of a Pharisee. He valued also his *achieved* honors: advanced in training beyond his peers, zealous for traditions, and a persecutor of the church. These things were honored by his community (the Pharisees). After he encountered Jesus and came to belong to the followers of Jesus, Paul valued this new community's *ascribed* honors: being a slave of Christ (Rom 1:1), of humility and weakness and of his reliance on Christ (1 Cor 12:9), and being called an apostle to the Gentiles (Rom 11:13). These are very different values. He also changed his *achieved* honors: suffering for Christ (2 Cor 11:30-33) and being the patron and father of congregations (1 Cor 4:15). Paul's values had changed. He boasts about these new values. He now considers them more important than the values of his former way of life.

CONCLUSION: HONOR WAS EVERYWHERE BUT NOT EVERYWHERE THE SAME

Honor was used by different groups to enforce different values. What earned you a high seat at the banquet table in one group might have no impact on your seating by another group. When members of different collective groups interacted, honor could be at play, but it was rarely as simple as some books might suggest.

Why does this matter? Well, it helps us read the Bible better. For example, we might assume that all Jews in Palestine shared the same values. They were Jews living in the same land and culture, after all. But this is not the case. There were Sadducees, Pharisees, Essenes, and Zealots. Some values were shared, but others were not. So when we read of a clash between two groups in the New Testament, is it correct to read it as an honor contest? Well, it depends. If they shared the value, then honor was at stake between them. When they didn't share the value, they might bicker, but no honor contest ensued. So the Pharisees and Sadducees clashed over different beliefs, such as whether there was resurrection from the dead (Acts 23:8) but no honor was at stake. The Sadducees lost no honor if Pharisees taught about resurrection, because the Pharisees used texts and quotations from sources the Sadducees did not value. The Sadducees only honored the five books of Moses. They might have sneered but wouldn't have had an honor contest over interpreting Daniel.

When Jesus argues for resurrection using *their* books, it is a different matter, and we see that Matthew reports it as an honor contest:

> That same day the Sadducees, who say there is no resurrection, came to him with a question . . . "Now then, at the resurrection, whose wife will she be of the seven, since all of them were married to her?"
>
> Jesus replied, "You are in error because you do not know the Scriptures or the power of God. At the resurrection people will neither marry nor be given in marriage; they will be like the angels in heaven. But about the resurrection of the dead—have you not read what God said to you, 'I am the God of Abraham, the God of Isaac, and the God of Jacob'? He is not the God of the dead but of the living." When the crowds heard this, they were astonished at his teaching. (Mt 22:23, 28-33)

So groups could struggle over honor. Scholars call those honor contests, which we'll discuss in the next chapter. For now we see honor is at stake in this scenario because Jesus is disputing with the Sadducees over the public interpretation of a text that both Jesus and the Sadducees consider sacred (Ex 3:6).

Of all the things that went without being said, honor might be the biggest one. Collective honor often explains why biblical characters act as they do. Jesus was killed over honor.

9

HONOR CONTESTS

HONOR KILLINGS HAVE BEEN AROUND for millennia and mystify
most of us raised in an individualist society. Coincidentally, many collectives condemn honor killing in stronger terms than any Westerner. In reality, the main reason we individualists shake our heads, thinking, *I wonder
how anyone could ever do that,* isn't moral outrage but because we can't
understand the motivation. Often it seems to us the wrong person was
killed. Many of us might (privately) admit that we are mystified why
someone would want to kill Jesus. He went around preaching, "Love one
another." How could masses of people celebrate him on (Palm) Sunday,
and then just five days later, the same folks yell "Crucify him!"?

Honor is always complex and deeply collective. We oversimplified in
the previous chapter when we stated that if groups clashed over something
that wasn't a shared value, there was no honor at stake. It is true one side
couldn't care less because they didn't value it. But often when they clashed
some part of the conflict touched on a shared value. People clashed over
honor all the time. We need to consider what it was they were clashing
over. Was it a shared value, or some shared and some nonshared values, or
was it just a conflict? This helps us understand whether, and how, honor
was motivating the contest.

Collective honor is such a difficult topic for most individualists, first,
because we don't have words for it. Our English word *honor* is woefully
inadequate. It is an etic word (see chap. 3 for our discussion on the term
etic). We hope you have seen that. Second, collective honor just isn't in
our DNA as individualists. While we individualists talk about honorable

things, honor isn't a subconscious, motivating, daily drive in most of us. Our discussions are inevitably hypothetical and detached, while honor is actually deeply contextual and intensely personal for collectivists. For us it is an intellectual concept, not a group of people looking expectantly at us. Yet, a challenge over honor strikes to the very core of collectivists, like a slap in the face. It's difficult to turn the other cheek. The existence and flow of honor drives much of their thinking and actions, just like Western values (guilt, change, efficiency) subconsciously drive so much of mine.[1]

THE ELEMENTS OF AN HONOR CONTEST

Besides honorable deeds, the other very common way people achieved honor in the ancient Mediterranean world was through honor contests with others. In honor contests, someone challenges another person, and if successful, they come out of the contest having gained honor at the other's expense. Scholars like to identify three different phases at work in these contests.[2]

One party challenges another. A challenger can contest the honor of another in many ways. Perhaps he says something, or does something, or perhaps even does not do something, toward the other party. The point is that the challenger implies he (or she) believes he has higher honor than the other party considers them to be due. If the other party recognizes the challenger as demanding more honor, then a contest occurs. Scholars have called this the honor game. As an etic term it is terrible. *Game* belies its seriousness. One's place in society, one's vocation, the family business, a child's marriage options, all could be at stake. People (including Jesus) have been killed over honor contests. It is scarcely a game.

It is difficult to understand honor contests in the abstract, so let's suppose an illustration. Mason is from the town of Tiom in the Baliem Valley of central Papua, Indonesia (one of the most remote regions of the world). As

---

[1] For a fuller discussion, see E. Randolph Richards and Brandon J. O'Brien, *Misreading Scripture with Western Eyes* (Downers Grove, IL: InterVarsity Press, 2008).

[2] We are indebted to Bruce J. Malina for his work on honor contests for the following description. See Malina, *The New Testament World: Insights from Cultural Anthropology*, 3rd ed. (Louisville, KY: Westminster John Knox, 2001), 33-36. We have modified his description.

a Dani tribesman, his culture is very collective. He excelled in the Tiom grade school and was sent off to middle school at the provincial capital, Wamena. Upon excelling, he was sent to high school at Jayapura, on the north coast of Papua. Eventually he found his way to the seminary on another island, where Randy taught. Mason earned his master's degree and was ordained to ministry. A few years later, word arrived that a prominent member of his family was getting married, and Mason decided to return to Tiom—no easy journey. He knew it wouldn't just be a quick trip. Likely his family would arrange a marriage, and he would serve in ministry there.

Upon arrival, at the next banquet, as an adult member of his family, he was offered a seat about halfway up the long table of over a hundred seats. Mason moved past the offered seat, walked up the table, and stood behind a chair nine seats down from the head of the table, where the village chief sat. The chief looked at Mason, and the entire room went quiet. Mason was the challenger, claiming that his village had not recognized all the honor he had achieved.

Before we shrug it off and say, "Just sit down, Mason!" we need to recognize what was at stake. If Mason sat, that person would have to move down a chair, as would the next, and so on. His claim to honor would impact nearly half the village. "Those who sit near" the chief had places at council, rights to village assets, and the respect of the town. The number of families that might offer a daughter in marriage to Mason could triple. Someone else's options would be reduced. The banquet table truly is a picture of one's standing in the community. More than that, it was the standing of Mason's entire family in the community.

The challenged person responds. If the challenged party acknowledges the other as claiming more honor, then they can either concede the additional honor is due to the other party or confront the claim. In order for an honor contest to occur, the two parties have to be viewed as within an acceptable circle or range of honor. Generally, a peasant cannot challenge the honor of a king. They are too far apart. Someone with no honor cannot challenge the honor of a person of rank. In the ancient world, if a member of the Sanhedrin were in the market and a blind person shouted out a question, the ruler could ignore the question with no loss of honor. Jesus is not honor-bound to respond to the blind men who call out, "Have mercy on us, Son of David!" (Mt 9:27). There is no honor at stake. This makes Jesus' actions all the more compassionate. When Job demands an audience with God, there is no honor contest. God's honor is beyond challenge by humankind.[3] (It is *mercy* that leads God to respond to Job's angry outbursts.) Assuming that a challenger's challenge is acknowledged by the challenged, the contest comes into effect.

In our example, the village chief was the one challenged. He had options. He could have just nodded and accepted Mason's claim. He could have insisted that Mason retake his lower seat. He could have done it unkindly, with a frown, or kindly, by making some jest that Mason has been gone so long he has forgotten where to sit. The chief could have offered some seat in-between. He could have made some derogatory snort or gesture that would shame Mason into leaving the banquet.

The court of reputation weighs in. In addition to the challenger and the challenged, honor contests usually need a third party. Scholars generally call this third party "the court of reputation" because this party acts as the judge. A contest over honor has to have a verdict in order for honor to be exchanged. While usually individuals challenge one another, they are collectives, and so their group's honor is involved. None of this is about individuals. Since honor contests are almost always public, people are watching. Without a collective audience to recognize that honor has or has not flowed to another, it is hard for there to be an honor contest at all.[4] In some ways, they are actually the ones who determine whether an honor challenge has been made. They murmur and otherwise publicly express displeasure if they feel one person is trying to ignore the legitimate challenge of another.

---

[3]Technically, for this reason, the Gospel writers might conclude (postresurrection) that Jesus was never in a true honor contest with anyone. As God-in-the-flesh, his questions to others and their questions of him were not true honor contests. Yet, during his ministry, those encounters were viewed by the others and by the crowds as honor contests.

[4]Some scholars argue it is impossible for an honor contest to occur in private. We disagree. The actual contest might be private, but if at least one person thinks that one day the news might reach their people, it is seen as an honor contest. Nonetheless, in general, honor contests need to be public.

In our example, the entire room was the court of reputation. Whatever response the chief provided would be weighed by the room. If it seemed justified, the crowd would nod approvingly, hum appropriately, and so on. If they did not agree, the crowds would grumble. If the chief ignored the grumble, they would gossip about him later. In Mason's case, the chief asks, "Why have you not taken your family's seat?"—a somewhat neutral response. Mason recounts to the entire room all that he had achieved. The crowd nods approvingly, and after a thoughtful pause, as if weighing the case, the chief also nods. Mason takes his seat. The entire community is actually happy. Why? Because now they *all* could boast that their village had a minister with a master's of theology, who had studied off-island. The language that scholars use can sometimes allow us to fit honor contests into an individualist grid, but they are not about individuals.

HONOR CONTESTS IN THE BIBLE

The New Testament often notes how the crowd responds to an honor contest. Sometimes the crowd is amazed and sometimes it grumbles.[5] For example, Jesus claims the honor of being a teacher, and Matthew tells us, "When Jesus had finished saying these things, the crowds were amazed at his teaching" (Mt 7:28). We should not be surprised, then, that Jesus is afforded the title "Teacher" by another teacher after this point in Matthew's Gospel (Mt 8:19). Jesus' status as a teacher has been acknowledged by the community.

On another occasion, John recounts that Jesus claims the (what seems to them ridiculously) high honor of being the heavenly bread of life. The crowd does not support his claim. Note how John's account is replete with honor: "At this the Jews there began to grumble about him because he said, 'I am the bread that came down from heaven.' They said, 'Is this not Jesus,

---

[5]The court looks at the honor of the challenger (both ascribed and achieved, and various balances depending on context) and decides whether the person merits the respect (honor) they are claiming. The so-called court of reputation will deem whether the challenger's behavior is appropriate and their new amount of honor is accepted. If the court agrees, the challenger has successfully defended his (or her) assertion to have more honor. If, however, the challenger's response is lacking in the eyes of those watching, then this court of reputation will reject this claimed honor. This may even move him down in their estimation, if his actions failed to embody their community's values.

the son of Joseph, whose father and mother we know? How can he now say, "I came down from heaven?"'" (Jn 6:41-42). They assume being the heavenly bread of life is an ascribed honor. Like the manna that God miraculously provided, Jesus would need to be ascribed this honor by God. They point to his known ascribed honor—his family of origin. His claim doesn't match his ascribed honor, in their view. In this case, the court of opinion begins to rule against Jesus. He makes it worse by adding, "Does this offend you? Then what if you see the Son of Man ascend to where he was before!" (Jn 6:61-62). Wow, Jesus has now claimed an even higher honor: the Son of Man who ascends (Dan 7:13-14). John tells us the court's verdict: "From this time many of his disciples turned back and no longer followed him" (Jn 6:66).

Between the Lord (Yahweh) and Baal. The Old Testament text often gives God the name Yahweh Elohim. English translates the Hebrew "the Lord God," as in, "This is the account of the heavens and the earth when they were created, when the Lord God made the earth and the heavens" (Gen 2:4). Scholars sometimes call this a double name, but it more likely just meant "the God Yahweh." For modern Christians, *God* just means "God." But in the ancient world, where there were many gods, the text wanted to be very clear it was talking about the Lord God, the God Yahweh. The Lord (Yahweh, I AM) is the name he gives himself on Mount Sinai:

> Moses said to God, "Suppose I go to the Israelites and say to them, 'The God of your fathers has sent me to you,' and they ask me, 'What is his name?' Then what shall I tell them?"
>
> God said to Moses, "I AM WHO I AM [YHWH, Yahweh]. This is what you are to say to the Israelites: 'I AM [Yahweh] has sent me to you.'" (Ex 3:13-14)

Now to the contest on Mount Carmel in 1 Kings 18. It would be easy to misunderstand this encounter as a contest between Elijah and Jezebel, but they only speak for their gods. The contest is clearly between Yahweh, the Lord (the traditional God of Israel), and Baal, the god that Ahab (through Jezebel) is pushing to supplant Yahweh. The contest begins with the Lord publicly challenging Baal. Baal was the god of storm and rain. His statues often showed him holding a lightning bolt.[6] When Elijah announces there will be no rain, the LORD is challenging Baal's right to send the seasonal rain (and thus the crops). As moderns, we think in terms of low-pressure systems and atmospheric movements. To all ancients, rain was a gift from the gods. The Jews were no exception:

> Sing to the LORD with grateful praise . . .
> He covers the sky with clouds;
>   he supplies the earth with rain. . . .
> He provides food for the cattle. (Ps 147:7-9)

> Your father in heaven . . . sends rain on the righteous and the
>   unrighteous. (Mt 5:45)

So, does rain comes from God or from Baal? Ahab insists Baal, who lives on mountains, sends the rain. Elijah announces the LORD will send no more rain, and, importantly, no more rain comes.

So the honor contest begins and is held on Baal's best territory: on a mountain. This is not just any mountain but Mount Carmel, the mountain on the border between Baal's established land (Phoenicia) and the land Baal is now claiming (Israel). The LORD gives every advantage to Baal to underline the difference in power. Baal is offered his place, his choice of bulls (1 Kings 18:23), and his weapon of choice (lightning). Once Baal fails, then the LORD further shows off, dousing the altar with water (which was in short supply). With every advantage given to Baal, it is the LORD who sends down fire to light the offering. The conclusion is clear. The verdict of the court of opinion is announced: "When all the people saw this, they fell prostrate and cried, 'The LORD—he is God!'" (1 Kings 18:39).

Between Jesus and the religious authorities. Individualist readers may think that the religious authorities challenged Jesus because of the content of his teaching. Sometimes that was the case. But it wasn't always. Other times they were responding to Jesus' claim of honor, such as the right to

---

[6]Most surviving statues show his raised hand, but what he was holding is lost. A stele (engraved image) shows him holding a lightning bolt. See "Baal with Thunderbolt," Wikipedia, https://en.wikipedia.org/wiki/Baal_with_Thunderbolt (accessed December 12, 2018).

teach the people on a prominent or even the premier public stage. It was one level of honor to teach peasants in a field or standing in a boat in Galilee. It was quite another to claim the honor to teach in the temple (Lk 20:1). The religious authorities valued being able to teach the people. Jesus is claiming to have that honor.

An honor contest ensues. Jesus claimed the honor by his actions, and they respond to his challenge: "The chief priests and the teachers of the law, together with the elders, came up to him. 'Tell us by what authority you are doing these things,' they said. 'Who gave you this authority?'" (Lk 20:1-2). The chief priests and elders had the honor to teach in the temple. Like my friend Mason, marching up to take a higher seat at a banquet in Papua, Jesus is publicly claiming a higher honor. They set the tone by insulting Jesus. They ask (in front of everyone), "Who gave you this authority?" Had they asked, "What have you done that gives you this right?" Jesus could have countered by telling of his miracles. Instead, their question shows they have ruled out the possibility that Jesus has achieved enough honor. They set the stage by asserting that Jesus could only have enough honor if it had been ascribed (given) to him. Tell us, they say, Who has ascribed this honor to you?

Jesus responds, "I will also ask you a question" (Lk 20:3). We might want to know what the rules of these honor contests were, whether Jesus was allowed to respond to a question with a question. It depended on what those watching, the court of reputation, considered to be honorable. They were the judges. Their collective opinion determined what they collectively accepted about you. If they thought it was honorable for you to respond with a question, then you could. Evidently, the crowd does in this case (perhaps because the leaders' question is so insulting). Jesus asks, "Tell me: John's baptism—was it from heaven, or of human origin?" (Lk 20:3-4). In other words, "Okay, let's talk ascribed authority. So who ascribed the authority to John the Baptist? God or people?"

The religious leaders are stumped. As a result, they lose honor because they must admit (publicly) they can't (publicly) answer the question. The court of reputation knows the answer. The crowd is thinking, *Even we*

know that John the Baptist was from God. Worse, the crowd is likely to conclude that if the leaders can't decide whether John is from God, when
everyone present knows, who are they to claim to be able to teach or judge
Jesus (or anyone else)? The leaders lose honor because they are clearly
seen to be afraid to take a stand on what they think. They are not acting as
brave teachers of Israel, as having no concerns higher than the law of God.
They fail to embody a community value. Jesus concludes, "Neither will I
tell you by what authority I am doing these things" (Lk 20:8). Jesus is
saying, "If you won't publicly say whether John is from God or not, who
are you to decide publicly whether I am?" Jesus is noting the temple
leaders don't get to rule on John the Baptist's authority. The court of reputation does. So also Jesus is refusing to allow them to rule on his authority.
Let the court of reputation do it.

Then the religious leaders ask about paying taxes to Caesar. The
question is designed to trick. They are placing Jesus between two courts
of opinion: the crowd (the oppressed) and the Romans (the oppressors).
It is impossible for Jesus to answer without offending one of them and
incurring their wrath. The crowd would have recognized that they were
only asking Jesus the question to trap him. It is unlikely that Jesus would
lose honor for refusing to answer a trick question. But Jesus says, "Show
me a coin." One of his challengers pulls out a silver denarius.

As soon as he does, the issue is settled. Jesus has won. The rest is expo-
sition. A denarius had an inscription calling Caesar "Savior and God." The
whole reason to have moneychangers was that Jews were not supposed to
have coins like that *in the temple.* Other coins were available. About thirty-
eight cities in that region had the right to issue their own coins. Thieves
often shaved off or snipped off small amounts of the metal from the edges
of coins, reducing the value of the coins. A silver denarius was, however,
made from (theoretically) a denarius's worth of silver, and Rome protected the integrity of its own coins. Rome aggressively (and violently)
crushed any attempts to devalue (shave or snip) its coins. Thus, a Roman
coin was more likely to be whole, which is why Roman coins were preferred over local coins and why this devout Jew has a denarius in his

pocket. So Jesus is pointing out, here is a guy who likes to use Caesar's coins because they are secured, but he doesn't want to pay for the empire to secure them. The leaders are being hypocritical. The Jews like Caesar's money and his roads and his safety from bandits and pirates, but they don't want to pay for these things.[7]

The leaders are unable to catch Jesus in his words. Moreover, the questioners are seen to lose honor. They decide not to continue: "They were unable to trap him in what he had said there in public. And astonished by his answer, they became silent" (Lk 20:26). Jesus has proven his superiority in the court of reputation.

Nicodemus: not an honor contest. Questions were often a means to make an honor challenge, as in the example above. The result was a verbal joust as each side tried to show they were the ones who embodied in a superior way the values the community held. This is likely why, in John 3, Nicodemus comes to Jesus at night. Nicodemus probably thinks that if he asks Jesus a question in public, it could become an honor contest. Nicodemus doesn't want to get into an honor contest. He has a genuine question. Similarly, when the disciples can't figure out what Jesus is talking about, they remain quiet until the crowds leave: "After he had left the crowd and entered the house, his disciples asked him about this parable" (Mk 7:17; see also Mk 10:10). They want clarification, not honor. That's why the Gospel writers take the time to tell us they don't ask in front of the crowd. Nicodemus is likely doing the same thing.

Jesus has just cleared the temple in John's story. He is asked to produce a sign, and he doesn't do one—at least not one the authorities or the crowd like (Jn 2:18-19). It is in this context that a member of the Sanhedrin (Jn 3:1; 7:50) enters the picture. It is likely the market had been recently relocated inside the temple because of a squabble within the

---

[7]Jesus' response, to give to Caesar what is Caesar's and to God what is God's, is difficult to interpret. It seems unlikely that Jesus is dividing the world into parts that belong to God and other parts that do not (although this is a traditional interpretation). Rather, Jesus may be saying that there are two ways to have honest money and safe roads: Caesar's way (by force) and God's way (by being part of his kingdom). In heaven, there will be no need for police to enforce the rules.

Sanhedrin.[8] It is easy to see why some wouldn't like this and why at least some would have initially applauded a prophetic denunciation. They would have cheered at Jesus' public critique of putting the market within the temple walls. They would have liked the symbolic action of turning over tables. It looked like something Elisha might have done. But they would also have been very disappointed Jesus produced no miraculous sign to demonstrate he had this authority.

Nicodemus represents others ("we know," Jn 3:2), possibly those who opposed the market's new location inside the temple. Nicodemus was a Pharisee, and Pharisees cared a lot about ritual purity. Nicodemus notes Jesus is a teacher *come from God* who does miraculous signs, such as what the crowd demanded publicly. Nicodemus comes at night because he wants a private meeting to sort out their confusion. Perhaps Nicodemus and some colleagues are mystified, even frustrated, because Jesus failed to defend himself with a miraculous sign, which they know he can do ("the signs you are doing," Jn 3:2). They are unsure whether Jesus was *unable at that moment* or *unwilling at that moment* to perform a sign. Nicodemus's reasoning might be: "If God withheld a miraculous sign, perhaps it was because Jesus had overstepped his bounds, which would mean God doesn't mind the market being inside the temple." Nicodemus has a genuine theological question. The Gospel of John doesn't delve into Nicodemus' theological quandary. The Gospel tells the Nicodemus story for another reason. John has just noted: "But Jesus, on His part, was not entrusting Himself to them, for He knew all men, and because He did not need anyone to testify concerning man (*anthrōpos*), for He Himself knew

---

[8]Evidence suggests the market with its animals was moved into the temple precincts that year (or at least recently). While the moneychangers had a longstanding presence, Victor Eppstein argues the animals were moved into the temple as part of a squabble among temple leaders. See Eppstein, "The Historicity of the Gospel Account of the Cleansing of the Temple," *Zeitschrift für die neutestamentliche Wissenschaft und die Kunde der älteren Kirche* 55 (1964): 42-58, esp. 56-57. Eppstein contends the high priest Caiaphas fell out with the Sanhedrin in AD 30 and withdrew permission for the Sanhedrin to use the Chamber of Hewn Stone. The owners of the traditional animal market (on the Mount of Olives, which was considered an extension of the temple area) gave the Sanhedrin a room to use. In revenge, Caiaphas gave their competitors permission to place their animals in the Court of Gentiles for the first time in history. Jesus' response may suggest that he reacted the first time he saw it (whether one sees one or two clearings).

what was in man (*anthrōpos*)" (John 2:24-25 NASB). Then in the next sentence, John writes, "Now there was a man (*anthrōpos*) of the Pharisees, named Nicodemus, a ruler of the Jews" (John 3:1 NASB). Nicodemus becomes the first example of Jesus knowing what's in the heart of man (*anthrōpos*). The Samaritan woman in John 4 becomes another.

At Jesus' trial. The trial of Jesus pivots around the issue of honor. Jesus has been winning honor from the Jewish leaders (at least in the eyes of the leaders and the crowds).[9] The leaders want their honor back. In the triumphal entry, Jesus claims the honor of being the Messiah, the Christ, the King of the Jews. Jesus is asked to deny the honor, and he *refuses*:

> As he went along, people spread their cloaks on the road.
>
> When he came near the place where the road goes down the Mount of Olives, the whole crowd of disciples began joyfully to praise God in loud voices for all the miracles they had seen:
>
> "Blessed is the king who comes in the name of the Lord!"
>
> "Peace in heaven and glory in the highest!"
>
> Some of the Pharisees in the crowd said to Jesus, "Teacher, rebuke your disciples!"
>
> "I tell you," he replied, "if they keep quiet, the stones will cry out." (Lk 19:36-40)

The crowd understood the Messiah to be like David; after all, another name for the Messiah was "Son of David." How did David establish his kingdom? With a sword. Everyone—even his disciples—expects Jesus to lead an armed revolt against the Romans. On that fateful night, the disciples bring swords (Lk 22:38) and ask when to draw them (Lk 22:49). Peter actually does pull his out and use it (Lk 22:50). Jesus refuses to lead an armed revolt (Mt 26:55). This is unfathomable to every Jew. How can anyone be a Messiah (like David) if he won't lead an army? Impossible, the crowd thinks. (Hindsight is twenty-twenty. Now, we understand how.)

---

[9]Again, we argue those really weren't honor contests because Jesus was God. Jesus didn't need or want to draw honor from the Jewish leaders. Actually, even by accepting Jesus as Messiah (king), they likely could be excused from the honor contests. But in their culture and with their understanding, it seemed to them that Jesus had taken their honor.

When Jesus volunteers himself to be arrested, no one sees anything Davidic in his actions. They honored him on (Palm) Sunday and now regret it. Their honor is at risk, in their minds, since they backed the wrong candidate.

The trial is partly over whether Jesus has the necessary honor to be designated Messiah. Clearly, in the eyes of the leaders and the people, Jesus does not have the *ascribed* honor. Jesus was anointed, sure, but by a *woman* (Jn 12). That doesn't count—in the court of public opinion. No king or court has recognized him as the Messiah. The crowds ascribed it to him on Sunday, but they changed their mind by Friday. By Friday, the clear verdict of the crowds is that Jesus is no David: "Give us Barabbas!" Unlike Jesus, at least Barabbas had *tried* to fight the Romans (Lk 23:18-19).[10] If Jesus has the honor, it wasn't ascribed. (Luke later argues that angels and even God himself ascribed the honor to Jesus; Lk 2:9-14; 3:38.)

Behind the trial is the question of whether Jesus has *achieved* the honor to be king. The leaders cannot dispute his miracles. His teachings have impressed the crowd. But King David didn't perform miracles or teach the crowds. In the eyes of the Jewish leadership, while Jesus may have achieved the honor of being called a teacher or miracle worker, it seemed clear that Jesus had not achieved the honor of being King. How could they demonstrate this fact to the crowds, who weren't so sure? If Jesus blasphemed the temple or otherwise was a lawbreaker, then to any Jewish crowd it would be clear Jesus did not have the necessary honor. It is evident at the crucifixion that the crowd agrees Jesus doesn't have the honor. Even passersby ridicule Jesus. We should not fail to add: a wonderful side effect for the religious leaders is that if Jesus is convicted and *publicly* executed, then any honor they lost to him in honor contests will be restored. Honor killings then and now are usually to restore honor. Proving to the people that Jesus had no honor was a win for leaders of both the Pharisees and the Sadducees. They defended their position and honor, and their values.

---

[10]Luke is being richly ironic in telling us the name the Romans had given to the criminal. Barabbas in Aramaic means "son of father." The Romans, not speaking Aramaic, didn't recognize it as a pseudonym: "a son of a father." The Romans assumed it was a legitimate name. Luke is ironic and expects us to catch it: the crowds ask for "a son of a father" instead of "the Son of the Father" (Lk 3:38).

A public execution publicly shamed Jesus for claiming more honor than he had deserved. The resurrection, among other things, demonstrated the Father's vindication of Jesus' honor (Phil 2:6-11). But we should not downplay the interim impact of the trial and execution. We may easily concede it affected the disciples, but what of Jesus? He was a man of his culture. Crosses publicly shamed. Hebrews insists that Jesus despised (not denied) the shame of the cross (Heb 12:2).

Yet, God corrected the verdict of the court of reputation, both that of the Jews and the Romans. His is the final word (Heb 1:1-4). The resurrection, among other things, demonstrated the Father vindicating Jesus' honor. Jesus is raised, yes, but raised to sit at the right hand of God. Restoring Jesus' honor means also validating the values Jesus embodied. These values become values we are to honor in the body of Christ. This is more significant than we might first think. Paul writes to the newly founded church in Philippi, "Do nothing out of selfish ambition or vain conceit. Rather, in humility value others above yourselves, not looking to your own interests but each of you to the interests of the others" (Phil 2:3-4). We do well to read this passage in the context of honor and honor challenges in the Greco-Roman relational world around the Philippians. People tended to look out for their own interests and in pride sought to value themselves above others. These were the values behind many of their honor contests. Paul tells them not to live on this basis. Rather, they are "in humility" to "value others above yourselves" (Phil 2:3-4).

This would mean those who had status might move down the pecking order. In the Asian example we discussed earlier, it means offering the seat you (and your family) have long had to someone lower down the table, because you value them higher than yourself. You move down as a result. This is a challenge to those who are high up. The Philippians might well ask, "Why would I want to do that, Paul?" Paul goes on to outline the values behind this action, the values God honors.

> In your relationships with one another, have the same mindset as Christ Jesus:
>> Who, being in very nature God,
>>> did not consider equality with God something to be used to his own advantage;

rather, he made himself nothing
by taking the very nature of a servant,
being made in human likeness.
And being found in appearance as a man,
he humbled himself
by becoming obedient to death—
even death on a cross!
Therefore God exalted him to the highest place
and gave him the name that is above every name,
that at the name of Jesus every knee should bow,
in heaven and on earth and under the earth,
and every tongue acknowledge that Jesus Christ is Lord,
to the glory of God the Father. (Phil 2:5-11)

In his death on the cross, Jesus didn't consider defending his status something of importance. This is *not* a repudiation of honor. Note that God *honors* Jesus for having this value (Phil 2:9). Jesus is modeling a new value: one-downmanship. The world values one-upmanship and honors those who pursue it. The world thinks about who should submit to me. The Christian message is to ponder to whom should I submit. Rather than thinking of those under my authority, we should be only thinking of those under whose authority I am. While modern theologians are arguing about whether the Son is subordinate to the Father, the New Testament paints a different value system. The Father has placed all things (his things) under the Son's feet (Jn 3:35; Eph 1:20-22). The Son only does what the Father says (Jn 5:19). The Son allows many to disrespect him, but he says no one should disrespect the Spirit (Mt 12:31-32). The Spirit only glorifies the Son (Jn 16:14). While we might argue who is greater in the Trinity; the New Testament asserts that each part of the Trinity honors the other.

We should follow Christ's example. In humility, Jesus, who was high in status, made himself nothing. He gave up his status to serve others, as Paul is asking those with status to do in Philippi.[11] Jesus allowed himself to be

---

[11]Joseph H. Hellerman, *Reconstructing Honor in Roman Philippi: Carmen Christi as Cursus Pudorum* (New York: Cambridge University Press, 2005), 166.

brought down so low as to die on a cross. "Therefore God exalted him to the highest place" and gave him a name over all other names. God honored his Son. God also honored his Son's values: humility, love, and self-sacrifice. These are the kind of values the heavenly court of reputation values and honors. Paul says we are to let *these* values underlie our relations with others in our community. And he reminds them that God honors these values, even if the world does not. The Philippian Christians (and we today) should be pursuing honor, but for the right values.

10

HAVING SHAME

It Is Good for Everyone

"A member stole a book from our church library." It seemed an odd way to end an evening meal. I was enjoying coffee by the sea in Beirut with my friend Arman. "The book is not worth a lot," Arman continued, "so the cost of the book is not important, but this could split the church." This Armenian pastor-friend now had my full attention. How could a five-dollar book split a church? "This situation is serious," Arman explained, "because there is the potential for accusations or exposure, and this will bring shame on the man. If the shame is too strong, it will destroy the relationship between him and the rest of the church, and one of our church families could be lost." He was a shepherd worried for a sheep.

I wanted to help. "How do you solve this?" I asked. "Do you ignore the missing book?" "You can't ignore a stolen book," Arman smiled, "but it would need to be handled delicately. I will find a way to meet him. I will talk about other things. Then I will say, 'Oh, someone has stolen a book from the church, and I am worried that the neighborhood will think we have no morals and everyone in our church will get a bad name. So I just hope that whoever stole the book will bring it back soon.'"

Arman had two problems. He was worried that a sheep would get lost, but also that the entire flock would get a bad name.

Arman taught me it was important to use indirect speech and not to accuse directly. The man knew he took the book. He also knew that Arman knew he took it. So why beat around the bush? Shame. The man would see that his deed was pulling the entire church into disgrace. His sin was not limited to himself. He would feel shame because "he is we." He could imagine the flock's faces. They would be shamed because of him. But the man also would see that Arman, his pastor, was being careful to use indirect speech and to not accuse him directly. Arman would be reminding the man that his sin was affecting the entire group, and Arman would also be demonstrating respect and love by dealing with the situation in a kind and sensitive way. The man would not be forced to admit (or deny) the deed. (In the West, we would think the problem is that the man hasn't confessed his sin. In the East, they see the problem as broken relationships.) The man would see that Arman was providing a way to return, to restore the relationship, with the minimum amount of shame. His sin would be covered by his caring pastor: "love covers over all wrongs" (Prov 10:12). Peter reminds his leaders, "Above all, love each other deeply, because love covers over a multitude of sins" (1 Pet 4:8).

The next Sunday the book was there. The man was shamed but not disgraced. Nobody else knew about the matter, because love had covered the transgression. The pastor didn't directly accuse him but instead protected him from humiliation. Arman said, "We use the tool of shame because it is the best tool to use in this situation. If I label him a thief, he must fight or flight. Both would ruin the relationship. I don't shame him to condemn him, but to restore him." It worked. The man was repentant, and the church was protected. My Indonesian pastor-friends would approve: everyone saved face (preserved honor).

WHY WE GET SHAME WRONG AS INDIVIDUALISTS

People in the ancient Mediterranean world likewise used shame, just as they used honor, as a tool to enforce and reinforce their collective group's values. The biblical writers were well aware of the power of collective shame. Sometimes they use it, and sometimes they challenge its misuse. In both cases, Westerners may struggle to see what's happening. Many English-language theological dictionaries don't even have an entry on *shame.* Those that do lump it together with honor and imply shame is bad, the opposite of honor.[1]

While there is a lot about honor that we don't understand well as individualists, we at least have some reasonably good language for it, and it's all positive. Shame, however, is categorically bad in modern Western culture. In another book I describe worldview as an iceberg, most of which is underwater. Some parts are deeply underwater, nearly completely out of sight; yet, they are still there (and sometimes the part that sinks the ships).[2] "Shame as wrong" is likely one of those ideas that is deeply submersed in our Western worldview. To even question the idea probably riled you up. I have often heard Western ministers encouraging Christians to "let go of shame." Most Western Christians would assert that it would be wrong to shame someone else. The problem is Paul does it: "I say this to shame you" (1 Cor 6:5). He encourages the Thessalonian church to shame a disobedient member (2 Thess 3:14). Even God chose to "shame the wise" (1 Cor 1:27). Our culture tells us shame is bad, and yet God is doing it.

While Western culture rejects shame as *always* inappropriate, many of us grew up in an individualist culture where guilt is used to reinforce values. Consequently, we see an immediate and—in our view—obvious connection between sin and guilt. Growing up, the message was, *When you sin, as a Christian, you should feel guilt.* In fact, many Bible dictionaries even include "Sin, Guilt" as a single article. One scholar writes that Paul "makes very little use of the 'guilt' terminology in the psychological sense, but it may be fairly said that many of the things he says about sin include the thought that sinners are guilty people."[3] To this theologian, it seems obvious that Paul is thinking about guilt, even though Paul rarely writes it. This is because, to us, sin and guilt are connected. But guilt is just our cultural tool. Easterners have other cultural tools. The Spirit uses all of them

---

[1] For example, F. Gerald Downing calls shame "the flip side of the pivotal Mediterranean value, honor." See Downing, "Shame," in *New Interpreter's Dictionary of the Bible*, ed. Katharine Doob Sakenfeld (Nashville: Abingdon, 2009), 5:212.

[2] E. Randolph Richards and Brandon J. O'Brien, *Misreading Scripture with Western Eyes* (Downers Grove, IL: InterVarsity Press, 2008), 155.

[3] Leon Morris, "Sin, Guilt," in *Dictionary of Paul and His Letters*, ed. Gerald F. Hawthorne, Ralph P. Martin, and Daniel G. Reid (Downers Grove, IL: InterVarsity Press, 1993), 877.

to convict sinners to repent. Yet the obvious link that biblical cultures saw with sin was shame. Daniel says, "We and our kings, our princes and our ancestors are covered with shame, LORD, because we have sinned against you" (Dan 9:8). Shame was an important aspect of both the Old and New Testament worlds. It's important to note that while Bible dictionaries published in the West have extensive articles on guilt, they have very little on shame, even though Daniel, David, and Paul use shame language.

SHAME, SHAMED, AND ASHAMED: MUDDLED ENGLISH AND MUDDLED UNDERSTANDINGS

One reason we get shame wrong is that we have such a limited vocabulary to discuss it, and that vocabulary is almost entirely negative. In the relatively recent past, Americans had a cultural understanding that was closer to the collective concept of shame. My grandmother once said, "Your friend is shameless." I asked what she meant. She explained, "He has no sense of shame." I still wasn't sure what she meant, but I wanted to defend my friend. I retorted, "I don't see what's wrong." She replied, "Have you no shame?" In my grandmother's time, to have a sense of shame was to know the difference between right and wrong. If you "had *no* shame," it meant you didn't know the difference between the right and the wrong way to act. Someone was "shameless" when their actions suggested they didn't know the proper way to act. If the person did finally realize what they were doing was wrong, they felt "ashamed." So, in the old days, shame was somehow connected with doing the right things, knowing the proper way to act. It was used to help us stay within the lines. This matches better the Eastern (and biblical) understanding of shame: the sense of shame warns that someone has or is about to transgress a boundary.

Today, however, in most of the West *shame* has generally lost this sense of meaning. We can use *shameless* (lacking shame) and *shameful* (full of shame) to mean the same thing. Moreover, *shame* is strictly a negative word. "To have shame" is no longer a positive trait, meaning that you know the proper way to act. Now, "to have shame" means you are ashamed, or worse, you have been shamed (and probably shouldn't have been). It is often used only in a punitive way. As we shall see, God wants to set people free from this kind of shame. The biblical writers also appealed to shame, but in a very different sense. Our word *shame* just obscures all these differences.

For example, we use *shame* today to mean dishonored, embarrassed, and so on. Perhaps speaking about people being devalued and disgraced might be a little clearer than shamed. How do you deal with someone who is devalued? Value them. How do you deal with someone who is disgraced? Grace. To say that we want to remove their shame in this situation might just be about removing their feelings or perceptions. Several writers today on shame, popular in the West, are addressing primarily this aspect. We absolutely agree that God wants to take away any feelings of being devalued or disgraced. The church can and should be involved in this too.

In some cultures a woman who has a child out of wedlock is described as having shame or maybe being shamed. Removing her shame would be more than taking away feelings, important as that is. It would actually mean to provide a path for her to be restored to herself, to her family, and to her community. The church can be involved in this too. These are different scenarios.

Using the one English word shame for both things is quite confusing.[4] No wonder we don't understand it when we see it in the Bible, and no wonder we struggle to help those experiencing shame around us. It's clear we need a more biblical understanding of shame.

SHAME LANGUAGE

Many languages in collectivist cultures recognize the difference between different shame tools and how they work, often with a rich vocabulary,

---

[4]English speakers don't have the exclusive right to muddle language. Others can do it too. "Saving face" is a common expression in many collectivist cultures. I remember a wife whose husband, a pastor, was accused of adultery. She exclaimed to us, "Where can I put my face?" As young missionaries in Indonesia, we didn't know the answer, but we were also surprised that this was her biggest complaint. Over time we discovered that saving face applied to two different situations. Sometimes, a person was trying to find a way to *retain honor* in a situation where her honor was at risk; she was trying to save face. Other times, a person was trying to *find a path back from shame* or a way to reduce shame; he was trying to save face. They knew the difference between honor and shame, but saving face was used in both scenarios.

much of it positive, giving the different ideas different words. English, as we have seen, clumps all these nuances together. We struggle in this chapter because we have to use one inadequate word to describe all the distinctions we're going to show. For example, Arabs, by contrast, use different words to describe some of the things we're going to show. They have some words that refer to a shameful act being made public. When shame is applied to these situations, it condemns. This kind of shame happens after a shameful act is made public and is a form of condemnation. As Christians, we should never use *this kind of shame*, this negative kind of shame. We should offer forgiveness and restoration, not condemnation.

What we are missing in our culture is the positive kind of shame, so of course we don't have a word for it. This kind of shame leads to virtue. People feel this shame *before* doing something shameless. For example, Arabs have *haya*, a shame that monitors one's behavior so one doesn't violate the community norms. Everyone should feel *haya*. It keeps us within the lines. When a young man leers at a woman on the street, people will tsk their tongues and say, "Ah, he doesn't feel *haya*." (My American grandmother would have agreed, saying, "He has no shame.") *Haya* should have stopped him from doing it. Someone who has *haya* (shame) doesn't want to lose it. You certainly wouldn't want God to take away your shame (*haya*).

Preachers will sometimes say, "The Greek language has at least four different words for 'love': *agapē, philia, eros,* and *storgē.*" It is more accurate to say that English uses one word for four different emotions: a lofty kind of love, friendship, sexual passion, and parental love. It isn't just a theoretical vocabulary problem. Greeks kept these separate, but English clumps them together. I sometimes hear someone say, "What's wrong with two men loving each other?" Well, there is nothing wrong with two men who love (*agapē* or *philia* or *storgē*) each other. In fact, it is good, Christian behavior. We should encourage it. Combining four different and strong emotions into one word can easily lead to confusion, or worse, to combining four different feelings into one idea. It is a problem with the English word "love" and also with the English word "shame."

Different kinds of shame and shaming. Both Hebrew (Old Testament) and Greek (New Testament) use multiple words for the different nuances and ways of using *shame*. The Old Testament has at least ten distinct terms for *shame*. These are not ten different words for the same thing. Hebrews saw at least ten different things that we in English lump together as one thing. They thought it was important to know whether they were talking about this kind of shame or that kind of shame.[5] Likewise, the New Testament contains numerous words relating to shame. Two of them, *aischynē* and *aidōs*, were quite distinct from one another. *Aischynē* usually referred to the kind of shame someone felt after committing an act the community saw and frowned upon. The person felt *aischynē* and was condemned by the community. *Aischynē* is what we think of when we think of the misuse, improper use, or negative use of shame. The New Testament has another word, *aidōs*, which usually describes the sense of shame people felt *before* transgressing a boundary. Like Arab *haya*, this sense of shame helped to steer them away from sin.[6]

Someone in the Mediterranean said to me, "I feel shame about lying to my parents." He hadn't yet lied. He wasn't condemned. No one was accusing him. At the thought of lying to his parents, he felt shame. This uneasy feeling in his gut forecasted how he would feel if he did lie and if his actions were discovered. It is not a pleasant feeling, but it is good for him to have it. This kind of shame led him to change course and to avoid committing a shameful action (lying to his parents). This sense of shame kept him within the boundary lines. Other kinds of shame had the same result but worked differently. While he would describe this kind of shame to me as an uneasy feeling in his gut, he would say *āb* (shame) wasn't a feeling at all. He says it's like an alarm bell. If he interrupted his father, he would suddenly hear the word *āb* in his head, even if his parents said or

---

[5]It is interesting to note that words for shame and shaming are primarily in the poetic books such as Psalms. Narrative books just describe the actions, expecting the reader to recognize the actions were shameful. See Yael Avrahami, "בוש in the Psalms—Shame or Disappointment?," *Journal for the Study of the Old Testament* 34, no. 3 (2010): 295-313, who suggests at least eighteen words in the construct for shame.

[6]See Joseph Roisman, *The Rhetoric of Manhood: Masculinity in the Attic Orators* (Berkeley: University of California Press, 2005), 65.

did nothing. Interestingly, we might lump the gut feeling and the head alarm together as my conscience speaking. I certainly wouldn't distinguish between them, but my friend clearly saw (felt) a distinction.

Honor versus shame? Even if we sort out the vocabulary, we will still misunderstand shame and shaming if we think it is the opposite of honor. When we make shame a negative thing, we can imagine that honor is the opposite or the solution to shame. It isn't. If by shame we mean feeling devalued, then giving honor certainly can make a person feel more valued. If they are disgraced, they need grace—to be shown favor and brought into community. Likewise, we can affirm, respect, and cherish an unwed mother, just as we would all believers, but how would honor help her out *practically*? (You may be thinking of a path back into the community, which is a goal of good shame, as we will see later.)

It may be important to bring honor into a situation involving shame, just like bringing compassion in, or providing assistance, or adding in any number of other good things to help. Nonetheless, honor isn't the opposite of shame. Yet many English Bible translations try to make shame the opposite of honor. For example, the New International Version translates Proverbs 3:35, "The wise inherit honor, but fools get only shame." Proverbs is describing opposites, but the problem is the translation.[7] The New American Standard Bible translates it better: "The wise will inherit honor, but fools display dishonor." Dishonor is the opposite of honor. Respect is the opposite of disrespect. Grace is the opposite of disgrace. But honor is not the opposite of shame.

Let's be really clear in all this: no matter what causes shame, the biblical solution is always restoration. Paul is appalled at the behavior of a particular churchman. His behavior is so immoral that even pagans disapprove: he has been sleeping with his father's wife. Paul's solution is to shame the man. He is to be excluded from the church. Paul does not do this to condemn his brother but that he might be restored (1 Cor 5:1-5). Whether it was this same man or another Christian brother who sinned

---

[7]We like the NIV, but it doesn't handle honor or shame well.

and was excluded, Paul later writes to the Corinthians that when such a one repents, the church should not only forgive but comfort and restore him. The goal of shaming is to show the person that they have crossed the line, so they might repent and then be restored (2 Cor 2:5-11).

Shame used badly only does half of this. It only tells people they have moved beyond the boundaries of the group; it offers no path of restoration. It offers no hope. It pushes out, rather than pulls back. People who have experienced this misuse of shame can be crushed or become hardened. Paul does not endorse any use of shame that causes someone or some people to be devalued, disgraced, or unwanted. The Bible calls this condemnation, not shame. Shame used properly provides a path of restoration.

SHAME IN THE MODERN MEDITERRANEAN

Modern Mediterranean cultures have largely retained the ancient Mediterranean tool we call shame. This tool—or really, set of tools—deals with those who have not embodied the values of the community. These tools can be misused to condemn someone by pushing them away, but they can be used well to restore someone to a group's values and to pull them back. Like honor, these tools we call shame are a collective culture's way of shaping behavior. It is the community's conscience. It is like my grandmother's idea that "having shame" means you know the proper way that "we" the group believe you should act. It is not that I am guided by my values but that we guide one another by our values.

In the Arab world, when children fail to embody the community's values by being disrespectful to others, or failing to greet someone, or not sharing their things, Arab parents will often say āb (pronounced abe, meaning "shame"). When we were newly married in the Middle East, we saw this happening and declared, "We will never say āb to our children." Of course, we planned to correct them when they did things wrong, but not by saying āb. Fast-forward six years. We had an eighteen-month-old son. My wife was in the grocery store, where the man who worked there routinely gave our son a banana. We often remarked on how kind and generous he was. Our toddler son had become used to this man's generosity. One week, my wife was shopping for vegetables, and our son pointed to a banana and said "Nana." The man hadn't yet offered him one. The shopkeeper felt embarrassed. My wife looked down at our son and found *āb* on the tip of her tongue. She loves our son and wanted to protect both him and the man from embarrassment. Her heart was for "we," the community, including both of them. The man felt embarrassed for not offering a banana and thereby appearing stingy. Our son should have felt embarrassed for asking before it was offered. My wife felt embarrassed by the old women who were clucking their tongues. (Judgmental moms and grandmothers are not just an American phenomenon.) Saying *āb* to our son would protect everyone. My wife would be protected because it would show the neighborhood that she understood the proper way to act. It would protect our son by showing that he was being trained in values. The man would be protected from embarrassment, and our son would be protected from growing up impolite. Saying *āb* saves the entire community.[8]

We were talking about this incident with Diana, a good Arab friend in Beirut. Diana said her parents had often said *āb* to her. She found it unhelpful because it had caused her to feel she was somehow lacking. Digging a bit deeper, we noticed the examples she gave. She was told *āb* for annoying her parents, for making noise in restaurants, and for appearing weak. These are hardly biblical values we would want to train our children to embody. They were not values Diana admired. As a cultural tool, shame can be used to collectively remind and enforce values in members of our group. Tools such as honor and shame are neutral. Their meaning depends on which values are being reinforced. As tools, they need to be used properly. When shame is used to pull someone back, it needs to be done with love, affirmation, and a willingness to stand with them on the journey. Arman pulled the man who stole the book back to the values of the church while affirming him and helping him feel Arman was for him. Shame was used on Diana to reinforce values that weren't

---

[8]Like anything, a good thing can be misused. *Āb* is no exception. It is applied improperly in Arab cultures and used to suppress other people. But its misuse does not invalidate the point.

important nor was it used to affirm her or to help her feel that her parents were for her.[9]

Shame used properly restores. Shaming done right pulls back toward the center. Every culture (or subculture) has some agreed-on ways of treating another person with respect. Imagine this shared understanding as a circle. The ideal way to treat someone with respect would be the center of the circle. Obviously, no one does this, but people are expected to be close to the center. When I say or do something that is too far from this ideal—act rude or disrespectful—my actions place me nearer the edge of the circle, and my community is alarmed. This is true of individualist as well as collectivist cultures. All societies guard their ideal behavior; otherwise, they begin to break down as a culture.

While Westerners often use guilt to shape behavior, collectivist cultures more often use shame. While individualists might use guilt to shape *my* behavior, collectives use shame to shape *our* behavior. My grandmother would try to make *me* feel guilty, because I (as an individual) had drifted too far from the center of ideal behavior and was too near the boundary. Collectivist cultures think collectively. It is not that the community is alarmed that I (as an individual) have moved too far. Their thinking is more alarm that I have pulled *all of us* off center. I am part of us, and I am influencing all of us. We could be known as a community that has drifted away from the proper way to treat someone with respect! My community will use shame to make me aware that I have drifted. The goal—and this is critical to understand—is to *pull* me back toward the center, for everyone's benefit. We have rescued me *and us.*

Rami is a close friend. He grew up in a village in Syria. I noticed Rami was always hospitable, quick to invite people in to drink coffee. One day I asked Rami, "How did you learn to be so hospitable?" He told me a story.

---

[9]Shame was misused on Diana. Likewise, the individualist tool of guilt can be misused. Both tools are to maintain values. Shame and guilt can both be used and abused. Parents can put harmful guilt-trips on their kids, and we can all point to times this has been done for things the Bible would not say are wrong. An American parent making a child feel guilty for not getting good enough grades, or for not doing the dishes, or for not calling their mother, is no different than how shame was misused by Diana's parents.

When Rami was a young boy, a neighbor knocked at the door and asked for his father. "Everyone is out," Rami replied, "but I will tell my father that you came to visit." As Rami promised, he told his father that a neighbor had come by. "Why did he leave already? Did you offer him more coffee?" Rami replied, "I didn't offer him any coffee." His father replied, "*Āb*. If any neighbors come to visit, you should always compel them in to have coffee." To be a member of their tribe meant to be hospitable. This is important: Rami wasn't just told *āb*; he felt *āb*. It pulled him into line with the community's values. Today, Rami takes pride in being hospitable. *Āb* taught him how to live out hospitality. This lesson was ingrained in him, and it shaped his character and behavior. Because he treasures the value *āb* taught him, he doesn't resent his family's use of *āb*, unlike Diana, our friend in Beirut. Shame as a tool was used on both Rami and Diana to enforce and reinforce a value. The difference was which value.

Shame misused ostracizes. We Westerners may still be uncomfortable with the idea of *āb*. How can shame ever be used properly? In Scripture, when Israelites bring a lamb for sacrifice, it is to be perfect. Arabic translations say it is to be a lamb without *āb*.[10] If we translate *āb* as "defect" instead of "shame," we understand why Arabs would use that translation. In fact, we Westerners probably feel better if we translate *āb* as "defect." Perhaps, for us, it would *feel* better to describe a behavior as "defective" rather than "shameful" when we correct our child. Likewise, as a Western reader, you feel better about *āb* when we offer "defect" as a translation rather than shame. This shows just how rooted in us is the negative perception of shame and shaming.

As authors, we believe shame is viewed negatively in our culture because shame is almost exclusively misused in our culture. Shame and shaming is misused when instead of *pulling* you back into the group, it *pushes* you away. Shame is misused when it is applied too strongly and/or too publicly. My Armenian pastor was careful to stress this distinction to me. When shame is misused, the shamed one can feel that they have

---

[10]In Ex 12:5, the lamb must be *tā-mîm* (perfect).

drifted too far to be restored; they can see no path of return. Shame misused is a terrible thing.

Shame misused almost always breaks relationships. If Arman had simply gone to the man who took the book and said, "I think you took a book from the library, and please could you put it back so people don't think we are all thieves," the man would likely simply have withdrawn from relationships in the church. He and his family would have been lost to the church. Such would be the improper use of shame. Westerners often prefer a direct approach. We don't beat around the bush; we cut to the chase. We confuse this with honesty. Such a direct approach easily leads to the *misuse* of shame. It may lead us Westerners to apply shame too heavily, especially in crosscultural situations where we don't understand the power of our actions and words.

In addition to an overly direct approach, a careless use of words or actions can misapply shame. An American friend of mine was pastoring a small church of Arab men in Europe. One day, a member told him that another man could not come because he was busy that night. My friend replied, "Oh, that's a shame." The brother who had not come that night never came back. He had been publicly shamed by the pastor. He didn't know how to show his face again. Obviously the American pastor didn't intend to shame this dear brother. He was using a common idiom to express his disappointment. But the power of words and actions can be very strong in shame-based societies. James warns of the power of words (Jas 3).

This pastor's careless use of words could have been repaired. The solution would have been an approach like Arman did. The pastor needed to be indirect and provide a path of restoration. He could have gone to visit the brother and say he was there to check the man was not sick because he missed him at the meeting last night. Or, he could have asked another member to mediate for him, explaining how he had misspoken. Either approach would have provided the path of restoration. The individualist pastor did not realize the power of shame and did not chart a path of restoration, and alas, the man was lost. Furthermore, the rest of the flock probably internalized that the value being reinforced was attendance rather than relationship. So, as individualists, what do we do with shame and shaming? We certainly don't want to superimpose modern Arab (or my grandmother's southern American culture) understanding.

SHAME IN THE BIBLE

We saw above that Paul uses shame. When he writes to the Corinthian church he says, "Come back to your senses as you ought, and stop sinning; for there are some who are ignorant of God—I say this to your shame" (1 Cor 15:34). My individualist signposts confuse me here. Paul is not using shame here to condemn the believers. It is intended in a positive way to *pull* the Corinthians back into acting in line with their values. A survey of English commentaries shows modern writers struggle with how to translate Paul here. One commentator says, "Paul eschews shaming other Christians."[11] Since *eschew* means "to avoid using," we wonder how the commentator can say Paul avoids shaming other Christians in a verse where he is explicitly doing it. The commentator is reflecting the modern English understanding of shaming as a negative thing to do. We agree that Paul would abstain from using shame in the negative way we have come to use it today. We are certain Paul would not condemn the Corinthians. He calls them saints (1 Cor 1:2). Paul himself argues there is no condemnation for those in Christ Jesus (Rom 8:1). There is always a path of restoration. Nevertheless, Paul is clearly participating in the Mediterranean system of shaming in positive ways, pulling people back to their values.

Let's look at another example. This time, our cultural signposts can mislead us in several directions. In 1 Timothy 2:9, Paul encourages women to dress "with shame" (*aidōs*). A literal translation doesn't work at all in English. It is commonly translated "with modesty." Here Paul is using a positive term for shame. This is the positive kind of shame that told someone the proper way to act. Paul is saying that women should dress in a way that wouldn't cause the voice in their head to say "shame" or for the

---

[11]David Garland, *1 Corinthians*, Baker Evangelical Commentary on the New Testament (Grand Rapids, MI: Baker Academic, 2003), 722. Garland notes Paul "vigorously objects to the 'haves' shaming the 'have-nots' at the Lord's Supper" (722). Yet, this is public, condemnatory shaming. We will discuss this later.

community to think "shame." Again, let's avoid being too individualistic. It is not that an individual woman should determine for herself what is proper but that the women in the community, as a "we," should determine proper dress. We help we.

Translating *aidōs* as "with modesty" can mislead in other ways too. In America, we assume Paul is talking about dressing in sexually modest ways. Paul is actually talking about economics, being economically modest. Women are not to dress lavishly, with expensive clothes, gold, and pearls. In antiquity, these were ways of dressing that said, "I have more money than you."[12] Paul says the women's sense of shame, or knowing what was right, should discourage dressing lavishly. It didn't embody the values at the heart of the gospel. It weakened the community. If Christian women today were tempted to dress in ways that flaunted their wealth in the faces of poorer church members, Paul would say *aidōs*. Their sense of shame (knowing the proper way to act to protect community) should keep them from crossing that boundary. Paul isn't targeting women or clothing. It is a family issue and ultimately a community issue. *Aidōs* should have kept the entire church from doing this. Paul is using shame to reinforce a value: everyone has an equal seat at the Lord's Table.

As an individualist, I need to be careful not to read into this passage an individual sense of guilt or right versus wrong. It's a collectivist value. Dressing lavishly when there are poor people around damages the community. It's about we, not me. Does that mean it's wrong to wear expensive jewelry? It depends on who is around. In some settings, wearing fine things would be dressing appropriately. A sense of shame (the proper, positive sense of shame that seeks to guard and strengthen community) helps someone to know when it is appropriate. *Aidōs* guides the hearts of the community to avoid hurting (and driving away) other members of the community.[13] In 1 Timothy 2:9 Paul is describing one way shame works.

---

[12]See the discussion in Richards and O'Brien, *Misreading Scripture with Western Eyes* (Downers Grove, IL: InterVarsity Press, 2012), 43-44.

[13]Aidos was "the Greek goddess of shame, modesty, respect and humility. Aidos, as a quality, was that feeling of reverence or shame which restrains men from wrong." See "Aidos," Wikipedia, https://en.wikipedia.org/wiki/Aidos (accessed February 19, 2020).

He says shame is what guides a godly woman. It's important to make this distinction. Last, we should see the compliment in what Paul says. He thinks Christian women could and should be able to govern what is proper.

We mentioned that English is a muddled mess when it comes to using the word *shame*. Shame is a tool collectives use to enforce and reinforce their collective values. In the Bible, when one doesn't embody our values, we can use shame to pull them back, because they are we. It's an insider tool. But, alas, shame can be misused, to push them away, where they become no longer we. Shame used properly happens before someone moves too far from the values of the group and can center them. As with other social tools, such as honor or guilt, this assumes the values we want to enforce and reinforce are good ones.

11

SHAMING
Done Right (and Wrong)

AMIRA'S HUSBAND WORKS FOR A COMPANY IN THE GULF. He makes a lot of money. Amira's sister, Mariam, married a painter. Mariam's family is not well off, so Amira passes on to Mariam lots of her own used clothes. There was a big family wedding, so Amira came back from the Gulf. As the family were sitting around talking excitedly about the wedding, Mariam said she was planning to get herself a new dress. Amira laughed and said, "Oh, so this time, you're going to buy your own clothes." Mariam was shamed in the bad sense. Actually, Amira had misused shame to devalue her sister. Mariam was very upset with her sister, but she didn't show it there and then. Over the next week, though, as Mariam and Amira messaged on the phone, Mariam accused her sister of saying cruel things, shaming her sister (but not offering a path of restoration). Amira felt shamed but couldn't remember what she could have said to cause it. They quit talking to each other. Amira's misuse of shame had pushed Mariam away, and Mariam's misuse of shame did the same.

A few days later, Mariam's dad (the mediator) came to Mariam's house. He said, "Mariam, my love, I know you're upset with your sister." She replied that she wasn't upset with her sister. The next week Mariam's dad came around again. He said, "Come on, get the kids ready and come to our house. Your mum and I have cooked your favorite dinner." Mariam dressed and went to her parents' home. Her sister was there. She didn't want to enter. Her dad said, "For my sake, because you love me, come in and eat." He was gently appealing to her sense of shame. She should eat with her father (because he's her father) and especially since he and her mum had troubled to prepare a special meal. Shame was pulling on Mariam to draw her back inside the boundaries. She couldn't say no; it wouldn't be in keeping with their family values. Over the meal, she talked with her sister. Her sister said she was sorry, and so did Mariam. They both cried, and the family was restored. By the way, this is how the parable of the prodigal son could have ended, when the father invited his son in to the feast. Yet, Jesus leaves it hanging; we don't know what the elder son decided (Luke 15). It is possible the parable was initially aimed at Peter, who may have been upset that Jesus had invited the local tax collector, Levi, to join the disciples (Lk 5). Levi had surely stolen from Peter, collecting more tax than was fair. If so, Jesus is honoring Peter by calling him the elder brother who had been doing right all along but now was resenting the return of the prodigal Matthew.

In our story of Amira and Mariam, we see kinship and brokerage in the story, but we also see shame working in different ways. Amira misused the tool of shame to push her sister away, to devalue and dishonor her. She did this because her sister didn't have wealth—but wealth is not a biblical value. Mariam responded by misusing shame, accusing her sister of cruelty, pushing her away. She did this because of unforgiveness—but unforgiveness is not a biblical value. Her father properly used shame to pull them back. He knew it would shame them to refuse his hospitality—but hospitality is a biblical value. He used shame as a cultural tool to pull the sisters back together. Shame is used and misused in their story.

Paul heard that some members of the Corinthian church were taking other members to court. This meant they were getting judgments from the wrong sources and exposing the trouble of the church to sinners. Paul writes, "If you have disputes about such matters, do you ask for a ruling from those whose way of life is scorned in the church? I say this to shame you. Is it possible that there is nobody among you wise enough to judge a dispute between believers?" (1 Cor 6:4-5). Their unwillingness to submit to the judgment of a member of their community is causing the entire congregation to be subject to unchristian values outside the church. Paul is trying to use shame to call the entire congregation back to one another and to embody the values of God.

BIBLICAL EXAMPLES OF SHAMING DONE RIGHT

Instead of pushing them away, toward the edge of the group, shame used properly pulls people toward the center, as we stated above. This is the goal of confronting the brother in Matthew 18.

The church shames a member. A church member has sinned and is not yet repentant. A fellow Christian needs to confront the sinning member. Alas, even after two thousand years, we still don't always do this well. Sometimes we act as if the member's problem is ignorance. For example, a man comes and says he is thinking of divorcing his wife. We open the Bible to show a verse where Jesus discourages divorce (Mk 10:11), as if we expect the man to slap his forehead and exclaim, "Wow, brother, I had not realized that I should avoid divorce. Thank you." Problem solved. Hardly. In Matthew 18, Jesus teaches, "If your brother or sister sins, go and point out their fault, just between the two of you. If they listen to you, you have won them over. But if they will not listen, take one or two others along, so that 'every matter may be established by the testimony of two or three witnesses.' If they still refuse to listen, tell it to the church; and if they refuse to listen even to the church, treat them as you would a pagan or a tax collector" (Mt 18:15-17).

What went without being said is that good shame is being used in this passage. It is applied as gently as possible. Initially it is done as privately as possible, just one on one. There is no need for others to know. Shame is kept to its absolute minimum to reach its goal. Arman took this approach with the missing library book. What if the brother here fails to respond appropriately to this gentle shaming? What if he does not repent? Now, we are to bring another member of the community. Influential eleventh-century Arabic theologian Ibn al-Tayyib, who lived in a culture that understood collectivism and shame well, comments on this, "Jesus said take one or two with you in order to urge him to good action for maybe the group of people will cause him to feel shame."[1] It is still done privately, but now the sense of shame is increased. Ibn al-Tayyib goes on to speak of this as being like a doctor who increases the dosage of medicine to heal the patient. The community is speaking, but two is the smallest form of the community. Jesus is encouraging the minimal number of people to be involved and still represent the community. If the brother still does not listen, then the entire community is brought to bear. The goal is still restoration, not condemnation. The goal from beginning to end is to find a path for the person to return or move back toward the center, to be restored and healed.

The final stage of shaming is "If they still refuse to listen, tell it to the church; and if they refuse to listen even to the church, treat them as you would a pagan or a tax collector" (Mt 18:17). In other words, treat him like he is no longer a member of the community—because, as we said earlier, this brother's sin is not an individual problem. He is not just pulling himself away from the center of the group; he is pulling the whole group off center. An unrepentant member endangers the group, and it's not just the group's reputation at risk. Even our culture recognizes that one bad apple can spoil the whole bunch. This person's behavior could contaminate and mislead others in the group: "our" group could become confused about what our values are. It's not me; it's we. Matthew 18 offers an example of shame used appropriately. This is a far cry from the misuse of shame, which tends to apply the maximum amount of exposure and does not seek restoration. Again, this is the kind of shame that Christians such as Dr. Brené Brown rightfully critique.[2]

Jesus shames a Pharisee. It may be hard for you to believe that Jesus would shame anyone. Well, he did. But only in the good, restorative sense of shame. To a religious leader named Nicodemus, Jesus asks, "You are Israel's teacher and do you not understand these things?" (Jn 3:10). This

---

[1]Ibn al-Tayyib, *Tafsir al-Mashriqi*, ed. Yusif Manqariyos (1908), 1:311, author's translation.

[2]E.g., Brené Brown, *Braving the Wilderness: The Quest for True Belonging and the Courage to Stand Alone* (New York: Random House, 2019). This very helpful book is clearly targeting individualists with "the courage to stand alone." Brown has published many helpful books for overcoming the misuse of shame; see also her TED talk.

is a very mild and gentle shaming. It is not public, but it is shame, and it works. Nicodemus is changed. He later is willing to defend Jesus in front of his peers (Jn 7:50-52). After Jesus himself is publicly shamed on the cross as a criminal by the Romans and as a blasphemer by Nicodemus's peers, Nicodemus honors Jesus by anointing Jesus' body with about seventy-five pounds of spice (Jn 19:39), an astonishingly large amount.[3] In both John 7 and John 19, we are reminded that Nicodemus originally came to Jesus by night. The Gospel wants to show how Nicodemus has changed. Jesus pulled him toward Jesus' new values.

In Luke's Gospel, the Pharisees present themselves as the guardians of social norms.[4] They act as if they know and protect the proper ways to act. Simon the Pharisee honors Jesus by inviting him to a public dinner. Luke tells us they are reclining to indicate it is a special meal. The larger community is allowed to participate by leaving open the door, permitting them to listen in.[5] As they are reclining, "a woman in that town who lived a sinful life" (Lk 7:37) approaches Jesus with an alabaster jar of perfume. "As she stood behind him at his feet weeping, she began to wet his feet with her tears. Then she wiped them with her hair, kissed them and poured perfume on them" (Lk 7:38). Simon, and probably everyone else in the town, knows this woman's sinful past.[6] Jesus isn't a local, so he doesn't necessarily know. Simon says to himself, "If this man were a prophet, he would know who is touching him and what kind of woman she is—that she is a sinner" (Lk 7:39). Since Jesus permits the woman to touch him, Simon concludes that Jesus does not know about her. Jesus corrects Simon by using shame, but he begins gently with a story that indirectly shames, like Arman with the stolen library book.

---

[3]Jouette M. Bassler, "Mixed Signals: Nicodemus in the Fourth Gospel," *Journal of Biblical Literature* 108, no. 4 (1989): 642.

[4]Anthony J. Saldarini, *Pharisees, Scribes and Sadducees in Palestinian Society: A Sociological Approach* (Grand Rapids, MI: Eerdmans, 2001), 179.

[5]Darrell L. Bock, *Luke 1:1–9:50*, Baker Evangelical Commentary on the New Testament (Grand Rapids, MI: Baker Books, 1994), 694.

[6]In our Western world, when we hear "sinful woman," we usually assume a sexual sin, such as being a prostitute. While this was one option, a woman who practiced healing with incantations, such as many forms of midwifery, would also be considered sinful. King Saul specifically requests a female medium (1 Sam 28:7). In other words, there were lots of sinful professions in the ancient world for women (and men).

Jesus begins by honoring Simon by asking his religious opinion. Jesus says, "Two people owed money to a certain moneylender. One owed him five hundred denarii, and the other fifty. Neither of them had the money to pay him back, so he forgave the debts of both" (Lk 7:41-42). Five hundred denarii would be nearly three years of pay for a working man.[7] No debt collector would simply write off such a large sum of money. Jesus asks Simon, "Now which of them will love him more?" Simon replies, "I suppose the one who had the bigger debt forgiven." Jesus honors Simon again by saying, "You have judged correctly" (Lk 7:43). This honor will take some of the sting out of the shame Jesus is about to deliver.

Simon thinks of himself as a guardian of social norms, but Jesus points out that Simon has failed to live up to them. He has not shown hospitality to his guest:

> Then he turned toward the woman and said to Simon, "Do you see this woman? I came into your house. You did not give me any water for my feet, but she wet my feet with her tears and wiped them with her hair. You did not give me a kiss, but this woman, from the time I entered, has not stopped kissing my feet. You did not put oil on my head, but she has poured perfume on my feet." (Lk 7:44-46)

This woman, Jesus notes, provided all the respect Simon did not. She has become a better host than Simon. Jesus has reversed their status. Simon is worried her presence is polluting his reputation. Jesus points out the woman is saving Simon's reputation.

Why does Jesus shame Simon at all? Because Simon has not worked to restore this woman to their community. Simon has been shaming her for not embodying the community's values, but he was doing it in the wrong way. He has been pushing her away. Yet she is the one actually upholding the hosting requirement of their community—an important value. We need to remember what everyone there already knew: that *she and Simon belong to the same community*. Simon is confident that this woman needs

---

[7]A day's wage was about a half-denarius. It is common to say a denarius was one day's wage, but the only basis is the parable of Jesus (Mt 20:2). Jesus is portraying a very generous man paying high wages at harvest time. See E. Randolph Richards, *Paul and First-Century Letter Writing* (Downers Grove, IL: InterVarsity Press, 2004), 51-52.

forgiveness. Jesus agrees that she needs forgiveness more than Simon. Yet Jesus' story reminds Simon that he also needs forgiveness. She comes and gets forgiveness. We are not told whether Simon does.

We can miss the point if we forget that the early New Testament audience would have seen Simon and the woman as connected. This is not a story of two unrelated individuals needing forgiveness who happen to encounter Jesus on the same evening. As a Pharisee, Simon claims the responsibility of protecting the community (which includes her), and he has failed. Jesus shames Simon when he says, "Do you see this woman?" (Lk 7:44). Simon had quit seeing her as we.[8] They both need to repent, but Simon needs some additional shaming to get there.

The Pharisees shame other Pharisees. Jesus isn't the only one who shames Pharisees. Sometimes the Pharisees shame each other, because they are guarding "we," their community of Pharisees. The Pharisees send a delegation to confront Jesus. When the delegation returns, they are mildly complimentary of Jesus. Some of the temple officers were supposed to arrest Jesus and come back honoring him: "No one ever spoke the way this man does" (Jn 7:46). The Pharisees shame them by suggesting they have been led astray, and they note that unlike the officers, no ruler or Pharisee has believed in Jesus (Jn 7:47-48). John expects us as readers to say, "Wait, one of them has!"—Nicodemus. He speaks up in Jesus' defense. They respond by also shaming him: "Are you from Galilee, too? Look into it, and you will find that a prophet does not come out of Galilee" (Jn 7:52). They suggest that Galileans are gullible and that Nicodemus is as well. Incidentally, the Pharisees are also wrong in claiming that no prophet arises out of Galilee. Actually, five did: Jonah, Nahum, Hosea, Elijah, and Elisha. Also, Jesus isn't from Galilee but from Nazareth. John expects us as readers to add shame to their actions.

---

[8]I was in a village in Borneo, and a single woman in the church was pregnant. The entire church was embarrassed, all the more because a guest was there to see it. It reflected poorly on the morals of the entire Christian community. Since I had seen it, I asked, "What are you going to do?" The elders looked at me, stunned, and said, "She belongs to us, and the child belongs to us, and we will take care of them." There was never a second in which she was not "us." She was never without a community. One of their own had stumbled, and the community was gathering around her, helping and restoring her. The church felt more that they had failed her than she had failed them.

Paul shames lots of people. People from South Galatia absolutely did not want to be called Galatians. That term was reserved for the Celts living in North Galatia. The Celts didn't speak Greek, and they had a reputation for being religiously gullible. This is why Luke is careful in Acts to call those living in South Galatia, "residents of . . . Cappadocia, Pontus and Asia, Phrygia and Pamphylia" (Acts 2:9-10). He would not have wanted to insult these new believers by calling them Galatians. Yet Paul is more than willing to insult them by bringing up gullibility (Gal 1). Is Paul just being racially insensitive? No.[9] What we are supposed to remember is that Paul is one of them. He was from Tarsus in South Galatia.

An insider can use language that would be an insult on the lips of an outsider. At a conference recently, during a break, we heard someone talking about "the problems with ministering to Colombians." At least one of the Latinos in the group became angry. He stood and asked (a bit loudly), "What do you have against us Colombians?" The man replied, "I am a Colombian. Both of my parents are Colombians." The man replied, "Oh," obviously mollified, "then that's OK." The two proceeded then to commiserate about how hard it was to minister to Colombians. But they were speaking as we, as fellow insiders. Similarly, what would be a racial insult on the lips of an outsider is not for Paul. As an insider, Paul is reminding them that they are being religiously gullible. He says they are quickly exchanging the true gospel for a false one (Gal 1:6). Paul is speaking as we to his fellow Galatians. As an insider, Paul is referring to this slur (which he shares in common with them) to shame them, to pull them back by reminding them to think again.

In another instance, Paul shames Peter. The apostle Peter had been participating actively in the ministry of the new church in Syrian Antioch. Gentiles there were not God-fearers (Greeks who had spent a lot of time around synagogues and usually complied with many Jewish kosher expectations). Most of the Gentiles so far in the book of Acts who came to faith had been God-fearers and those who had close relationships with Jewish communities. Presumably, they were complying with Jewish kosher

---

[9]See the discussion in E. Randolph Richards and Brandon J. O'Brien, *Paul Behaving Badly* (Downers Grove, IL: InterVarsity Press, 2016), 58-61.

expectations. Antioch was different. This church had plowed new ground by aggressively evangelizing run-of-the-mill pagan Gentiles. The Antiochian church shared one table, and the Lord's Table welcomed all believers. This might seem unremarkable to us, but this was new territory. Suddenly, in Antioch, a Jewish Christian was expected to share a meal with a pagan Christian whose breath stank of pig fat. As far as we know, such a thing had not happened previously.

Peter was participating as well; the lesson God taught him in Acts 10 he is able to actualize in Acts 11. Then some members of the Jerusalem church (which was primarily if not exclusively made up of Christians from the Jewish community) come to Antioch. We get a hint of their attitude by a comment James and the other elders of the Jerusalem church later make to Paul, "You see, brother, how many thousands of Jews have believed, and all of them are zealous for the law" (Acts 21:20). James's comment indicates that there were many Jewish Christians who maintained the commands of the law, which were Sabbath observance, circumcision, and table fellowship (kosher laws). Yes, they were believers in Jesus, but they kept their Jewish cultural customs. The challenge was that the Antiochian church shared one table with both Jews and Gentiles, with each presumably following their cultural food customs.

The group from Jerusalem are shocked at the shared table. They have never seen anything like this. They think that, to maintain purity, believers must still not share a table with those not following kosher laws. They persuade Peter to stop eating with the Gentile believers. Peter's prestige as a premier, if not *the* premier, apostle carries all the other Jewish Christians in the church along. Paul is alarmed. It looks like Peter thinks the cross of Christ is not sufficient to earn a seat at the table. What was a beautiful picture of the future kingdom of God has devolved into ethnic division.

Paul confronts Peter. Because Peter's actions have already moved the congregation away from the central values of the gospel message, Paul shames him back toward the center: "When Cephas (Peter) came to Antioch, I opposed him to his face, because he stood condemned. . . . When I saw that they were not acting in line with the truth of the gospel, I said to Cephas in front of them all, 'You are a Jew, yet you live like a Gentile and not like a Jew. How is it, then, that you force Gentiles to follow Jewish customs?'" (Gal 2:11, 14). It needs to be in front of them all because the whole church community is involved. All of them need to move back toward the center. The shaming of Peter is actually the shaming of all who followed him. It is as private as it could be. Paul doesn't take an ad out in the local paper, gossiping about it around town. We read later that the church in Antioch continued to strongly endorse Paul's mission to the Gentiles, so we may assume that Paul restored the community back to the heart of the gospel, believing that the cross is sufficient.

Asaph tries to shame God. On one occasion, the psalmist Asaph is frustrated because it seems to him as if God has rejected Israel and won't rescue them. God is not, in Asaph's eyes, doing the right thing. It is not surprising that he uses his culture's socially acceptable way to urge someone to act properly. As a Mediterranean, Asaph would have used shame to urge a friend to change their actions. It might surprise us that he tries to shame God, and it might even offend us, but Asaph is treating God like a beloved and trusted friend. He is trying to urge God to do what Asaph thinks is the right thing, to rescue his people. Asaph reminds God that their enemies have burned down God's temple (Ps 74:7). He reminds God that they have ridiculed his name. He suggests it is shameful for God to ignore their taunts and not respond:

> Remember how the enemy has mocked you, LORD,
> > how foolish people have reviled your name.
> Do not hand over the life of your dove to wild beasts;
> > do not forget the lives of your afflicted people forever.
> Have regard for your covenant,
> > because haunts of violence fill the dark places of the land.
> Do not let the oppressed retreat in disgrace;
> > may the poor and needy praise your name.
> Rise up, O God, and defend your cause;
> > remember how fools mock you all day long.
> Do not ignore the clamor of your adversaries,
> > the uproar of your enemies, which rises continually. (Ps 74:18-23)

Modern theologians say God accommodates himself to culture. What they mean is that God adjusts himself to *our* understanding. So in a time when people thought the world was flat and held up on pillars, God points out to Job that he (God) is the one who established those pillars. When humans thought snow was stored in giant rooms in the sky, God says only he knows where those rooms are (Job 38). Likewise, God accommodates himself to a shame-based culture's way of speaking. He understands Asaph is asking him to rescue Israel. Just like God accepts laments (Lamentations) or the anger of Psalm 137, so also he understands the heart and motivations of Asaph (and includes this psalm in Scripture).

We see another example when God wants to destroy the Israelites in the wilderness and Moses basically argues, But what will the nations think of you if you bring the people out only to kill them yourself? Moses is using a gentle form of shaming in his argument to rescue the Israelites. Moses was a man of his culture, and God accommodated (Ex 32:11-14). Most scholars think that God did this to teach Moses to forgive, for he was about to have his own anger against the Israelites for being a laughingstock to their enemies (Ex 32:25).

The Pharisees try to shame Jesus. Levi was a wealthy man from a business that most Jews considered unclean. He was a tax collector for the Romans. After Jesus calls him, Levi throws a big reception to honor Jesus. When the Pharisees see Jesus at the banquet, they want to remind him that the people he is eating with are sinners and one should not desire their honor. After all, Proverbs 23 cautions against that very thing, desiring the delicacies of the rich man's banquet. "When the teachers of the law who were Pharisees saw him eating with the sinners and tax collectors, they asked his disciples: 'Why does he eat with tax collectors and sinners?'" (Mk 2:16). By saying something to the disciples, the Pharisees are being polite and sensitive. They want to apply the minimum amount of shame by posing the question to Jesus' disciples, but within Jesus' earshot. The proper response, and what they expect, would be for Jesus to pretend he doesn't hear but to change his behavior and to leave the banquet. In this way, they have not publicly rebuked Jesus. They are treating Jesus as we.

After all, despite their differences, Jesus and the Pharisees were one community over against Levi and his Roman-loving friends.

But Jesus does not do as they expect. He does not object to their method, only their message. Like with honor, the problem is which *value* were they honoring. Jesus' concern was that they were shaming to achieve the wrong value. Jesus uses the same level of gentle shaming in return. He does not publicly rebuke them. Rather, he speaks indirectly through a metaphor that should lead them to draw the correct conclusion, to the correct value, and to change *their* behavior: "On hearing this, Jesus said to them, 'It is not the healthy who need a doctor, but the sick. I have not come to call the righteous, but sinners'" (Mk 2:17). Jesus identifies himself with the Pharisees (in a way) as those who are healthy. But he points out what the Pharisees have neglected: Levi and his friends are also we. They are also members of the community. They are sick and need restoration. The Pharisees were pushing Levi and his group out (the bad kind of shame). The Pharisees no longer considered people like Levi to be *us*.

BIBLICAL EXAMPLES OF SHAMING DONE WRONG

While shame can be used appropriately, it is often not. Rather than pulling someone back into the group, it pushes them away. Jesus tells a parable of a Pharisee and a tax collector: "Two men went up to the temple to pray, one a Pharisee and the other a tax collector. The Pharisee stood by himself and prayed: 'God, I thank you that I am not like other people—robbers, evildoers, adulterers—or even like this tax collector. I fast twice a week and give a tenth of all I get'" (Lk 18:10-12). We should note that the Pharisee's prayer would be heard by the tax collector—and everyone else. Rather than pulling the tax collector back into the community, the Pharisee further pushes him away. The tax collector feels it. He stands at a distance. He won't even look up to heaven (Lk 18:13). Luke uses this parable to introduce the Zacchaeus story, where a tax collector is lovingly forgiven and restored—not by the efforts of the Pharisees, or the village, but by Jesus.

In Jesus' parable, there is nothing wrong with the behaviors the Pharisee mentions. Fasting and giving are commendable behaviors. But by standing by himself, he indicates he does not want the tax collector as part of his community. He considers the tax collector to be other and not us. His rebuke of the tax collector is not a positive use of shame but a negative one. Luke loves divine reversal stories, and this is another one. Jesus flips it over: it is the tax collector who is reconciled with God; the Pharisee is not. Jesus tells this story to shame those in his midst: "some who were confident of their own righteousness and looked down on everyone else" (Lk 18:9). Jesus is using this parable to gently shame them, trying to pull them back. They were supposed to be trying to restore folks such as Zacchaeus.

In another story, Jesus is in a debate with leaders in the temple. Jesus has been contrasting his Father and their father: "I am telling you what I have seen in the Father's presence, and you are doing what you have heard from your father" (Jn 8:38). They don't like the way the conversation is going, and so they reference Jesus' unusual birth. They say to him, "We were not born of fornication" (Jn 8:41 NASB). This is one of the worst biblical examples of shame used improperly. It does not provide any path of restoration. It is a public condemnation. They are trying to push Jesus away from the community. We know Jesus' birth was a miraculous event. Clearly, they assume otherwise. But even if it were true, how would that have been Jesus' fault? No child born out of wedlock should be blamed for the actions of their parents. Such a comment provides no path for restoration. It is not the words of a community seeking to restore someone. There is no place in God's kingdom for such misuse of shaming.

When Paul was in the city of Corinth, "the Jews of Corinth made a united attack on Paul and brought him to the place of judgment. "This man," they charged, "is persuading the people to worship God in ways contrary to the law" (Acts 18:12-13). The Jews lost the case, and it seems they blamed Sosthenes, the synagogue leader. Apparently, he is considered responsible for the way the case against Paul was presented to the Roman authorities. They do not handle the matter privately. "Then the crowd there turned on Sosthenes the synagogue leader and beat him in front of the proconsul" (Acts 18:17). If this (very public) shaming were done properly, Sosthenes would be restored to his community. We have a hint that this shaming was condemning, too public and too harsh. Paul later writes to the church in Corinth, and his cosender is a man named Sosthenes. If it is the same man (and it's quite possible), then the Corinthian Jews' inappropriate use of shame did not restore Sosthenes to them but pushed him away.

The Romans designed the cross to shame people in the most public and harsh way. It functioned to make people reject the crucified person as not one of their own. The cross was used by the Romans on Jesus and many early Christians to shame them and to encourage others to break their ties with the movement. This would have been a fearsome force to discourage people from following Jesus. The writer of Hebrews writes to Christians facing persecution and says, "Let us run with perseverance the race marked out for us, fixing our eyes on Jesus, the pioneer and perfecter of faith. For the joy set before him he endured the cross, scorning its shame" (Heb 12:1-2). This is the proper response for anyone who has been improperly shamed: scorn it. We should not allow shame improperly used to push us out. *And* if other people experience this kind of shame, it is our responsibility to pull them back into the community. It is good for the (mis)shamed person but also for our community. Not only do we gain back our brother or sister, but we protect *us* and our godly values.

CONCLUSION: A LITTLE SHAME GOES A LONG WAY

Shame is a powerful tool. Wood can be carved with a whittling knife or a chainsaw. Both have their role. A chainsaw can be very, very useful. But it must be handled with special care, because it is so powerful. Used wrongly, it can cause serious damage. Shaming can be like a chainsaw. It can be the best tool, but it can also do a lot of damage when used improperly. Just like a chainsaw, some people will never want to use it. And perhaps this is wise (for them and us). Inexperienced hands, not the tool, make the result bad. If you saw a friend carelessly swinging around a chainsaw, it would be appropriate to urge them to stop. We would say the same to anyone using shame improperly. You may have experienced this yourself. Wounds from a chainsaw are rarely minor. You as a reader may have been the victim of shame used wrongly. Again, we are very sorry. God wants to pull you back into his community and to comfort and heal you.

Nonetheless, we have seen biblical stories where shame is used in a different way—properly, correctly, and by God—to restore people. As individualists, we may try to use guilt to bring people to repentance. But we don't like to use shame. Why? Partly this is because we think of shame only as the negative kind of shame, which condemns. We rightly refrain from wanting to use that kind of shame on people around us. Guilt can be used to teach; so can shame. But only the right kind of guilt and the right kind of shame, in the right kind of situations. However, when we dismiss all shame as wrong, we miss a lot of what is going on under the hood of Bible stories. As we saw in the stories of Levi and the sinful woman, no explicit shame words are used. They didn't need to be. The Pharisees felt Jesus' pulling on them to think and act differently. The Bible has stories of shame used well, gently, and to restore. Shame can be a tool to pull back into our community those who have wandered beyond the boundaries. But like a chainsaw, it needs a prominent sign: Danger. Handle with care.

12

HAVING
BOUNDARIES

Us and Them

"WHERE ARE WE?" I ASKED MY BEDOUIN FRIEND as we were driving through the desert. "Oh, we are on the land of the Beni Sakhar." It looked like desert to me. A while later, he noted, "Now, we are in the land of the Beni Hamideh." It looked the same to me. He pointed off in the distance and said, "That land over there belongs to the Alabadi tribe." I asked how he knew. He said, "*Everyone* knows." After I pressed him more, he explained that most of the time people use landmarks. They know that, from this valley to that mountain, the land belongs to a certain tribe and so on. I exclaimed that I would never remember all these landmarks. He assured me the easiest way was to look at how they lived. Each tribe and clan live on their own land. Each clan has its own customs and traditions. By looking at how people behaved, I would know which tribal land I was on. Easier said than done.

I find it much easier in Beirut. I live near an Armenian neighborhood. The Armenians came to Beirut around a hundred years ago, so today almost everyone in the neighborhood speaks both Armenian and Arabic fluently. Most choose to speak Armenian as their community language. Armenians tend to wear much brighter and more Western-style clothes than other communities in the area. The shops sell Armenian food. It is easy to know when I am among the Armenian community. I just need to look around. It is also easy to tell a member of the Armenian community when I meet them elsewhere in Beirut.[1] I use the Armenian community as an example, but my friend in New York City does the same thing. He lives in a Puerto Rican neighborhood and thinks it is obvious. There are clear landmarks, such as Spanish store signs, the smell of mofongo, or old men playing dominoes. As we will see, landmarks are a key tool that collectives use to mark between us and them.

WE AND THESE AND THEY AND THOSE

We individualists think of ourselves as individuals, and so we tend to think of the people we meet as individuals. Collectives tend to think of themselves as members of groups and tend to think of the people they meet as members of collective groups. Many times my Arab friends have expressed sympathy to me because of some tragic thing that happened in the Western world. I used to think, "What has it got to do with me?" When I lived in a multicultural city in Britain, my Pakistani friends used to speak to me in a similar way. While they lived in Britain, culturally they thought in a more collectivist way. An Asian friend at church once pointed out there were terrible storms and flooding in Asia at the time and asked if we could pray for it as a church. It seemed remote to me. He felt it was close and affected him in a very similar way, because it was his people. To him, it was happening one relative away.

As we know, people in collective cultures form their identity from the group to which they belong. Collectivist groups guide and protect one another. They use honor and shame to enforce and reinforce their values. Particularly in urban areas, there are often multiple collective groups in close proximity. Collectives are always aware which group they belong to.[2] One way Arabs speak about this is with the phrase "from us and among us." Those "from us and among us" share a common identity. They are

---

[1]Lebanese anthropologist Lara Deeb writes that many markers are used by people in Lebanon to determine religious and community identity, including dress, mannerisms, kinds of jewelry, regional accents, and which holiday lights people use, and that some people even claim they can tell someone's community identity from their looks. See Lara Deeb, *An Enchanted Modern: Gender and Public Piety in Shi'i Lebanon* (Princeton, NJ: Princeton University Press, 2006), 36.

[2]Some ethnic minorities in the West still do this. It is a chicken-and-egg discussion whether they do it because they are [fill in the ethnicity] or because they are (or were) collectivists.

expected to support one another and to behave in certain shared ways. They therefore view other people on the basis of whether or not they are from us and among us.

We see signs of people thinking this way everywhere in the Bible. When Jesus speaks to the Samaritan woman, she immediately marks each of them as a member of a distinct collective group. She says, "You are a Jew and I am a Samaritan woman" (Jn 4:9). Peter goes inside the centurion's house and said to them, "You are well aware that it is against our law for a Jew to associate with or visit a Gentile" (Acts 10:28). Paul says to Peter, "We . . . are Jews by birth and not sinful Gentiles" (Gal 2:15). The Samaritan woman, John's disciples, Peter, and Paul think of people as members of collective groups, not as individuals. As Peter notes to the centurion, the collective group to which he belongs shapes his behavior. This is foreign to the thinking of most of us individualists.

Because members of different collective groups live side by side in Beirut, New York, Palestine, and ancient Antioch, there is a danger that people could get confused about which group they belonged to. People might feel obligated to give loyalty to other groups. Worse, they might act in ways that benefit other groups over their own. Maybe they feel obliged to a patron who belongs to another group. When this happens, the collective group becomes weakened. Weakened groups lead to weakened values. So, as groups of collectivists begin to interact with others, how do they distinguish between who belongs to their group and who does not? Boundaries.

Boundaries are bad, right? In my individualistic world, when I think of boundaries, I think of limitations. "Put no boundaries on me!" In fact, the word *boundaries* often conjures up negative images among individualists. "Don't fence me in!" When collectivists think of boundaries, they think of protection, belonging, a people. Both individualists and collectivists are right here; boundaries have both elements. America has two common phrases associated with advertising: "the cost of membership" and "membership has its privileges." These different phrases capture both ideas well. Boundaries do have a cost. They do limit. Becoming a Boy Scout puts boundaries on you. You must dress a certain way (at least when you meet); you must behave a certain way (Boy Scouts don't lie); and you must abide by the rules of the group. But becoming a Boy Scout makes you a member of a group. You belong. You have friends who will look after you. You have a scout master, who will protect you. You have goals (badges), clearly defined ways to get to your goals, and a community that will praise you for reaching those goals. Boundaries have both costs and privileges. Boundaries make Boy Scouts. They also create honor. There is a sense of honor to be ascribed with the title of Eagle Scout.

Is it a crowd or a community? There I stood in a crowd of people bustling about. It was the mall at Christmas, and it was packed with people. I was shopping and felt very alone. In fact, I felt a bit buffeted by the masses, jostled and lost. Suddenly, people stopped and began to sing a Christmas carol. It was a flash mob. How fun! There in the middle of the horde of people was a distinct group. They belonged to each other. It was obvious who belonged and who didn't: there were no fences, but there was a boundary. In the midst of the crowd was a community. Boundaries make communities.

Some people, like my Bedouin friend, use physical boundaries such as land and landmarks to separate themselves from other collective groups. However, most of the time it is not possible for a collective group to *completely* separate itself from others.[3] Populations are intermingled in cities. It is often not possible to rely on physical boundaries, so communities use other kinds of boundaries.

In Beirut, different collective groups wear different clothes, speak different languages, eat different foods. There are many cultural differences, but they are not all boundaries. What makes something a boundary is that a collective group sees it as a significant part of establishing who they are. We must ask a community to find out which things they consider signs that show who belongs. The things a group view as boundary markers may be physical signs, but they can also be nonphysical things, such as the language *we* speak, traditions *we* follow, certain things *we* believe, lifestyle

---

[3]Sometimes people use other physical boundaries. We all know of times when people have attempted to use walls, fences, and barriers to separate one group from another. Their aim was to isolate other groups and their influence from their own group. Rightly or wrongly, people usually say they are doing this to protect their group.

choices *we* make, and food *we* eat or, more often, avoid eating. To an individualist it can seem like all of these differences are simply the result of people coming from far afield to live in the same city. While this may be true, *some* of these differences are choices groups make to help them maintain boundaries, to maintain who they are despite the changing world around them.[4]

What we are getting at is that not every cultural difference marks a collective boundary. Different collective groups may wear different clothes, eat different foods, and take different days off work. What makes some of these things act as boundary markers is when a collective group views them as being significant in distinguishing who *we* are. This is the case whether the group is kin, patronage networks, or religious groups.

The collectivists of the Bible distinguished between which groups they belonged to by using boundaries. These were sometimes physical and other times cultural. While these boundaries are very important in the Bible, we may miss them. If I am an individualist, I rarely realize the importance of collective boundaries. Furthermore, I often don't know what the collective groups in the Bible considered to be their boundary markers. As a result, I may not see boundary markers at work in the Bible even when the writers expect me to. When we are aware of the boundaries groups in the Bible used, we can better understand what is going on.

Boundaries we inherit. In our conversation with a talented young Puerto Rican minister, she shared that she was born in a poor, remote mountain village. It was not a respected place. According to her, people would drive a little farther in the car in order to avoid that village: "Don't go there, or they'll rob you." Nonetheless, it was her home. When she came back to her area, she felt she was coming home. She didn't see a village to avoid. That place others were taught to dread was the place she longed for.

She commented that other Puerto Ricans judged her: "You know how people from that village are." They connected values with land. People

---

[4]Fredrik Barth, *Ethnic Groups and Boundaries: The Social Organization of Culture Difference* (Long Grove, IL: Waveland, 1998), 10.

who live in that village have those values. What struck us was that she did not deny her heritage or hide it. She shared it openly. It was part of her identity. Identity, land, and values are tied together.

In some parts of the Old Testament, people used land boundaries to distinguish between collective groups. Perhaps like my Bedouin friends today, tribes and clans back then lived together on the same land. In their land, their values and way of life prevailed. Everyone knew it was their land. Visitors were expected to adapt to the customs and values of the people in whose land they were traveling. We can sometimes miss the significance of land when we read these passages. When someone was born into a clan, they would often live on that clan's land. They would share the values of their clansmen. So, when Abraham tells his servant to find a wife for his son Isaac from among his relatives, he naturally tells him to go to his people's land (Gen 24:3-4). That's where they *all* live. Abraham tells his servant not to allow Isaac to settle there. Abraham assumed Isaac might want to settle there because all his relatives are there. For someone who had spent all his life living as a stranger in foreign (though promised) land, it would have been pretty attractive to settle in his people's land, where there were shared family and shared values.

Those born in Nazareth inherited the community. They were raised knowing who they were. Let's imagine a Salome, born in Nazareth. In her town of a few hundred people, she belongs. Everyone knows her; she has a people who support her and protect her. Salome is the third daughter of Judah, an olive grower, and she knows how to act in the world. When she is sent four miles up the road to Sepphoris, suddenly she is in the large capital city of Galilee and a Gentile city. It is a beautiful, wealthy city, and she works in her uncle's house, part of an estate that encompasses a large city block. Her uncle's friend (a.k.a. patron) is a merchant who sells olive oil to Antioch. She has a place to live, but where is Salome supposed to hang out? Who will be her friends? How is she supposed to act? Roman soldiers are everywhere. Nazareth doesn't have them. They are the enemy, she is told, but Antonius seems nice. He is always smiling at her, and he is rather handsome. In this situation, her people's boundaries will tell her how to act and protect her. She doesn't need to make an individual decision. It isn't just up to her. Her group identity helps her maintain her values.

Boundaries we choose. Why would we choose a boundary? The decision doesn't work that way. We choose to belong to a group. With that group, that community, comes boundaries. Cornelius chooses to become a God-fearer. *God-fearers* was a term used to refer to Gentiles who had chosen to worship Yahweh and join in with the Jewish community. When Cornelius chooses that group, boundaries come with it. The Ethiopian eunuch chooses to follow Yahweh. He is so committed that he learns Hebrew. He travels to Jerusalem to buy a copy of some of the Scriptures. But he knew going in that he will never be a full Jew because Judaism had boundaries for people like him, a eunuch. He could not be baptized into full membership, nor could he enter the temple. If he wants to belong to the group, he has to accept the boundaries.

BOUNDARIES IN THE BIBLE: GOD'S TERRITORY

We tend to read the Bible backwards because we know the ending. We also do theology as a composite, combining verses from Deuteronomy and Luke. When we do, we miss the unfolding revelation of God. When God first spoke to Abraham, everyone "knew" there were many gods and that gods each had their own territory and expertise. There was no concept of one God who does everything. People imagined there were gods for baking bread and safeguarding wells, and bigger gods for protecting cities, and even bigger ones for countries. This was the world Abraham lived in when God first called him.

When God reached out to Abraham, he accommodated to Abraham's world, and the story unfolds that way. Abraham's god has no name and seems to focus on fertility. He promises Abraham a child. He also promises to give Abraham a land. The promised son shows up miraculously, but the land doesn't seem to work out. Then this god appears to Moses and promises to deliver Abraham's descendants, Israel, from bondage in Egypt. Moses politely asks the god's name. (One should always be polite with a god.) Up to that point, the god had just been called Abraham's, Isaac's and Jacob's god

(Ex 3:6). When we read that, we think of it as some majestic title for the God of the whole world. It actually meant the opposite. He was a god with no name, but he is the god these three men worshiped. It is an inauspicious beginning for the Lord of the universe to begin to reveal himself. (Reminds us of a manger in Bethlehem—another inauspicious beginning.) Moses is told his name is I AM (Yahweh). Moses is somewhat skeptical that this god can deliver what he promises. After all, the promise of a land to Abraham hadn't seemed to go anywhere. But ten plagues and a divided sea later, wow, does this god amaze or what? Israel is taken aback. They imagine this god is young. After all, the pyramids were five hundred years old when this god first appeared to Abraham. Yahweh seems a latecomer compared to the Egyptian gods. But Yahweh is clearly powerful, defeating the Egyptian gods. So, when the Israelites wrongly decide to make an image of him, they pick a young bull. Clearly, they should not have made any kind of idol of him, but why did they pick a young bull? Well, it's how they imagined God: young and powerful. Wait, we might insist. God is the Creator of heaven and earth and is omnipresent, omniscient, and omnipotent. Yes, but they didn't know that. God had yet to reveal most of this. God was slowly unpacking who he is, slowly revealing more and more about himself.

Later, when an outside empire, Assyria, threatens to conquer Jerusalem, it isn't just a battle of two armies. The people see it as a war between the god(s) of one army against the god(s) of another army. Jerusalem is part of Yahweh's territory, within Yahweh's boundaries. The head of the Assyrian army calls out to the inhabitants of Jerusalem and says,

> Do not listen to Hezekiah, for he is misleading you when he says, "The LORD [Yahweh] will deliver us." Has the god of any nation ever delivered his land from the hand of the king of Assyria? Where are the gods of Hamath and Arpad? Where are the gods of Sepharvaim, Hena and Ivvah? Have they rescued Samaria from my hand? Who of all the gods of these countries has been able to save his land from me? How then can the LORD [Yahweh] deliver Jerusalem from my hand?" (2 Kings 18:32-35)

The king of the Assyrian army is wrong. Yahweh does deliver Jerusalem (2 Kings 19).

But a hundred years later, Hezekiah is gone. Judah has forgotten Yahweh, and Yahweh hands them over to the Babylonians. The crisis of the exile comes. The Babylonians, whose god is Marduk, defeat Jerusalem and ransack Yahweh's temple (2 Kings 24:10-14). In the minds of most Israelites, Marduk has defeated Yahweh. To make it worse, the Israelites have been relocated to Babylonia. In the minds of most Israelites, Yahweh lives in the land of Zion, a *long* way from Babylon. They faced a religious crisis. They have been taken out of their land, their boundaries, and separated from Yahweh; they are outside the boundaries of his territory. Listen to the sadness in Psalm 137:1-4:

> By the rivers of Babylon we sat and wept
>> when we remembered Zion.
> There on the poplars
>> we hung our harps,
> for there our captors asked us for songs,
>> our tormentors demanded songs of joy;
>> they said, "Sing us one of the songs of Zion!"
> How can we sing the songs of the LORD [Yahweh]
>> while in a foreign land?

What use is it, they reason, to sing when Yahweh can't hear you? They imagine Yahweh is sitting in his land in Palestine, while they have been hauled away to Marduk's land in Babylon. Then God (once again) amazes them all. What is amazing is not just that God appears to Ezekiel, but that God does so *in Babylon*. The heavenly court of Yahweh is on *wheels* (Ezek 1). It can go wherever God wants, even to Babylon. Now, suddenly Yahweh claims what no other god has claimed, to be God over the whole earth, a god without geographical boundaries. For this reason, Daniel has to be obedient to God's commands *even in Babylon*.

At this point God starts being called the God of heaven. After all, a throne in the stars covers Palestine, Babylonia, and more. God has been revealing more and more of himself. His boundaries encompass all of creation: the heavens and the earth. He demands loyalty of his people, even outside the boundary of Israel's land. This was not the way the world worked. Such a claim surprised and offended people. If a Babylonian worshiper of Marduk visited a town in Philistia, he would have offered sacrifices first to Baal. After all, he was in Philistia, which was Baal's domain. Even though he was a worshiper of Marduk, how could he be so rude, ancients thought, as to ignore the host god?

Yahweh has different expectations of his people. They are to worship him first and only. Why? Because Yahweh claims every place falls within his boundaries. The whole world is his.

DEFINING VALUES TAKES BOUNDARIES

Defining *identity* takes boundaries, because identity and values are two sides of the same coin for collectivists. For example, growing up I was taught the value of respecting women. I was taught to say, "Yes, ma'am," to shake women's hands, and to look them in the eyes. Arab culture likewise believes that men should respect women. One way to show respect to a woman is by *not* shaking the hand of a woman who is not family. Where I lived in Indonesia, that Manadonese community also believes women should be respected. In Manado, men show respect by shaking the hand of a woman in public (but not looking them in the eye). I navigated both cultures adequately well until one week I was in Nazareth with some Arab friends. Behind me, I heard a group talking in Mandonese. I spun around and greeted them in Mandonese, and they were so pleased to meet an American who spoke Mandonese. They rushed up, and one of the women leaders reached out her hand. *Aaagh, what do I do? Do I respect her and disrespect my Arab friends? Or the other way around?* One group was going to feel uncomfortable or even offended. I was trying to maintain my value of respecting women. Clear boundaries in Arab culture make it easy, as in Mandonese culture. But when they mix on the street, it's a problem.

One of the major boundary markers in Judaism was monotheism. Monotheism was not the value; it was the boundary. The underlying value monotheism was defining was the value that Yahweh is our God and he set special rules for his people, including worshiping him alone as their patron. So defining that boundary defined Jews' relationship with God, but also their relationship together as a people. In John 8 the Pharisees say to Jesus, "The only Father we have is God himself" (Jn 8:41). Monotheism seems to us a reasonable assertion. It is polytheism that strikes us as odd. The ancient world felt the opposite. Monotheism was the strange idea.

MAINTAINING VALUES THROUGH BOUNDARIES

Boundaries mark out us from them. "We" have values that make us *us*. "Maintaining values" is the same thing as saying "maintaining identity" or maintaining boundaries. We keep repeating this because some of the biblical stories seem to focus on maintaining values, while others seem to focus on maintaining identity or boundaries. But they are ways of saying the same thing. In collectivist cultures, values are held not by individuals but by groups, and groups determine identity and boundaries.

We have already noted that Paul was raised in a Gentile city. The reason Paul grew up a Pharisee instead of a Gentile was that he was the son of a Pharisee (Acts 23:6). His family maintained its identity, which helped Paul maintain his values and gave him clear boundaries. As Paul maintained his boundaries, his values were reinforced. By keeping his values, he maintained his identity.

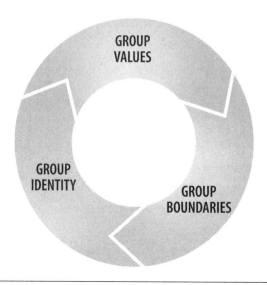

Figure 13.1. The self-reinforcing cycle

Maintaining a group identity is not a fundamental goal for most individualists. I think individually and choose my own values. Collectivists share their values. When the group dissolves, the values dissolve. When a group is absorbed into another group, it takes on the new group's values. They assimilate. When parents immigrate to a new country, they fear their children will assimilate. Why is this to be feared? When the boundaries are dissolved, the identity is lost, and (most importantly) the values are lost. My Armenian friends in Beirut are diligent about maintaining their boundaries. As an individualist, I can easily misunderstand this as a matter of preference or custom—they don't eat this or wear that—but collectives think it is an issue of identity: we don't want to lose who we are.

CONCLUSION: HAVING BOUNDARIES
KEPT ISRAEL "ISRAEL"

Maintaining boundaries and thus values and thus identity is part of what was going on in the period of the exodus and conquest. God took the Israelites out of Egypt to make them into a people. Part of forming their identity as a people was that God gave them their values (the Ten Commandments on Mount Sinai). But as they enter the Promised Land, these values come under threat. Losing the values leads to losing identity. They may be absorbed into Canaanite culture. They may not remain a people (of one God). Boundaries maintain their values and identity.

It's easy to misread the book of Judges and imagine a united nation of twelve tribes, but they are not. For this reason they demand of Samuel a king who will unite the twelve tribes. Samuel selects Saul, but not all of the tribes are initially persuaded that Saul is the right choice. We are told, "The people shouted, 'Long live the king!'" (1 Sam 10:24). This might convince us that everyone supports Saul, but the writer wants us to catch his subtle point in the next verses: not everyone brings a present to this new king (1 Sam 10:25-27). Clients were expected to give gifts to show their loyalty. As readers we are supposed to recognize that the writer is saying that words are cheap and in reality not everyone recognizes Saul as king. Saul ultimately became king when the town of Jabesh-Gilead was besieged by the Ammonites. The citizens appealed to their kin for help. Saul cut a yoke of oxen into pieces and sent these pieces of meat throughout Israel. The imagery was clear: a divided ox is of no use. The tribes saw the benefits of belonging to this larger group, which meant accepting the boundaries and accepting the king. The tribes united under Saul and delivered the city of Jabesh-Gilead.

This story is rife with boundaries. What went without being said—but is essential to notice—was that Saul changed the boundary. He was not a member of Jabesh-Gilead. They were not part of his we, not his tribal kinsmen. Under the old boundaries, he had no responsibility for them. They were not his people and thus not his problem. Yet, Saul gathered others (from yet other tribes) to rescue the town. Saul's actions said (much louder than words), "Those people belong to us." This act spoke the right message to each tribe. Each tribe understood that if their city were attacked, Saul would consider them us and rescue them as well. Saul *showed* that all of the tribes and towns were considered his people, within his boundary. Saul defined a new we that harked back to the we of the exodus.

13

GUARDING
BOUNDARIES

Keeping Us Us

LET'S PRETEND THERE WAS A TALENTED SCRIBE in Jerusalem around the year AD 50, named Judah. His wealthy relative, who heads the olive-oil business, has moved to Corinth. Judah's wealthy relative is now a patron for the synagogue in Corinth and arranges for Judah to be hired to copy new books. Note how patronage and kinship are blended. It is a grand opportunity for Judah, and his family is so honored. Judah's extended family in Jerusalem host a commissioning banquet for him. Judah enjoys the banquet and has no concern over the meat. In fact, it never enters his mind to be concerned. When he arrives in Corinth, there is another banquet, this time to welcome him (and as a thanksgiving to God for his safe travels). Unlike before, Judah is concerned whether the meat at this meal is kosher. His relative reassures him that the meat came from a Jewish meat market.

Such a dilemma might confuse us today, but in antiquity the customary place to buy meat was not at a grocery store but near a (pagan) temple(s). After an animal was sacrificed to a god or goddess, the family received a portion, often served at a banquet hosted by the temple. For example, one might arrange a wedding feast to be held in honor of Dionysus at his temple. For many people, it was no more than having the wedding catered. But for the more devout, the feast truly was in the god's honor. A portion of the cow (or whatever) was served at the banquet. The priests and temple staff received a portion, but the rest of the meat needed to be sold immediately, since there was no refrigeration. So the butcher shop was near the temple(s).[1] For many people, such meat had an extra benefit. It was blessed by that god or goddess. For Jews, however, the association with pagan deities rendered the meat unacceptable. How could you honor Yahweh and yet enjoy another god's food? That would be unfaithfulness to Yahweh.

Now imagine Judah later hears the preaching of Paul and believes Jesus is the promised Messiah. Judah now worships at Jason's house. There is still no problem, because even Gentile Christians buy their meat from the Jewish meat market so as not to offend Jewish Christians such as Judah. Sometime after Paul leaves, the city officials force the Jewish market to close. (Now we are not imagining. Historians suggest this occurred.[2]) What should Christians do? Perhaps Jewish Christians go vegetarian. The very thought of eating meat from a pagan temple makes them nauseated. Gentile Christians, whose stomachs aren't troubled—perhaps even rumble—at the thought are confused about what to do. Some Christians say meat sacrificed to idols is fine because "An idol is nothing at all in the world" and "There is no God but one" (1 Cor 8:4). Other Christians say eating that meat would be like dining at "the table of demons" (1 Cor 10:1-25). Suddenly a boundary problem has arisen. It's not really about the meat. It's about values. Living by different values means living by different identities, which threatens the church's having one single identity. After all, how can people with the same identity have different values? An individualist might try to argue, "I can." A collectivist would say we can't. After all, we are we. Different values would make some of we into *them*, that is, those who eat meat sacrificed to idols. It wasn't a theoretical theological dilemma. Could the church in Corinth share the one table?

---

[1] See, e.g., David Gill, "The Meat Market at Corinth (1 Cor 10:25)," *Tyndale Bulletin* 43, no. 2 (1992): 391-92; and P. R. Trebilco, *Jewish Communities in Asia Minor*, Society for New Testament Studies Monograph Series 69 (Cambridge: Cambridge University Press, 1991), 17.

[2] Bruce W. Winter suggests that after Paul left Corinth the first time, city officials withdrew the special permissions they had given to allow kosher meat. See Winter, *After Paul Left Corinth* (Grand Rapids, MI: Eerdmans, 2001), 287-301.

In collective cultures, group identity and values are two sides of the same coin. If you were to ask an Armenian (or an Indonesian), "Why does your grandmother live with you?" they would look aghast at such a stupid question. They would raise their hands and say, "Because we are Armenian!" Being Armenian means living by the values that Armenians value. It seems to us a cyclical argument. It is cyclical, and that's the point. One leads to the other, which in turn reinforces the first. It is the same thing to say, "We are Armenian because we respect our grandparents," or, "We respect our grandparents because we are Armenian." My Jordanian friend Hasan would say, "To be Jordanian is to be hospitable." But he could just as easily say, "To be hospitable is to be Jordanian." Once, when I was particularly hospitable, Hasan's mother said, "You are Jordanian!" She didn't mean my ethnicity had changed. Boundaries define values, and boundaries define group identity.

So let's go back to Judah's church in Corinth. Some of his church family are saying, "We are Christians so we *are not* able to eat meat sacrificed to idols." But others are insisting, "We are Christians so we *are* able to eat meat sacrificed to idols." It isn't ultimately a question about kosher meat. It is a question about who *we* are as Christians. If we have different values, how can we have the same identity? This question reaches Paul, and he responds with a letter, which we call 1 Corinthians. Paul answers that question in 1 Corinthians 8–10. Scholars often treat the problem of divisions within the church in 1 Corinthians 1–4 as a separate problem, as if the church in Corinth had multiple, distinct issues. Yet perhaps the divisions and the meat (and other issues) are symptoms of one problem: they are at risk of becoming different groups. Saying "I follow Paul" or "I follow Apollos" (1 Cor 1:12) is also a boundary marker.

ENFORCING VALUES BY GUARDING BOUNDARIES

Why enforce values? Why guard boundaries? Because to do so protects the group's identity. A collectivist would say, "The boundaries keep us *us*." We individualists might say, "The values keep us *us*." For collectives, these are ways of saying the same thing, because guarding boundaries protects identity. The term for leaving Judaism, leaving the community, was "casting off the yoke." A yoke tied oxen together and helped them to work together, to pull in the same direction. In people's minds, a yoke *helped* the oxen be better. So also a group's identity, values, and boundaries made their group better.

Phinehas enforces the boundaries. During the exodus, while staying in Shittim, the Israelite men began to "indulge in sexual immorality" (Num 25:1) with the local Moabite women. It is unclear in the story whether Israelite men were marrying Moabite women and adding their gods and practices to their household, or whether they were participating in the religious festivals of the Moabite people. Either way, God considered it "to play the harlot" (Num 25:1 NASB), using the common prophetic image of Israel as God's bride. We are told the Moabites seized this opportunity to deceive the Israelites and lead them astray to join in with the Moabites' sacrificial meals and to bow down before their gods. The Moabites were trying to change the boundaries. They were trying to incorporate Israel into their group, their community. The Moabite strategy was that once Israel was *us*, then there would be no more war.

Their plan is working. The people of God begin to follow Baal of Peor (Num 25:1-3). They are being absorbed into another people, which means absorbing their values and their gods. All Israel is at risk of losing *us* and becoming *them*. The Lord's anger burns against these Israelite men. God tells Moses to kill the leaders of these men. Moses is standing there delivering the sorry news to Israel's leaders; everyone is weeping at the entrance to the tent of meeting. Just then, "an Israelite man brought into the camp a Midianite woman right before the eyes of Moses and the whole assembly of Israel" (Num 25:6).[3] He is forcing a critical moment. If nothing is said, the assembly's silence will be endorsement. It will be approval for everyone. The boundary between us and them will be gone. The

---

[3] The interchange of *Moabite* and *Midianite* can be confusing in this passage. Some suggest *Midianite* is a more general term for a loose confederation of nomads in the area. See, e.g., William J. Dumbrell, "Midian: A Land or a League?," *Vetus Testamentum* 25 (1975): 323-37, esp. 324-25. In any case, the Moabites aligned with the Midianites against Israel during this time (Num 22:4). The Bible here treats them as one group: them versus us.

Midianites and the Israelites will be one, just as the man and woman are becoming one.

An Israelite called Phinehas sees this. He wanted to keep Israel *Israel*, so he needs to reinforce Israel's boundaries. Phinehas "left the assembly, took a spear in his hand and followed the Israelite into the tent. He drove the spear into both of them, right through the Israelite man and into the woman's stomach" (Num 25:7-8). We are told this gruesome detail to let us know what the man and woman were doing. Their act of becoming one was the very risk to the group. God's judgment against the man uniting with the woman is symbolic of God's judgment against Israel uniting with the Midianites. It is important to note how public are the actions of both the man and Phinehas. It is decision time for all of Israel. Phinehas is protecting the boundaries.

Later Israelites took Phinehas as an example of someone zealous to preserve the boundaries of God's people. Biblically, the word *zeal* came to refer to the use of violence to guard and enforce boundaries and so to preserve the values (and identity) of the people of God. In 167 BC, when Mattathias killed a fellow Israelite for publicly sacrificing to a pagan god, he was praised: "Thus he burned with zeal for the law, just as Phinehas did against Zimri son of Salu" (1 Macc 2:26 NRSV).[4] Both Phinehas and Mattathias were defending their group's identity. Although they killed fellow kinsmen, they thought this violence was necessary to protect the good of the whole group by guarding the boundaries and so maintaining values: the death of one to save the many. Paul describes his actions in violently persecuting the early church as zeal (Phil 3:6). This is because he felt he was defending the boundaries of God's people.

Synagogues enforce boundaries on Paul. Synagogues enforced the boundaries of common Judaism in many ways. One such way, used for people who had seriously broken the rules of Torah, was the corporal punishment of flogging, forty lashes minus one. This was based in part on the legislation of Deuteronomy for punishing lawbreakers: "If the guilty

---

[4]See also the discussion in Larry W. Hurtado, *Destroyer of the Gods: Early Christian Distinctiveness in the Roman World* (Waco, TX: Baylor University Press, 2016), Kindle loc. 361.

person deserves to be beaten, the judge shall make them lie down and have them flogged in his presence with the number of lashes the crime deserves, but the judge must not impose more than forty lashes. If the guilty party is flogged more than that, your fellow Israelite will be degraded in your eyes" (Deut 25:2-3). It seems that the goal of such synagogue punishment was to protect the boundaries *and* to restore the rule breaker.[5] This happened in two ways. First, boundaries were enforced so that everyone was clear that this serious violation of the law was not at all acceptable behavior to the synagogue community. Second, it seems they felt that the serious rule breaker, in agreeing to receive the punishment, was cleansed of his guilt and restored to being part of the community. One text explains how later Jews thought about someone who received the whipping, "All they that are liable to Extirpation, if they have been scourged are no longer liable to Extirpation, for it is written, 'And thy brother seem vile unto thee' when he is scourged then he is thy brother." The point is that the rule breaker has not been excommunicated; he is still a brother in Judaism. As Rabbi Hanina b. Gamaliel said, "If he that commits one transgression thereby forfeits his soul, how much more, if he performs one religious duty shall his soul be restored to him."[6] So in the case of serious rule breaking that threatened the community, the forty-minus-one lashing enforced the boundaries, and the brother remained a brother. Boundaries were enforced, and the brother was kept within the boundaries.[7]

In 2 Corinthians, among the things Paul suffered for the sake of the gospel, he includes: "Five times I received from the Jews the forty lashes minus one" (2 Cor 11:24). It seems that Paul received this severe punishment because

---

[5] We say "seems" because the Mishnah is later than the first century. Just as we are wary of reading modern Middle Eastern culture uncritically into the Bible, we are also wary of uncritically reading later Mishnaic texts into what first-century Jews thought and taught. Our reading seems likely since nothing in the New Testament indicates otherwise. Some texts (2 Cor 11:24 and possibly Mt 10:17) suggest it was practiced by synagogues in the first century.

[6] Herbert Danby, *The Mishnah: Translated from the Hebrew with Introduction and Brief Explanatory Notes* (New York: Oxford University Press, 1933), 408. This Tannaitic text likely dates from the first or second Christian century.

[7] In one sense, the public flogging was a public shaming that restored and pulled the offender back within the boundaries. Refusing the flogging and the shaming was a decision to go outside the boundaries.

he was challenging the boundaries of the synagogue in ways they thought were very serious. Note what goes without being said. Paul accepted the synagogue discipline, as painful as it was. He could have refused the discipline, but that would have meant he was refusing the value and thus refusing the identity. Refusing the discipline would be casting off the yoke. Paul accepted the beatings because he wanted to maintain his identity as part of the group. To stay a member of the group, he had to stay within the boundary. He was able to speak in synagogues as a brother. Clearly, he did not tone down what he proclaimed—he went through this process five times. Paul was willing to pay a very heavy price to retain the right to be part of *us*, members of the synagogue.

Pharisees (try to) enforce the Sabbath boundary on Jesus. We know the story of Jesus healing a man with a shriveled hand (Mk 3). It can be puzzling when Pharisees appear to become angry with Jesus for healing. They are not angry that Jesus heals someone. They are frustrated he does it on the Sabbath. This is not just some nitpicking, rule-keeping, over-the-top religiosity on their part. Their actions come from genuine fear. They consider that if the boundary of the Sabbath is lost, so might their values be lost. If their values are lost, so will their identity (as the people of God) be lost.

We are supposed to notice that the man's situation is not an emergency. We are also supposed to notice it is the Sabbath. We might think, "Well, it was a coincidence. You need to make the most of the moment." Yet there is no reason Jesus could not heal the man the next day or even after sundown on that day. The man is not dying of a fever. He has a withered hand. The Pharisees are correct to see that Jesus does it deliberately on the Sabbath and does it in the most public place, the synagogue. In fact, Jesus asks the man to stand up in front of everyone (Mk 3:1-3).

I was raised to see the objection by the Pharisees as a lack of compassion. Yet any one of them, including the man, would probably have been willing to wait a few hours for the sake of the group. As we have noted previously, for collectives the well-being of the group usually ranks above the well-being of the individual. We call it "the story of *a man* with a shriveled hand."

They might have called it "the story of the Sabbath in peril." For the Pharisees, Jesus' healing matters because forsaking the boundaries of the Sabbath is forsaking the Torah, which is forsaking the covenant, which is forsaking loyalty to God. It appears as casting off the yoke. To them it seems Jesus is putting the whole village's loyalty to God at risk. Clearly Jesus is not teaching disloyalty to God. Jesus had just taught that the Sabbath was made for humankind (Mk 2:27). In the very next story, Jesus asks what is permitted on the Sabbath (Mk 3:4). Jesus is teaching them about who he is. In Jesus' day, it was recognized that God worked on the Sabbath. After all, babies were born on Sabbath days. God is allowed to do good, to save life, to care for his people, even on the Sabbath.

THE DANGERS TO GROUP IDENTITY
FROM REDEFINING BOUNDARIES

Can a collective group's identity and values be maintained when boundaries are redefined? If the redefined boundary alters values, or causes new values, what happens to the group's identity? What keeps us *us* when the boundary has been moved?

The risk of lost values. As we have seen, Torah created boundaries, whether Sabbath, kosher food, or circumcision. These clearly marked those who were within the boundaries and those who were outside the boundaries. Jews would have said, "We are Jews because we keep Torah." They could equally have said, "We keep Torah because we are Jews." Could they lose Torah and still be the people of God? Most first-century Jews would have said no.

In the early years of the church, Paul completed a missionary journey planting churches in South Galatia. Paul wasn't the only Jewish Christian traveling around. The churches Paul started were on the major road, so we should not be surprised to learn that other Jewish Christians passed through the same towns. Naturally, they visited the young churches. To their dismay, they discovered that these recent Gentile Christians were not observing Torah. Torah obedience included circumcision of males. The Jewish Christians explained (in a rather convincing argument) that circumcision was required. This was a boundary that God had given: "Any uncircumcised male, who has not been circumcised in the flesh, will be cut off from his people" (Gen 17:14). This boundary had to remain. They had a persuasive point from Scripture: "My covenant in your flesh is to be an everlasting covenant" (Gen 17:13). To cast off the boundary, the practice of circumcision, was, in their minds, to cast off their identity as the people of God. The boundary equaled the covenant, which equaled identity, which equaled values, so to the Jewish Christians, if this boundary were gone, they would have no group identity and hence no values. It would be the classic slippery slope. The churches would have no boundary to keep us from them. Circumcision protected them. Without that boundary, they thought, these churches would inevitably become as immoral as the Gentiles around them. In their minds, a lawless Christianity (a Christianity without Torah) could not produce godliness.

So these Jewish Christians began instructing these young believers in Sabbath, kosher laws, and circumcision. When Paul hears, he becomes angry about this development, because boundaries define values. In Paul's view, these Jewish Christians were reinforcing the wrong boundary—a boundary that wrongly excluded Gentiles from Christian fellowship. These Jewish Christians were essentially arguing that salvation came by grace, but you stayed in the community by keeping Torah. Paul cleverly argues, "Did you receive the Spirit by the works of the law, or by believing what you heard?" (Gal 3:2). Paul argues that having God's Spirit, not circumcision, shows you are within the boundaries. Thus, the Gentile Christians were already "in" before they ever heard of keeping Torah. Torah obedience was no longer a boundary marker separating us from them. The presence of the Spirit, seen in the Spirit's work in the believers' lives, showed who was us.[8] Gentile Christians could have a law-free (Torah-free) Christianity, because the Spirit would produce godliness in them and thus they would arrive at the desired values, a boundary marking us from them.

---

[8]We are very aware of how much we have oversimplified a very complex Pauline argument, but we believe boundary marking is key to understanding Paul here. It is *not* boundary marking *instead of* justification. It is not an either-or. Paul is counting on the Spirit developing godliness in the lives of Gentile Christians.

The risk of altered values. In Acts 21, Paul has returned to Jerusalem. James and other Jerusalem Jews have heard distressing rumors that Paul has forsaken his Jewish identity, that he has cast off the yoke. Not only that, but Paul has been teaching other Jews to cast off the yoke—to forsake the laws of Moses (Acts 21:20-21). In the eyes of most Jews and perhaps many Jewish Christians in Jerusalem, the identity of the people of God is at risk. Forsaking the laws of Moses is forsaking the boundary, which is forsaking the values, which means you forsake the identity. Paul is putting *everyone* at risk, they would have reasoned.

James wants to assure those in Jerusalem that Paul still maintains his group (Jewish) identity. James needed a way for Paul to do something that can easily be seen in public. In this case, James asks Paul to take a purity vow, which likely meant shaving his head and publicly recording the vow at the temple. The reason this will work is that people will see Paul walking around town with a shaved head. People will say, "Oh, Paul is taking a purity vow." They will all "know that there is nothing to the things which they have been told" (Acts 21:24 NASB). The purity vow is a visual boundary marker. It indicates that Paul is keeping the boundaries, which means he is keeping the values, thus keeping the identity, and keeping us *us*. This seems a great practical move to calm fears. Jewish Christians in Jerusalem were still keeping within the Jewish boundaries. (Jewish) Christians were still seen as *us*: Pharisees, Sadducees, Essenes, *and Nazarenes* were viewed as us, part of the group, and all were staying within the boundary of Torah. James and the Jerusalem church need to show that Paul also is still within the boundaries.[9]

This vow means Paul will abstain from unclean things. It goes without being said to all readers of Acts that Paul takes the vow seriously. For most Jews, the list of unclean things to avoid would certainly have included Gentiles. In fact, a customary use of this vow was for Jews who had been out in the Diaspora, living among "unclean" Gentiles. When they returned to

---

[9]Paul has just written: "If it is possible, as far as it depends on you, live at peace with everyone" (Rom 12:18). He himself may be attempting to live that out. See the discussion in E. Randolph Richards and Brandon J. O'Brien, *Paul Behaving Badly* (Downers Grove, IL: InterVarsity Press, 2016), 32-34.

Jerusalem they would take this vow to purify themselves. Precisely because Paul's vow is quite visible, a problem arises. Paul is seen walking around town with Trophimus the Ephesian, a Gentile (Acts 21:29). Trophimus would be easily recognizable as an Ephesian because of his own boundary markers. It would be obvious to Jews that he dressed like an Ephesian, just as I can easily recognize a typical Armenian in Beirut or a Chinese Indonesian. To the great dismay of Jerusalem, they see a Jewish man under a purity vow, walking around with a Gentile. Obviously (in their minds), Trophimus is unclean. This could only mean (to them) that this Jew (Paul) is flouting, mocking, his purity vow. In their minds, this is not just Paul breaking his purity vow, but rather Paul is publicly mocking the vow.

In Acts, it goes without being said Paul would never mock a vow he had taken before God. Instead, Paul is trying to make a theological statement, that Trophimus is *not* unclean. Although Trophimus is a Gentile, he is a brother in the Lord, and therefore clean. Thus, Paul is arguing by symbolic action that he can *both* maintain his purity vow *and* walk with Trophimus at the same time. Paul's message collapses, though, because Paul assumed it would go without being said that he would *never* break a vow before the Lord. Since, in Paul's mind, that is obvious, Paul expects every Jew who sees him to conclude there must be some way in which the purity boundary is still being maintained. The crowds, however, merely assume Paul is ridiculing the vow, thus ridiculing the boundary and ultimately ridiculing them as a people. This makes it easy for them to believe that Paul would also break the boundaries of the temple by taking a Gentile inside. It is no wonder then the crowd is so angry (Acts 21:30-31). Paul's actions were not some individual act. Paul was putting the boundary at risk. Like Phinehas, violence was perhaps needed to protect the boundary and thus to protect *our* identity.

The risk of new values. One day in Galilee, some Pharisees and teachers of the law who came from Jerusalem see Jesus and some of his disciples eating with unwashed hands (Mk 7:1-2). Pharisees considered unwashed hands to be ritually defiled. In case we don't know, Mark explains this for us (Mk 7:3). When others see that Jesus does not follow this boundary marker, they ask, "Why don't your disciples live according to the tradition of the elders instead of eating their food with defiled hands?" (Mk 7:5). As when Jesus was "eating with sinners," the Pharisees were gently applying a low level of shame to Jesus by saying "your disciples" instead of "you." Their motivation in shaming is good (at least from their viewpoint). They want Jesus and his disciples to see they have transgressed a boundary and to be pulled back. Restoration is the goal.[10]

Jesus then calls the crowd (to move from a relatively private shaming to a public honor contest with a public verdict). Jesus tells the Pharisees the correct way to interpret the Scriptures regarding clean and unclean things: "Listen to me, everyone, and understand this. Nothing outside a person can defile them by going into them. Rather, it is what comes out of a person that defiles them" (Mk 7:14-15). Jesus is redefining the boundary and thus defining a new (correct) value: clean and unclean does not come from external things. This new value requires new boundary markers. Washing the hands no longer provides cleansing. Rather, another cleansing is required, that of the heart. Mark understood just how significant this was. It defined a whole new value (Mk 7:19). Jesus is redefining what constitutes the people of God.

CONCLUSION: GETTING THE BOUNDARIES RIGHT

Soon after Jesus' resurrection, Paul was zealously persecuting Christians. As individualists, my students often insist, "Live and let live," or, "You do you." Thus they often ask about Paul here, Why didn't Paul just let them get on with it? Why were the actions of these new Jewish followers of Jesus any of Paul's business? Boundaries. They were *we*. These new followers of Jesus were Jews; they belonged to Paul's group, and they were proclaiming that "the crucified imposter Jesus" was the Messiah. Paul understood that their change in values would change the boundaries of what it meant to follow God as his people. The Pharisee Paul saw this contagion was spreading. Paul was zealous for God, and so, like Phinehas, he began to use violence to enforce the boundaries. He thought this would protect the Jews (us) and honor God. He was involved in the violent execution of Stephen

---

[10]Of course, we can never be sure what their true motives were, but this is an acceptable and mild use of shaming.

(Acts 7:58; 8:1). In his zeal for the Lord, Paul was not content to settle for protecting the boundaries only in Jerusalem but even set out for Damascus, "so that if he found any there who belonged to the Way, whether men or women, he might take them as prisoners to Jerusalem" (Acts 9:2). Understanding the importance of boundaries helps us understand Paul's actions.

While traveling to Damascus, something happens to Paul. Understanding that event helps us to better understand Paul and his writings. Paul later tells King Agrippa the story and adds this interpretive element:

> [Jesus said,] "Now get up and stand on your feet. I have appeared to you to appoint you as a servant and as a witness of what you have seen and will see of me. I will rescue you from your own people and from the Gentiles. I am sending you to them to open their eyes and turn them from darkness to light, and from the power of Satan to God, so that they may receive forgiveness of sins and a place among those who are sanctified by faith in me." (Acts 26:16-18)

This appearance of Christ changes Paul. Within a short time, he goes to the synagogues of Damascus, but not to persecute followers of the Way but rather to proclaim their message (Acts 9:19-21). To fully understand Paul's change, we need to understand what Jesus said to Paul. The context of Jesus' command goes without being said, and we might have missed it.

Four passages in Isaiah are often termed songs about the Servant of the Lord (Is 42:1-9; 49:1-13; 50:4-11; 52:13–53:12). The songs refer to the time when the Servant of the Lord will come to open the eyes of the blind, set captives free, and establish the kingdom of God. These passages show God's salvation reaching beyond ethnic Israel:

> It is too small a thing for you to be my servant
>> to restore the tribes of Jacob
>> and bring back those of Israel I have kept.
> I will also make you a light for the Gentiles,
>> that my salvation may reach to the ends of the earth. (Is 49:6)

The New Testament writers came to recognize Jesus as the Servant of the Lord. Here, on the road to Damascus, Jesus commissions Paul to play a role within the fulfilment of these things. Paul comes to see that Jesus is the Christ, the Servant of the Lord, and that the time has come for salvation to include Gentiles as well as Jews. This is good news, a gospel, and Paul is now to be a messenger of this good news (Acts 13:46-47).

Did Paul lose his zeal? Did he decide that the boundaries didn't matter anymore? No. He was still operating within the boundaries, at least the ones that God set. While most Jews saw Gentiles as outside the boundary, Paul saw, in the words of Isaiah, God's plan to extend his offer of salvation to Gentiles as well. Just as not all physical descendants of Abraham are true children of Abraham, as John the Baptist asserted, insisting God could turn stones into children of Abraham (Mt 3:9), so also those who were not physically kin of Abraham could be adopted into his family. Adoption was a valid means for *they* to become *we*. Rather than kinship, though, Paul uses an agricultural metaphor: Gentiles can be grafted into Israel's tree (Rom 11:13-24). Nevertheless, Paul, like the Baptist before him, is redefining the boundary of God's people.

Paul did not set aside Judaism and start a new religion. He saw himself as fulfilling all God promised through Isaiah. During this first missionary trip to be a light to the Gentiles, Paul saw some pagan Celts come to faith in Jesus. Success! God's salvation was reaching "to the ends of the earth" (Is 49:6). Then some other Jewish Christians came along (Judaizers) and said Gentiles needed to keep Torah to be within the boundaries. These Jewish Christians wanted the Gentiles to join the people of God, but to be we, they needed to keep the original boundaries, including to be circumcised. Paul's anger wasn't over circumcision—he was circumcised—but over the definition of *we*. If Jesus was the Servant of the Lord (and if Paul was his emissary),[11] then circumcising Gentiles meant going back to the old boundaries, and therefore the old values. It was a denial of the good news that the Messiah/Servant had come.

---

[11]As the emissary of the Servant, he should bear the same mission and markers. In Paul's letter to the Galatians, we see many references to the Servant Song in Is 49. Like the Servant, Paul says he was set apart in his mother's womb for this purpose (Gal 1:15; Is 49:1). As such, he claims God is glorified in him and what he is doing (Gal 1:24; Is 49:3). He also worries, like the Suffering Servant, that he may have labored in vain to these purposes (Gal 2:2; 4:11; Is 49:4). See Susan Eastman, *Recovering Paul's Mother Tongue: Language and Theology in Galatians* (Grand Rapids, MI: Eerdmans, 2007), 67.

The definition of who is *we* had changed, so the boundaries needed to be in line with this new definition. Paul fought all his life both in person and in his letters to ensure that the Gentiles and Jews would be together one in Christ; both were inside the same boundary and thus were we. What I as an individualist may once have seen as quibbling about personal preferences of individual ethnicities was actually defining (redefining) group identity. Now that the Servant had come and God's salvation had come to Gentiles, then the collective people of God (the we for Jewish Christians) had changed, and the boundaries needed to change to reflect this.

Paul has neither lost his zeal nor relaxed God's boundaries. Rather, the Gentiles are now to be welcomed into the family of God. The value has not really changed: those inside the boundary (we) are clean.

Collectives use boundaries to protect community. While we individualists may frown on boundaries as something that limits us, collectives treasure boundaries. Without boundaries, there is no community. *We* becomes arbitrary, shifting with changing preferences, or even whom we are with at the moment. Biblical writers often mention a practice, expecting the reader to know it is a boundary. Yet, I as an individualist can miss this completely. I can assume certain practices were simply an individual's own choices and beliefs, rather than collective practices. I can miss the role of boundaries, keeping us *us*. When I miss the boundary, I can miss its importance in the story. I can end up describing Paul as crossing boundaries or even breaking boundaries, when in reality, he was their fiercest guardian—at least of the right boundaries.

PART 3

WHY DOES COLLECTIVISM REALLY MATTER TO ME?

"**THEY ARE GOING TO BE SO GLAD TO SEE YOU**," my Syrian friend said as we walked up a crumbling stairwell. We were taking a short-term team of Western Christians to visit a home in a poor area of the city. Many Syrian refugees had settled in this part of town because they didn't have relational connections elsewhere in the city and needed somewhere cheap.

We entered a small two-room apartment. The mother of the family warmly greeted us. Her family, a neighboring family, and some family friends were sitting on the floor with a plastic tablecloth spread out between them all. They gestured for us to sit down and asked us how we were. Someone thanked God for the food, and we began eating together. When we finished, our hostess removed the food and rolled up the tablecloth, and Bibles were passed around. One member of the group led a discussion on Jesus being the Word of God made flesh. Everyone chipped in their thoughts and ideas, and testimonies. After this, we began to pray. A couple of people thanked God for revealing himself to them. A few prayed to God for provision for the next day's food. One in our short-term team prayed for God to help these dear people now that they had lost their homes and their possessions and become very poor refugees.

When we finished, our hostess asked me to translate and tell my friends, "Thank you so much for praying. I just want to let you know that we actually thank God for what happened. Yes, I have lost my home and my business because of the war. We lost lots, but we have gained much more: Jesus. You see, I didn't know him personally when I lived in Syria, so we are very thankful." My friends and I were trying to hold back tears. "And even more than that," she continued, "I have actually gained a much bigger family, and they love me and care for me, like all of you." She hugged each one of us. Now, our team were crying. Still sobbing, we debriefed in a nearby cafe. The members on the team each said they weren't crying because of her story (sad though it was) but because they had come to see Jesus and what the church in the New Testament was like even more clearly.

Throughout this book, we have shared a lot of ways collectives think and live differently from individualists. Like apple and orange trees, these two cultures are not opposites. They are just very different. Not all oranges are the same, but they do share some characteristics common to oranges, and they are all very different from apples.

We have taken you on an exegetical journey, sometimes using examples from modern *collective* cultures. Any modern collective example is just an attempt to provide a story that might illuminate how their culture is different from mine to open possibly a new viewpoint as I read the biblical text. For too long, I have read the Bible solely from the viewpoint of a modern Western individualist. It's possible this has restricted my perspective and has allowed me to misread Scripture by unconsciously reading my own cultural systems back into the biblical text. Our goal is always to discern what the biblical text meant when it was written.

PRODIGAL SON

In Luke 15, Jesus tells a parable of a man with two sons. The younger son decides to take his father's inheritance and make a life for himself. Collectives expect his eldest brother to intervene as a broker to try to persuade him not to be so foolish and selfish. After all, this isn't just *his* money; it's *our* money, a huge piece of the family's inheritance. Everyone in the family, including the lowest slave, is poorer as soon as the younger son leaves with his part of the family inheritance. Lands and orchards that stood in the family for generations now belong to someone else. The younger son sold them for transportable cash. Next year's harvest will be smaller. Although sons were expected to be loyal to the well-being of the family, this younger son alienated himself from his community. What will the rest of the village think about this selfish son, who clearly isn't loyal to his family? What will they think about the family? Even in the midst of all this, there is no sign of his elder brother at this stage in the story.

When the younger son arrives home destitute and his father runs out to greet him, the community would have seen. His father has servants. They likely chased after him to see why he was running and what all the commotion was. As good slaves, they are expected to be loyal to their *pater* (father) and patron and to serve his every need. That's why the father doesn't have to go find them. When he makes his decision, standing there in the road with his son, he merely speaks to them (Lk 15:22). They have been standing and watching the whole event.

It's interesting the slaves prepare the banquet but don't bother to inform the eldest brother. As an important member of the family, he surely should be there too, right? Maybe they think he won't come. Perhaps he has already made it very clear that he has no brother (Lk 15:30). We don't know. It does appear, though, that the elder brother has alienated some of his community. We do know what happens when he comes home and hears the music and asks the slaves what's going on. They tell him his brother has returned home and his father has thrown a party to celebrate. He rushes to join his father and younger brother and celebrate as the eldest son, right?

Embarrassingly, no. He doesn't embody the values of commitment and love. Instead, the elder son flies into a rage. He refuses to enter the celebration. As a result, his father again humbles himself, seeks what is lost, and leaves the celebration, in front of everyone there. Growing up, I think my church did a good job of teaching me this much of the parable. But understanding collectivism helps me to see more. This elder son is ungrateful, which we have seen was considered one of the worst traits in ancient Mediterranean society. The cardinal vice in the patronage system was ingratitude. The elder son dishonors his father, but not only that, he *publicly* shames his father, by accusing him of being stingy (Lk 15:29), of being a poor patron. The father gently corrects his elder son, reinforcing the value of celebrating the return of those who were lost, and then asks him to come into the party and join in the celebration, to rejoin his community. The parable is about how the father restores *both* sons to their community. As a modern individualist, I might miss these signposts in the story.

As an individualist, I might misread in other ways. I can be tempted to think about the younger son venturing out into the world to make a living for himself, perhaps even privately admiring his desire to be independent and self-reliant. I might conclude that his sin is that he makes bad choices while on his own in a foreign land. We can be rightly saddened by his bad choices but then rejoice at the image of him repenting (privately). After all, he has only wronged his father by making poor (personal) lifestyle choices. If the younger son had gone out and become a successful businessman, and lived a life of personal godliness, then the story might have had a happy ending, right? Wrong. The story is about alienating oneself from one's community. In fact, that's the story of the Bible. That's what sin is and does. We alienate ourselves from God's community.

I might also imagine that the elder son has a good point to make. He is the lone brother standing for what is right, like a hero in a movie, right? He didn't attempt to mediate or correct his younger brother earlier in the story. Why had the brother not gone out to seek and restore his brother? He clearly thought he knew where his brother was and what he was doing (Lk 15:30). We can miss the importance of the way Jesus highlights the character of this elder son. The elder brother is no hero; he doesn't act honorably to his brother or his father. We misread if we think this story is all about the younger son and his mistake and how the father receives and celebrates him. We misread if we see a story about an individual prodigal son or even two individual sons.

I'M SAVED INTO WE

Jesus' parable of the prodigal son(s) has kinship, patronage, and brokerage running throughout. Tools such as honor, shame, and boundaries are used to maintain these values by people in Jesus' parable. The father seeks to honor both sons; yet both sons try to misuse shame to get what they want. Both sons transgress boundaries. Neither brokers for the other. Yet the father brokers (for himself) to pull both sons back inside the (family) boundary.

What's more, Jesus told this story to a collective culture. He told the parable in response to Pharisees and teachers of the law muttering, "this man welcomes sinners and eats with them" (Lk 15:2). Jesus was using the parable to gently shame them to pull them back to God's values. They are to think of the sinners as lost brothers (kinship) and are to celebrate their being welcomed back into the family. They are not to be the elder brother, who stands for the wrong values, is a sorry brother, a poor client, and a terrible broker. So, Jesus told a parable that contained kinship, patronage, brokerage, honor, shame, and boundaries to redefine who is the we.

This book has explored these collective social structures and tools, but a key goal is to look for the values that these social structures and tools are defining and maintaining. While God uses patronage, the system is not based on looking for worthy clients but on God's desire to graciously give, to bless. The Bible has been working all the way through to show that while kinship is a wonderful system, it doesn't end with just God as father of a bunch of lone individuals. The Bible begins by saying God created everything (Gen 1:1), so everything is part of his household, his community. God created us to live together with him *and* with one another in loving harmony. At each step, God announced that it was good. The first time God says something is not good is when he sees that Adam is alone. We need one another. (My sweet individualist grandmother used this verse to mean that I individually needed a wife.) Kinship, patronage, and brokerage are all based in community. Yet, our individualist signposts can sometimes obscure this.

One such way is the way we interpret salvation. God doesn't want to save me as an individual. God saves us into something: a community. Paul writes to the Corinthians, "Don't you know that you yourselves are God's temple and that God's Spirit dwells in your [plural] midst?" (1 Cor 3:16). In Revelation, John writes, "And I heard a loud voice from the throne saying, 'Look! God's dwelling place is now among the people, and he will dwell with them. They will be his people, and God himself will be with them and be their God'" (Rev 21:3). At the heart of these images is that we are a community of people where God dwells.[12]

It is so easy for me to read salvation as being an individual matter. "For God so loved the world that he gave his one and only Son, that whoever believes in him shall not perish but have eternal life" (Jn 3:16). More than once, growing up in church, I was taught to read my name into this verse: "God so loved *Rich* that he gave his one and only Son, that *Rich* shall not perish but have eternal life." It is true that God loves us, each and every one of us. Salvation is a deeply personal matter, and I as an individual am restored to God. He does love *me*. At the same time, it is also about we. The lost son is restored into a family. The shepherd brings the lone lost sheep back into the flock. God sent Jesus as a broker to reconnect us to him *and* to one another. The Bible teaches I'm saved—into a community. The new popular presentation of the gospel, the Three Circles, correctly emphasizes community and one's relationship to community.[13] All through the Bible, collective images are used to demonstrate, explain, and shape this reality. Now we want to put the pieces together in terms of how recognizing the collectivism in the Bible should shape the way I (we!) apply the Bible to my (our!) lives today.

---

[12]Robert H. Mounce, *The Book of Revelation*, rev. ed., New International Commentary on the New Testament (Grand Rapids: Eerdmans, 1998), 382.

[13]See, e.g., Dustin Willis, *Life on Mission: Joining the Everyday Mission of God* (Chicago: Moody, 2014). Note how it emphasizes how sin has broken relationships and salvation restores one to a community.

14

REDEEMING KINSHIP
AND BOUNDARIES

Who Is Our Family?

I WAS SITTING WITH SOME MEDITERRANEAN FRIENDS in my living room studying Mark's Gospel. We got to the story where Jesus' family hears all he is doing and decides to take charge of him.[1] This is a very collective way of dealing with such a problem, so everyone in the living room was nodding along with the story. We got to the part where it says:

> Then Jesus' mother and brothers arrived. Standing outside, they sent someone in to call him. A crowd was sitting around him, and they told him, "Your mother and brothers are outside looking for you."
>
> "Who are my mother and my brothers?" he asked.
>
> Then he looked at those seated in a circle around him and said, "Here are my mother and my brothers! Whoever does God's will is my brother and sister and mother." (Mk 3:31-35)

Suddenly my Bible study group went crazy. Ghaith stood up, arms in the air. "There is no way Jesus said something as offensive as that!" I wondered what all the fuss was about. It's a nice story about loving one another, isn't it? Nothing to get all worked up about. Months later the Bible study group remembered the story and said it was one of the most

---

[1] We cannot know the motive of Mary and Jesus' brothers, but it may have been to bring Jesus back under control before he could be accused of being "a stubborn and rebellious son" (Deut 21:18). Jesus is accused elsewhere of being a glutton and a drunkard (e.g., Mt 11:19). Nazareth's attempted execution may have been on this charge (Lk 4:28-30).

challenging stories in the entire Gospel of Mark. I had missed something: the foundational role kinship plays in organizing Mediterranean
society. Worse, I had glossed over a scandalous statement by Jesus about
how life altering the Christian message is to be. Mark probably had expected me to react like Ghaith.

The early church lived in a collective culture where kinship was a basic
building block of society and family defined what it meant to be me. They
had high expectations of family members to associate with and care for
one another. Kinship metaphors and terms were not lost on them. John
tells us of another time Jesus speaks to his mother about family being the
people of God: "Near the cross of Jesus stood his mother, his mother's
sister, Mary the wife of Clopas, and Mary Magdalene. When Jesus saw his
mother there, and the disciple whom he loved standing nearby, he said to
her, 'Woman, here is your son,' and to the disciple, 'Here is your mother'"
(Jn 19:25-27). Mary and the beloved disciple see the depth of Jesus'
statement and how this isn't just some nice metaphor for saying they will
be friends. Indeed, John tells us, "From that time on, this disciple took her
into his home" (Jn 19:27). Jesus chooses the family of faith to care for his
(believing) mother rather than James or Jude or some other physical relative in Nazareth or Bethlehem. This should not be underplayed.

GOD AS FATHER

I was drinking coffee with Hassan, a Mediterranean man. As an older man,
he was seeking to teach me (as a young man) some wisdom, but in a way
as to not overly shame me. He said, "I am in my fifties, but I still ask *baba*
for guidance, and I will always do as he says. It's not about my age. It's
because he's my dad and an older generation. He has more wisdom to
guide me with." He recognized the importance of collective help, especially coming from parents. At fifty, he still called his father *baba*, the
Arabic word for "father." He used the term because they had an intimate
relationship. Jesus speaks about God as "father." When Jesus teaches his
disciples how to pray, he begins with the Aramaic name for father: *abba*.[2]

---

[2]The Gospels were written in Greek, but Mk 14:36 quotes the Aramaic term. See Joachim Jeremias,
New Testament Theology, vol. 1, *The Proclamation of Jesus* (London: SCM Press, 1975), 64.

It is true that Israelite children used *abba*, but so did adult Israelite men—unlike with our English term *daddy*. Collective cultures value dependence on older generations. This understanding of God being our father was very important to the early church, so much so that Paul writes to the church in Rome and says, "The Spirit you received brought about your adoption to sonship. And by him we cry, '*Abba*, Father'" (Rom 8:15). This largely Gentile church in the capitol of the Roman Empire already knew the Aramaic term *abba*. Teaching God as Father was such a foundational aspect of the early church that Paul doesn't need to introduce it.[3]

A Korean friend moved to the United States as a child. He still tells this story: On his first day in school, the teacher asked him to tell the class about himself. He began by saying, "Our dad is a doctor." He recounts how the class burst out laughing: "Why did you say 'our,' not 'my,' dad"? one of them giggled. He had never thought of it that way. He was not an only child. He loved his dad, but so did his siblings. His dad belonged to all of them. His father was their father.

Jesus taught us to say "our Father," not "my Father." God is my father, and he loves me, but it is more biblical to say God is *our* father and he loves *us*. We have all become a family, with God as our father. Let's explore some of the ways the biblical writers teach this, picking up collective systems, images, and metaphors from their time, taking care to avoid following individualist signposts.

When I read about Paul telling the church in Rome that through the Spirit we cry out *abba*, I need to avoid my individualist signpost that leads me to think only about "me and my Dad." When *we* cry out *abba*, we are supposed to think of siblings. This is Paul's point. It is how he culminates a long argument about how Jewish Christians and Gentile Christians are one family.[4] The picture is of a community calling to *their* one Father:

---

[3]Paul is introducing the idea that the Spirit is how we are adopted. This is part of the same argument he uses against Judaizers in Galatia. It is by the Spirit (and not Torah) that believers are part of the elect of God. His argument assumes the Roman Christians are already using *abba* in their worship.

[4]Obviously, we are simplifying Romans, a complicated book. Scholars debate about the central theme of Romans. See, e.g., Karl Donfried, *The Romans Debate*, rev. ed. (Grand Rapids, MI: Baker Academic, 1991).

For those who are led by the Spirit of God are the children of God. The Spirit you received does not make you slaves, so that you live in fear again; rather, the Spirit you received brought about your adoption to sonship. And by him we cry, "*Abba*, Father." The Spirit himself testifies with our spirit that we are God's children. Now if we are children, then we are heirs—heirs of God and co-heirs with Christ, if indeed we share in his sufferings in order that we may also share in his glory. (Rom 8:14-17)

We are not brought into the household as slaves (no subgroup of the church is brought in as slaves). God has chosen to adopt us to sonship. Paul is teaching God as father (and patron) will care for us. We are (all) fully legal inheritors of the family, and as part of that we are responsible for our fellow family members. We are co-heirs with Christ. We can expect to suffer with him but then also inherit a share in his glory! This is why the Spirit in us cries out "*Abba*."

CHRISTIANS AS SIBLINGS

All over the world, Christians describe themselves as family. In the country church where I was called to preach, I was called "Brother Randy." We said we were a church family; yet, I didn't live as family with them. I would loan my car to Tammy, my actual sister. Recently, we were both visiting my folks. I was sleeping late, and she needed to dash over to the grocery store to buy some milk. She took my car without asking me. She knows me and knew I wouldn't want her waking me up to ask. She can borrow my stuff, and I can borrow hers—because we're siblings.

While my sister is my blood sister, my Indonesian Christian brothers and sisters saw our relationship just the same way. One morning in Indonesia, I woke up and walked into our living room, and all our furniture was gone. I walked into the kitchen, where my wife, Stacia, was cooking, and said, "Our furniture is gone." Without even looking up from cooking, she said, "Yeah, I noticed that, too." I went off to teach class at the seminary where I was serving. When I got home for lunch, the living room was still empty. Later that afternoon, a truck pulled up with all our furniture. People unloaded it, put it back, and started to leave. "Wait a minute," I said, coming in from the kitchen. "Where has our furniture been?" One of the men on the way back to the truck, said over his shoulder, "At a wedding." When I still looked confused, he added, "It was early this morning, and you were still asleep. We knew you wouldn't mind." Christians are family, and families loan things. Perhaps churches in the individualist West have forgotten how to be family. One church owns a church bus. If another church needs it, are we family? "Our insurance policy won't allow it," my deacon protests. I know, I know. But if we were really family, wouldn't we find a way?

John writes to the believers, "See what great love the Father has lavished on us, that we should be called children of God! And that is what we are!" (1 Jn 3:1). Later in the passage, John goes on to say, "This is how we know what love is: Jesus Christ laid down his life for us." We may expect him to continue here, "We ought to lay down our lives for Christ." He doesn't say that. Rather, "And we ought to lay down our lives for our brothers and sisters" (1 Jn 3:16). While many of us would sacrifice for our biological family, we might protest that church family is another matter. John argues otherwise. John has high expectations of how Christ's love will change our hearts toward our Christian brothers and sisters. Christ's love has a call on our time, our ambitions, and our wallets. John continues, "If anyone has material possessions and sees a brother or sister in need but has no pity on them, how can the love of God be in that person? Dear children, let us not love with words or speech but with actions and in truth" (1 Jn 3:17-18).

Years ago, I invited a dear Indonesian colleague, Joubert, to spend a semester teaching at my Christian college in the United States. When Joubert and his wife arrived, I loaned him my truck the next day to run some errands. He kept it for the entire semester. The evening before they flew home to Indonesia, he returned it. He didn't say, "Thank you," though he is a gracious Christian gentleman. Indonesians are quick to be thankful. Rather, he didn't say thanks because it never occurred to him. We are Christian brothers. I had two vehicles, and he had none. What would family do? We were family.

Acts 2 often confuses Christians in individualist cultures. I've heard it described as failed communism. My collectivist friends find Acts 2 no mystery. The believers were acting like family. The kinds of things believers were doing for one another were the kind of things they would have (ideally) done for their family members. If we call God *Abba*, then we cannot think of one another as brothers and sisters merely with empty words, as John notes. We must treat one another as brothers and sisters, because we are family under a new heavenly Father.

NEW FAMILY BOUNDARIES

Today I teach young ministers at a university in the United States. I often tell them, "Your biggest challenge will be to make a Christian family out of a congregation of individualists." As Westerners, we may try to excuse ourselves by saying early Christians were collectives and not individualists like us, so it was part of their culture to care for one another. Actually, this was not so. Ancient Mediterranean people were indeed collectives who had high expectations for *their* group to spend time and care for one another in *their* group. But they had no such expectations for other groups. In fact, their collective culture urged them to ignore the needs of outsiders. At a recent workshop, Jackson Wu, a scholar on collectivism in Chinese culture, shared a depressing tale. An older woman fell into a busy street. A stranger stepped forward and snatched her to safety. But the fallen woman then sued the stranger, arguing he must have been the one who pushed her; *otherwise*, he would never have helped her. A sad story. It became a depressing tale when Wu added that the court ruled in her favor, reasoning that clearly no one would help a stranger, so the man must have been the one who pushed her. If someone is not part of your group, then collectives have even stronger boundaries. Ancient Mediterranean cultures would not have encouraged redefining family. It was such a strange concept that Paul needed to use a metaphor they would understand: adoption. It was a way their culture understood for redefining family. (Marriage was the other, and the New Testament uses it as well.)

We have seen the importance boundaries played in collective cultures. This is because boundaries show who is inside the group (and to be cared for) and who is not; boundaries keep *us* from *them*. So when new churches were established, the old boundaries would have tried to pull them apart. How could these new believers be a group? They had different blood. They had a different collective history. They had a whole network of blood relatives who depended on them and had expectations on them. Collectivism didn't solve this problem; it aggravated the problem.

The challenge of building a Christian community is not an individualist or collectivist problem. It is the problem of living as God's family in a fallen world. It can be hard to form a deep community from individualists because individualists often do not understand the importance of community. At the same time, it can be hard to form a deep community from collectivists because collectivists understand the importance of community— the ones they are already a part of.

When Paul writes to the newly established church in Thessalonica, he emphasizes kinship: Paul calls these new believers his "brothers and sisters" (1 Thess 1:4). We can miss some of the weight of Paul's pastoral strategy. He is forming a new family with new boundaries. In fact, Paul impresses on them that they are brothers and sisters seventeen times, even in this short letter.[5] He also reminds them he is a father to them and they are like his children (1 Thess 2:11). He also says he is like a mother to them (1 Thess 2:7). Paul speaks about a father instructing his children, children obeying their fathers, a nursing mother caring for babes, brothers living in harmony, and, of course, family loving one another. Even when Paul shames a church member who is unruly, in order to draw him back within the boundaries Paul describes the person as a brother (2 Thess 3:6). This was not just a strategy in Thessalonian culture. In 1 Corinthians, writing to a church divided in a number of ways, Paul's strategy remains the same: reminding them they are kin. For example, he shames the church (as a whole) for allowing a brother to take a brother to court, and in front of unbelievers (1 Cor 6:6). Paul shames them for taking *we* to them instead of to *us*.

Paul uses the language and metaphor of kinship over and over to shape the way his audience thinks about one another. Defining the boundaries

---

[5] 1 Thess 1:4; 2:1, 9, 14, 17; 3:2, 7; 4:1, 6, 10, 13; 5:1, 4, 12, 14, 25, 26, 27.

defines the values. He intends the kinship language to transform the way they behave toward one another.[6] Paul sees this as the outworking of the gospel: in Christ they all call God *abba,* so they are family. This shapes the way they care for one another, stand with one another, restore one another, overlook offenses, challenge one another, have authority to speak into one another's life. The intimacy of kin underlies and runs through all of this. Paul wants them to understand this. It will heal the Corinthian church's divisions if they do. Paul practices what he preaches. Paul explains that he urged Apollos to come to them, but Apollos refused. Nonetheless, Paul emphasizes "our brother Apollos" (1 Cor 16:12). Paul is reminding the Corinthians they are family and that they are to understand Paul's and Apollo's relationship in the context of family.

Familiarity breeds contempt.[7] We read kinship language so often in the New Testament that we skim over it rather than read it for how scandalous it was. The gospel was plowing new ground. Understanding the role kinship played in the collective culture of the Mediterranean makes us better able to understand the responsibility of Christians to love one another, care for one another, and live in harmony with one another.

WE SHARE A TABLE

Households figured prominently in the first-century Mediterranean world and in the New Testament. Let's explore households by envisioning what happened when Paul visited Lydia of Philippi in Acts 16.

When Paul and his team entered the city of Philippi, they found no synagogue. Paul went down to the river, where Jews would gather on a Sabbath.[8] Luke recounts:

> On the Sabbath we went outside the city gate to the river, where we expected to find a place of prayer. We sat down and began to speak to the

---

[6]Kar Long Lim, *Metaphors and Social Identity Formation in Paul's Letters to the Corinthians* (Eugene, OR: Pickwick, 2017), 192.

[7]This is an old saying. Chaucer is the first recorded instance: *Tale of Melibee,* one of the Canterbury Tales, circa 1386.

[8]Perhaps this custom went back to the time of the exile in Babylon. A psalmist writing from exile in Babylon says: "By the rivers of Babylon we sat and wept when we remembered Zion" (Ps 137:1).

women who had gathered there. One of those listening was a woman from the city of Thyatira named Lydia, a dealer in purple cloth. She was a worshiper of God. The Lord opened her heart to respond to Paul's message. When she and the members of her household were baptized, she invited us to her home. "If you consider me a believer in the Lord," she said, "come and stay at my house." And she persuaded us. (Acts 16:13-15)

So we find Paul in the household of Mrs. Lydia.[9] The homes of wealthier merchants, such as Lydia, typically were the size of a small city block, called an *insula*. The front of the house held the public shop; behind it was a large open room, usually with a dining hall to the side; and behind that was an open-air courtyard, with various sleeping rooms on at least one side and perhaps another dining room. The kitchen, stable, and privy were at the back of the courtyard. We should not imagine a modern, private Western home. While the bedrooms might have been more private (and they were very small, dark rooms), the rest of the house was more public than we individualists typically imagine of a home. When I was living in Indonesia, it was not uncommon for me to wake up at about 5 a.m. and go into the living room to find a pastor and his family sitting there waiting for me. They had come from the village with some need. Other times I would come home for lunch, and there would be a few strangers in the kitchen cooking. I would ask my wife, Stacia, who they were, and she would shrug and say "I don't know." Our bedrooms were very private, but the rest of the house was (far) more public than was our custom in Texas.

Further, there could have been thirty or more people in Lydia's household. Not just her family members (blood), but also her clients and

---

[9]We deliberately chose this nomenclature. We note several facts Luke mentions about Lydia. We should assume she is a widow. A husband is never mentioned, and she is clearly the head of the household. Luke's custom is to refer to characters by the third part of the traditional Roman tripartite name (praenomen, nomen, and cognomen), what we might call their family name. Luke also tells us she is from Thyatira. What went without being said was basic Roman geography: Thyatira was the largest city in the Roman province of Lydia. Thus, *Lydia* was likely the cognomen, the family name, chosen by their ancestor in Thyatira when they achieved Roman citizenship and earned a tripartite name. This was common. Thus, we do not know Mrs. Lydia's praenomen or personal name. We should not immediately assume she cannot be Euodia or Syntyche, two women in Philippi whom Paul calls out by name (Phil 4:2). See E. Randolph Richards, "Roman Names," in *The Baker Illustrated Bible Handbook*, ed. J. Daniel Hays and J. Scott Duvall (Grand Rapids, MI: Baker Academic, 2011), 719-20.

slaves. Recent excavations in Pompeii show wealthy homes with adjacent (or attached) houses of poorer clients. It shouldn't surprise us that in the days before public transportation a patroness would need her clients and slaves close at hand.

Paul's being invited into Lydia's home would not have been unprecedented. There were many itinerant philosophers plying the roads of the Roman Empire.[10] Paul's speaking in the market in a city square (Greek *agora*; Latin *forum*) would not have seemed uncommon, and in fact he might not have been the only speaker that day. Philosophers who impressed were invited into homes, like Lydia invited Paul to her home. She honored Paul by inviting him in, so it would likely have been expected for Paul to reciprocate her gift by speaking (performing) at one or more dinner parties. This was not demeaning but rather honoring (for all involved). Even elite rhetorician Cicero was asked to read something he had recently written.[11] Other invitations would follow. It is quite possible the church spread in Philippi (and elsewhere) by Paul speaking in homes such as Lydia's. For example, we read Paul was hosted in the home of Jason in Thessalonica (Acts 17:7).

Through these meetings, Lydia's and Jason's networks would be reached. The reciprocity system inherent in patronage facilitated the spread of the gospel from one patron's network to another. Because Lydia invited her friends to her house, they would need to reciprocate. Lydia would bring her guest with her. When that home welcomed Paul as a guest, then he would be expected to reciprocate their hospitality by sharing something. The gospel would then spread through this new patron's network.[12]

---

[10]It appears some traveling speakers adopted the Christian gospel as one of the messages they marketed. Paul is not complimentary of them, calling them peddlers (2 Cor 2:17).

[11]On one occasion, Cicero is hesitant to read something before Pompey, an honored guest, because Tiro, his secretary, has not yet proofread it. See Cicero, *Letters to Friends* 16.10.2; see also E. Randolph Richards, *Paul and First-Century Letter Writing: Secretaries, Composition and Collection* (Downers Grove, IL: InterVarsity Press, 2004), 45.

[12]Likely another significant method of evangelism was women, slave and free, who took children to the meeting. See Margaret Y. MacDonald, *The Power of Children: The Construction of Christian Families in the Greco-Roman World* (Waco, TX: Baylor University Press, 2014). Slave women responsible for children could not leave them at home. The children would likely have been a mix from her own slave marriage, those fathered by the owner, and the owner's legitimate children. Paul appears to credit women for Timothy's conversion (2 Tim 1:5).

Dinner parties provided a great platform but created at least two problems. First, these dinner parties were commonly called *convivia*, or wine parties.[13] They were known for certain common forms of misbehavior. Several Greco-Roman philosophers wrote treatises denouncing the licentiousness, drunkenness, and gossiping that went on in these parties. The second problem was that these parties reflected the social stratification of the Greco-Roman world. The patrons feasted, while slaves stood silently watching. Seneca famously describes it:

> The master eats more than he can hold, and with monstrous greed loads his belly until it is stretched and at length ceases to do the work of a belly; so that he is at greater pains to discharge all the food than he was to stuff it down. All this time the poor slaves may not move their lips, even to speak. The slightest murmur is repressed by the rod; even a chance sound,—a cough, a sneeze, or a hiccup,—is visited with the lash. There is a grievous penalty for the slightest breach of silence. All night long they must stand about, hungry and dumb.[14]

As Christian communities were formed, they shared a meal in common. It was not to be the meal of a wine party but the shared table of a family household. But the old boundaries pulled at these new Christians. Boundaries define values. Their pagan friends ridiculed them for eating with those of lower (or higher) social status. When a peer, perhaps a fellow patron, invited a Christian to dinner, the problem wasn't just the issue of avoiding the vices. The person would be expected to reciprocate the invitation. We see Paul dealing with these very real problems. In 1 Corinthians some—perhaps most or even all—of the problems occurring in the church were the problems of these wine parties. Paul calls the issues immorality, drunkenness, and division: vices. Roman pagans might have referred to these same issues as virtues: sexual privilege, the blessings of Dionysus (the god of wine), and social stratification.

---

[13]Technically, the Greek *symposium* was an after-dinner wine party, while the Roman *convivium* focused on food and was a meal. In practice, the meal flowed into drinking afterward.

[14]Seneca, *Epistle* 47.2-3. See Richard M. Gummere, *Seneca: Epistles. [Ad Lucilium epistulae morales]*, Loeb Classical Library (Cambridge, MA: Harvard University Press, 1917), 1:302-3.

Seneca describes how hosts were expected to provide escorts for their guests. Often, these would be some of the slaves from their household.[15] What was the church to do? The answer may seem simple, but it was very challenging. When Jason or Lydia was invited to a friend's home, they could turn down the offered escorts. But when they reciprocated and hosted a dinner at their home, their pagan friend would expect them to provide an escort. Their reputation as a gracious host was at risk. To make it worse, what if those slaves were now their Christian brother or sister? Paul warns the Thessalonians: "It is God's will that you should be sanctified: that you should avoid sexual immorality; that each of you should learn to control your own body [possess one's own vessel] in a way that is holy and honorable, not in passionate lust like the pagans, who do not know God" (1 Thess 4:3-5). The Greeks idiom "possess [one's] own vessel" was a blunt expression that translates well into an equally blunt modern idiom: keeping one's toga zipped.[16] Paul may well be targeting the common sin of a slave owner sexually abusing young (often male) slaves, tragically known as a *delicium*.[17] Note that Paul in the next verse says that by abstaining from sexual immorality a Christian man can avoid wronging a *brother*: "that no man transgress and defraud his brother in the matter because the Lord is the avenger in all these things, just as we also told you before and solemnly warned you" (1 Thess 4:6 NASB).

The old boundaries (and values) were trying to pull Christians back. "Shouldn't an owner have the right to do as he wills with his own property?" a Christian's pagan friends would argue. Boundaries define values. Paul is giving a new value. These slave boys are now your Christian brothers.

---

[15]Seneca, *Epistle* 47.7: "Another [male slave], who serves the wine, must dress like a woman and wrestle with his advancing years; he cannot get away from his boyhood; he is dragged back to it; and though he has already acquired a soldier's figure, he is kept beardless by having his hair smoothed away or plucked out by the roots, and he must remain awake throughout the night, dividing his time between his master's drunkenness and his lust; in the chamber he must be a man, at the feast a boy" (Gummere, *Seneca*, 304-5).

[16]Paul's cleverness is twice over. The Jews used the same idiom to mean "gain a wife" (since, I suppose, a wife was a vessel of children). Thus, with both Gentile and Jewish Christians, Paul is using a blunt phrase to jar his readers out of their complacency with sin.

[17]The term refers to a pet child in both positive (favorite) and tragically negative (sexual) ways. See, e.g., Christian Laes, *Children in the Roman Empire: Outsiders Within* (Cambridge: Cambridge University Press, 2011), 284.

Moreover, as we saw from Seneca, the masters ate while the slaves served. Slaves ate what was left over. When Christians sat down to a meal, old boundaries said the rich ate first. After all, they would argue, wealth shows God's favor. Slaves ate afterwards. Paul notes this, saying:

> In the following directives I have no praise for you, for your meetings do more harm than good. In the first place, I hear that when you come together as a church, there are divisions among you, and to some extent I believe it. No doubt there have to be differences among you to show which of you have God's approval. So then, when you come together, it is not the Lord's Supper you eat, for when you are eating, some of you go ahead with your own private suppers. As a result, one person remains hungry and another gets drunk. (1 Cor 11:17-21)

Despite being believers and sharing in the same household, they were maintaining the old boundaries between wealthy and poor, owners and slaves. These old boundaries maintained the old values—as boundaries are supposed to do. To counter, Paul argues they all call the same God *Abba*. Children all sit at the same table together. The church is supposed to reflect new values as brothers and sisters in one household. This is why Paul is passionate. There cannot be unity in this new collective group if they maintain the boundaries that enforced and reinforced their old groups and the former values they were built on.

Paul deals with this by providing new boundaries: "So then, my brothers and sisters, when you gather to eat, you should all eat together" (1 Cor 11:33). What went without being said was that family all ate together. By sharing corporate meals, including the Lord's Supper, boundaries were being established and reinforced around the new values: *one* family in Christ.

CONCLUSION: A SHARED FAMILY HISTORY

We noted in chapter eight that genealogies are important to collectives. Genealogies show who is *we*. Growing up in a church in the southern United States, as children we sang, "Father Abraham had many sons.... I am one of them and so are you." There is amazing theology in this song. We have been grafted into Abraham's tree. So, the exodus is part of *my* family history. I have been adopted. So have you, and we all share in the promises God gave to our father Abraham. As an individualist, I get that part, but I forget that I was adopted into a *family* with family responsibilities. I have new brothers and sisters, new boundaries and new values.

This also has implications for the gospel. For a long time, individualist cultures have focused on the gospel's impact on me or you as an individual person. The gospel affects me as an individual. I am forgiven; I am saved; I am restored to God; I am adopted into God's family. The end is community, but the message has focused on reaching me as an individual. What about the New Testament world? When the Philippian jailer asked Paul and Silas,

> "Sirs, what must I do to be saved?" They replied, "Believe in the Lord Jesus, and you will be saved—you and your household." Then they spoke the word of the Lord to him and to all the others in his house. At that hour of the night the jailer took them and washed their wounds; then immediately he and all his household were baptized. (Acts 16:30-33)

Paul and Silas had a view to reach his household, not only him. They also understood that when they came to faith in Jesus, they joined God's family.

One night I had been hanging out with some people I didn't know well. They knew I taught the Bible and were asking me some questions about Jesus. I shared some stories, and we discussed them together. When I got up to go home, one of them offered to walk with me for a while. As soon as we were alone together, he asked, "Do you think I can become a follower of Jesus?" I replied that yes, anyone can. He was silent for a while. I wondered whether he might next ask, "What do I need to do to be saved?" He didn't. Instead, deep in thought, he asked, "But how would that work, because nobody in my family has ever been a Christian?" I was silent for a while. I'd never been asked that question before, but I understood how important it was to him. He thought in "we." He was thinking how the stories of Jesus and the good news I had shared that night affected him as a member of a group.

A lot of theology is produced and published in the Western world (such as this book). Apples and oranges are different, but they are both delicious.

We think theology and biblical studies done by members of the Western church can offer much to the body of Christ. It has, and we hope it will continue to do so. We also recognize that the powerhouse of Western publishing and training centers has also spread a gospel that is more focused on the individual and applied to individuals than communities. There are many times where someone has come to understand the gospel as how it relates to *me*, but received little teaching on how it applies to *we*. Thankfully, believers in collective cultures are also studying the Bible, listening to God, and engaging with their communities. As Western authors, we have learned a lot from brothers and sisters in collective cultures. We have benefited from their insights, and we hope this book will also benefit them with some of our insights. The body needs all its members. As Westerners who have long focused on the individualistic implications of the gospel, we can learn a lot from the body of Christ in collective cultures. Many Lebanese, Syrian, Chinese, Columbian, and Congolese brothers and sisters have long been explaining the good news in collective cultures.

Part of the good news is that it is addressed to communities and that it calls all people, regardless of ethnicity, into God's family, a new community. We believe that the more we get hold of the collective nature of the biblical world, and of the nature of salvation as being people brought into God's family, then the more we might begin to bring out these aspects of the gospel and address them in a way that makes sense to communities: families, tower blocks, neighborhoods, colleagues, friends, and other ethnic groups. What does it mean to announce the good news that King Jesus has invited us to join his kingdom?

15

REDEEMING PATRONAGE AND BROKERAGE

GOD AS FATHER WITH THE KINGDOM AS family and household is a beautiful image. Understanding the people of God as family is an important Old Testament theme (Gen 12:1-4 onward). The people of God were the children of Abraham. But the ancient Mediterranean world understood kinship as blood kinship. Despite stories such as the book of Ruth, we see Jewish people in the Gospels who had restricted kinship to the blood lines of Abraham. We saw in the previous chapter how the New Testament writers took up many kinship images from their collective culture to help Christians to see that we are family. We are all adopted into God's family.

Here in the individualist West, we are fairly comfortable with the idea that Christians are family. We get the basic idea, whether or not we actually live it out with our brothers and sisters in Christ. We are less familiar with patronage and brokerage, and so we can miss the way the biblical writers draw on these systems too, often incorporating them with kinship, to help Christians understand their relationship with God and one another. In this chapter, we want to explore some of the ways the biblical writers draw on patronage and brokerage and some of the related aspects of these systems, sometimes combining them with kinship, to help believers live out who they are.

GOD AS PATRON

Throughout Scripture, God is described as a shepherd. We saw previously that a shepherd was a common metaphor for explaining patronage relationships. The shepherd is the patron, who cares for, protects, leads, and feeds his flock. The flock are the clients, who depend on, follow, and trust the shepherd. When the Bible speaks of God as shepherd and his people as his flock, ancient readers weren't thinking pastures but patronage. Likewise, the Old Testament is filled with kingdom imagery. God created the earth. It's logical he is king of it. When God brings his people out of Egypt, he establishes a community, where he is king (*pater*).

The shepherd cares for a flock, not a single sheep. The Bible speaks throughout of God as shepherd and his people (plural) being his flock. Yet, my mental image of the Good Shepherd has me draped over his shoulders as he walks through a green field (which looks a lot like an English meadow). While Jesus did tell the parable of the shepherd going to find the one lost sheep (me), he did it to bring me back to the flock, to join my ninety-nine brothers and sisters. The problem with my image is not that I am draped over Jesus' shoulders (a good place to be) but that there aren't any other sheep in my image. Somehow I squeezed God as shepherd back into my individualist "me and Jesus."

In my individualist world, I preach the gospel. Good. But "my" gospel is about personal (i.e., individual) salvation. Acts tells of the spread of the gospel. Luke begins with the disciples asking the risen Jesus, "Lord, are you at this time going to restore the kingdom to Israel?" (Acts 1:6). He ends Acts by describing Paul: "He proclaimed the kingdom of God and taught about the Lord Jesus Christ—with all boldness and without hindrance!" (Acts 28:31).

My collectivist friends hear the word *kingdom*, and they think about people. They ask, "Who is the king? Where is the community? How big is it?" My individualist signposts can lead me down the wrong route when I hear kingdom imagery. I think about the king and about his rules, which teach me how to live my individualized life. I even think in terms of inviting the kingdom of God into my heart—an odd image.[1] Paul writes of "giving joyful thanks to the Father, who has qualified you [plural] to share in the inheritance of his holy people in the kingdom of light. For he has rescued *us* from the dominion of darkness and brought *us* into the kingdom of the Son he loves" (Col 1:12-13).

The book of Acts is the story of the kingdom of God spreading from Jerusalem to the ends of the earth: "But you will receive power when the Holy Spirit comes on you; and you will be my witnesses in Jerusalem, and in all Judea and Samaria, and to the ends of the earth" (Acts 1:8). Luke tells his story from that viewpoint. He recounts stories in Jerusalem, then in Judea and Samaria, and then to the ends of the earth. Ancients thought the earth had four ends. The southern end of the earth was in Ethiopia, which is probably the reason Luke tells the story of the Ethiopian eunuch. The western end of the earth was at Gibraltar, which is likely why Paul wants to go to Spain (Rom 15:28). The first disciples took Jesus' command quite seriously. They were witnesses to all sorts of people all over world with the goal of spreading the kingdom to cover the entire world.

When I close my eyes and imagine the kingdom of God, I am not supposed to see just me and Jesus. How does Jesus portray the kingdom? His people are gathered together, feasting at a banquet, hosted by King Jesus. We should be imagining a banquet table with people from Brazil, Canada, the United States, Europe, Kurdistan, India, Nigeria, and China, sharing a banquet table together with our King.

PUTTING PATRONAGE BACK INTO PAUL

As we have seen, patronage, reciprocity, gratitude, and faith connected all kinds of people together in the ancient Mediterranean world. Paul expected his hearers to understand these dynamics very well when he used the patronage language *charis* and *pistis* to explain the work of God, Christ, the cross, and grace in believers' lives. We want to continue to dig even deeper into the way Paul used patronage to explain the gospel.

---

[1] I know the image likely comes from Rev 3:20, but there Jesus is standing at the door of the church of Laodicea. Anyone in the church can respond and invite Jesus back into the *church*.

God is a wronged patron. Paul wrote to the church in Rome to draw them into his mission to the Gentiles. He wants them to understand how Jews and Gentiles are reconciled to God in Christ, as well as to gain their support to help him continue farther afield to share the gospel with the Gentiles in Spain. Paul begins by explaining how Jews and Gentiles are reconciled to God. It will not surprise that the thought and language in Paul's letter to the Romans is deeply collective and has as a backdrop kinship and patronage. After an introduction, Paul begins to explain the gospel by saying, "The wrath of God is being revealed from heaven against all the godlessness and wickedness of people, who suppress the truth by their wickedness" (Rom 1:18).

My neighbor Ali and I were sitting in the morning sun by the gate of our parking lot one day. One of our neighbors came out of the building dressed for the beach. We sat watching her as she walked past us, across the parking lot, got into her car, and slowly drove back toward us. As she waited in the car beside us for the gate to open, I waved to her. She didn't see me, and then slowly drove out into the road. "How dare she!" Ali said furiously. "She didn't greet us or say goodbye!" I said, "Maybe she didn't see me wave." "Oh she saw," Ali said. "And she saw us sitting here too as she walked right past us. She only sees herself. This is the problem with the world. People are so sinful!"

I certainly agree that people are sinful, but not based on what had angered Ali. Collective culture is based in relationships, and so it is very important to collectives to acknowledge others. For this reason, my students are careful to thank me. They point out whenever other students have helped them. They call students who are not in class in order to tell them they noticed they weren't there. In Indonesia, when someone walks into a crowded room, they will shake the hand of everyone there. They will do it again when they leave. As I learned, they noticed if I (accidently) skipped someone. They corrected me, "Already! Already!" if I tried to shake their hand a second time. In collective cultures, people matter, thanking them matters, acknowledging them matters. If relationships are not constantly honed (or polished, to put it in Indonesian vernacular), then the glue of community could weaken or fall apart.

Failing to acknowledge others in your life means failing to honor them. It is considered a great insult. Paul continues his description of sinful humanity in Romans: "For since the creation of the world God's invisible qualities—his eternal power and divine nature—have been clearly seen, being understood from what has been made, so that people are without excuse. For although they knew God, they neither glorified him as God nor gave thanks to him" (Rom 1:20-21). Paul highlights the way people have not acknowledged God, not honored him, not thanked him. As we see, in the collective world of the Mediterranean these were not merely impolite actions. Paul is not saying people were rude. He is saying humankind has failed to recognize and honor God. Humankind has wronged our patron. Darkened hearts mean people honor manmade idols in place of God, and this lack of recognition is demonstrated in their sinful behavior (Rom 1:22-32). The example of my neighbor Ali being furious with our neighbor pales in significance compared to the insult felt by God. In a Mediterranean way, Paul is providing an easily understandable explanation for why God's wrath is on all people (Rom 1:18).

Paul's Jewish audience would surely have agreed that the Gentiles were under God's wrath. Isaiah 40:18-20 and Psalm 115:1-8 speaks of the way pagans create false gods with their hands rather than acknowledge Yahweh. Around the time of Paul, there was a very popular Jewish book called the Wisdom of Solomon. One part of the book talks about the way people marvel at creation but don't come to recognize the Creator. It ridicules a woodcutter who creates a tool from wood. That night, he picks up a piece of leftover wood and starts carving it. He fashions a little figure, then he paints it. Eventually, he places this little figure in a niche in the wall of his house and starts asking it for help and protection (Wisdom 13:11-19).[2] It criticizes Gentiles, "them," for idolatry and says "we" know better:

> But you, *our* God, are kind and true, patient, and ruling all things in mercy.
> For even if *we* sin *we* are *yours*, knowing your power; but we will not sin,

---

[2]Scholars have long remarked on the similarities between Wisdom 13 and Rom 1. See Joseph R. Dodson, *The "Powers" of Personification: Rhetorical Purpose in the "Book of Wisdom" and the Letter to the Romans*, Beihefte Zeitschrift für die Neutestamentliche Wissenschaft (Berlin: de Gruyter, 2008), 5-13. Our understanding here is heavily reliant on Dodson's work.

because *we* know that you acknowledge *us* as yours.... For neither has the evil intent of human art misled *us* ... whose appearance arouses yearning in fools, so that they desire the lifeless form of a dead image. Lovers of evil things and fit for such objects of hope are those who either make or desire or worship them. (Wisdom 15:2 NRSV)[3]

The Wisdom of Solomon is very collective in its language: Jews will receive mercy, while Gentiles will receive judgment. Jews know better, while Gentiles do not. Paul's Jewish audience may have nodded along when Paul said people who denied God were without excuse and deserved wrath, assuming Paul meant Gentiles. After all, they were probably thinking, *we* Jews are an exception to this, since *we* are the descendants of our father Abraham and those whom God protected in the exodus. Furthermore, *we* have the law (Torah) and so know the one God and his will. In Romans 2, Paul challenges who belongs in the we, by suggesting that just hearing the law read doesn't make us we: "All who sin apart from the law will also perish apart from the law, and all who sin under the law will be judged by the law. For it is not those who hear the law who are righteous in God's sight, but it is those who obey the law who will be declared righteous" (Rom 2:12-13).

Paul attacks the idea of who we the righteous are. Jews were given the law, while Gentiles were not, but Jews will therefore be judged by the law. Yes, God gave Jews the law (which is a good thing), but if Jews hear the law and still sin and disobey God, then what good is that? Paul agrees it's good to boast in having the law, since boasting means giving something honor and recognizing its worth. But while they boast about the law, this has only drawn more attention to their failure to obey it. By boasting and not following it, they end up bringing shame on God: "As it is written: 'God's name is blasphemed among the Gentiles because of you'" (Rom 2:24). Paul concludes that circumcision (the law) only "has value if you observe the law, but if you break the law, you have become as though you had not been circumcised" (Rom 2:25). Speaking as a fellow Jew, Paul concludes, "What shall we conclude then? Do we [Jews] have any advantage? Not at all!" (Rom 3:9). As an individualist, I miss some of

---

[3]Richard J. Clifford, *Wisdom* (Collegeville, MN: Liturgical Press, 2012), 65.

what Paul is doing here. Like his Jewish readers, Paul agrees the issue is collective: there are two groups. Paul's audience thinks, "Yes, Jews and Gentiles." Paul says no. One group is those under sin: "For we have made the charge that Jews and Gentiles alike are all under the power of sin" (Rom 3:9). The other group is those not under sin: "Therefore, there is now no condemnation for those who are in Christ Jesus" (Rom 8:1).

God is the patron, who magnanimously and generously desires to benefit sinful people. Despite all of this sin, God has generously decided not to show wrath to humankind but instead to offer them his favor, his benefaction, his *charis*, to be their patron. But God is not like the patrons of the world, who give patronage to people they think would prove to be worthy clients—those who will reciprocate by giving them honor and loyalty. God offers patronage in a very different way. This is a key part of the good news: "There is no difference between Jew and Gentile, for all have sinned and fall short of the glory of God, and all are justified freely [a free gift] by his grace [patronage] through the redemption that came by Christ Jesus" (Rom 3:22-24). All people have not been worthy clients and so do not deserve his favor. Rather, as ungrateful recipients of creation, they deserve his wrath. Yet, God has responded by generously offering all people his patronage. He acted to benefit us because he could. He offers us a *charis*: the life of his Son. Paul describes it as a patron's gift, because we the clients are not worthy or deserving. Paul is using the ancient system of patronage to stress—in ways ancient people readily understood—that God gives us this gift on the basis that he wants to benefit us because he can.

When clients accept a patron's gift, they are agreeing to be his clients. We have the choice of whether we want to accept what God has lovingly offered us. As we noted, patronage creates households. By accepting this gift, we move from being under God's wrath to standing in his favor. (Paul explains this further in Rom 5.) But Paul's use of patronage language adds a dimension that I often miss: a patron's gift creates an ongoing relationship.[4] I joined his household.

---

[4]Troels Engberg-Pedersen, "Gift-Giving and Friendship: Seneca and Paul in Romans 1–8 on the Logic of God's Χάρις and Its Human Response," *Harvard Theological Review* 101, no. 1 (2008): 27.

When we accept God's patronage and help, we enter into a patronage relationship with him. One Asian friend said, "This makes so much sense, but it feels so heavy. How will I ever live up to honoring God as he deserves as my patron!" This relationship is patronage, but God acts differently from the patrons of the world. We have seen that the New Testament is full of stories of how God treats clients who let him down: love and forgiveness. The cross demonstrates that (Rom 5:8). Yes, we want to love God and let our gratitude come out in service and allegiance to him, but not because of fear of what he will do if we don't fully live up to what he deserves. Our gratitude comes from love not fear, and not our love, but God's. He has shown us who he is and how he treats us if we don't honor him. We can rest in his loving character, as the Father who adopted us.

For Paul, Abraham was a faithful client (he trusted God, and it was credited to him as righteousness). Paul has shown that we have a relationship with God through trusting in his benefaction, his grace, to us. In fact, Paul argues that this is not a new development in how people relate to God and become his people. To explain this, Paul goes right back to the beginning of the story of the Jewish people: Abraham.

God promises Abraham a child in Genesis 12. Years pass, and Abraham still hasn't had a child, so he complains to God (Gen 15:2-3). God assures Abraham that the promise he gave him of offspring will come to pass. God tells Abraham to look up at the stars and count them, and he promises Abraham that his offspring will be more numerous. After hearing this, the text says, "Abram believed the LORD, and he credited it to him as righteousness" (Gen 15:6). Understanding this statement is key to understanding Paul. He writes:

> Against all hope, Abraham in hope believed and so became the father of many nations, just as it had been said to him, "So shall your offspring be." Without weakening in his faith, he faced the fact that his body was as good as dead. . . . Yet he did not waver through unbelief regarding the promise of God, but was strengthened in his faith and gave glory to God, being fully persuaded that God had power to do what he had promised. This is why "it was credited to him as righteousness." (Rom 4:18-22)

The key for Paul is that this declaration of Abraham being considered righteous, after he trusts God, comes in Genesis 15. Abraham doesn't bear a child until Genesis 16. God's promise is given without any evidence yet. There is a lot going against God's promise—Abraham's age and Sarah's barrenness. Yet, Abraham trusts the promise. For Paul, this is a beautiful image of how trust and righteousness are related.

Potential patrons can make promises to potential clients all the time. But this doesn't mean a patron-client relationship is formed. The relationship is only formed if the client decides to trust the patron and their promises. If the client is looking for other options, backup plans, the client doesn't really trust the patron. No relationship is established. The client isn't choosing to depend on the patron. Abraham trusted God, in the faithfulness of God. Abraham was considered righteous because he believed and trusted in what God had promised to do for him. This was key to Paul because Abraham's righteousness was declared before the law was given, and also before the son was provided. By choosing to trust God's promise, Abraham became dependent on God. A relationship was established. Righteousness here has absolutely nothing to do with works of the law, or works of any kind. It is about trust. For Paul, the beauty is that anyone, whether Jew or Gentile, can trust God. He continues: "The words 'it was credited to him' were written not for him [Abraham] alone, but also for us, to whom God will credit righteousness— for us who believe in him who raised Jesus our Lord from the dead. He was delivered over to death for our sins and was raised to life for our justification" (Rom 4:23-25).

Paul wants us to see that Abraham trusted God and so was considered righteous. Later the promise was fulfilled. Paul helps the believers in Rome to see all those who trust in the cross, both Jew and Gentile, are trusting in God's faithfulness as Abraham did. Like him, they will be considered righteous by faith: "The promise comes by faith, so that it may be by grace and may be guaranteed to all Abraham's offspring—not only to those who are of the law but also to those who have the faith of Abraham. He is the father of us all" (Rom 4:16).

We are members of God's people, the family of Abraham, not because we follow the law or because we share Abraham's blood. Abraham became a father by trusting God, and we become his children by trusting God. We honor it by boasting. We proclaim that we depend on the cross and God's faithfulness. We boast of receiving this hope. "Therefore, since we have been justified through faith [trust], we have peace with God through our Lord Jesus Christ, through whom we have gained access by faith [trust] into this grace [patronage] in which we now stand. And we boast in the hope of the glory of God" (Rom 5:1-2).

God, our patron, gives grace. Paul uses patronage to explain to the Roman church how Jewish and Gentile Christians are united. Part of his letter addresses how we are reconciled to God and to each other. Yet, my individualist signposts led me to read it as if it were written to me. The letter does not focus on how *I* am saved (though that is part of it) but how *we*—all believers in Christ, the people of God—are saved. Paul speaks with collective imagery. Our identity is *not* through shared blood or ethnicity but through *charis*, the gracious gift of our patron. Although we are all from different households, different genealogies, different ethnicities and networks, we all had a need that only this new patron could meet. He graciously gave us the gift we needed (salvation as justification, sanctification, glorification). As his new clients, we are to exhibit the proper loyalty, *pistis* (faith, trust). As clients, we are now part of a new household, his kingdom. Whatever differences we had no longer matter—"There is neither Jew nor Gentile, neither slave nor free, nor is there male and female, for you are all one in Christ Jesus" (Gal 3:28). Our loyalty, our allegiance, our trust, is in our new patron, who gives us new values (and boundaries).

By entering into relationship with God through faith (*pistis*), we become part of his household, his community, his flock. We individualists can miss this horizontal dimension of grace. We can imagine grace means *I* am reconciled to God. It does, but it also means we are reconciled to God and to one another. It is worth underlining again that Paul's argument in Romans is how Jews and Gentiles have both received reconciliation to God, and therefore to one another by grace, the gift (*charis*) that our patron has given all of us. Paul's point is addressing we, not me. Those others used to be *them*, but now they are *us*. All those who have been brought into relationship with God have been brought into relationship with each other.

Since this is based in God's *charis*, we cannot add or find some reason to distinguish between ourselves, whether different social status, different education, different ethnicity, or different cultural traditions. If we do, we have added something to the basis for our relationship with God. God gave us salvation by favor, *charis*, through Christ. We received this by trusting, *pistis*, in it. Nothing else. The same is true for all our brothers and sisters. We relate to God and to one another by grace: "For it is by grace [*charis*] you [plural] have been saved, through faith [*pistis*]" (Eph 2:8). We individualists might benefit from seeing the patronage and collectivism of Paul's words. A new household means new boundaries and thus new values as we seek to live in community.

Fellowship. The early church understood the collective dimension of salvation. They saw that, by trusting in God's gift of Christ, they had become a new community. As we have seen, collective communities depended on one another, shared resources, and enabled one another to survive. Church offerings are not membership dues but family members contributing to the family fund to take care of each other. In Acts, we read about the Jerusalem church, "They devoted themselves to the apostles' teaching and to fellowship, to the breaking of bread and to prayer. Everyone was filled with awe at the many wonders and signs performed by the apostles. All the believers were together and had everything in common. They sold property and possessions to give to anyone who had need" (Acts 2:42-45). This isn't some form of communism, where no own owned anything. To claim that misses the point on many levels. The believers continued to own property and possessions. But they chose to share so that nobody was in need, like a family does (or should). Patronage pulls clients, outsiders, into a household, into a family. In Acts, the Spirit comes in power on the believers, Peter boldly preaches, many come to faith, and the community cares for one another. This community devotion among believers is the natural outworking of the goods news of Christ. It is what happens when a new household is formed. Just like a family, the church is to depend on one another.

"One another" language permeates Paul when he talks about how believers are to relate in community. Paul writes, "So in Christ we, though many, form one body, and each member belongs to all the others [one another]" (Rom 12:5). Believers are to "be devoted to one another in love," to "honor one another above yourselves" (Rom 12:10), to "live in harmony with one another" (Rom 12:16). This is not *I* to *you* but *we* to *us*. For Paul, the church really is to be a family: "Let no debt remain outstanding, except the continuing debt to love one another" (Rom 13:8), "accept one another" (Rom 15:7), "serve one another humbly in love" (Gal 5:13). Likewise, Peter says believers are to "offer hospitality to one another without grumbling" (1 Pet 4:9). We often dismiss these commands as some sort of unattainable ideal. But these commands do not seem as outrageous if we imagine these are the rules for our personal family. In fact, we might expect our family to live by such rules.

Paul calls the church a body to illustrate this mutual dependency among members. The hand, eye, and feet cannot say to one another, "I don't need you" (1 Cor 12:21). The community of believers is to mutually depend on, care for, honor, love, support, and serve one another, with gifts constantly flowing back and forth among the believers. When people use every kind of gift they have received to serve one another, the recipients are made strong, and with that, the whole community is strengthened. This is true both spiritually and materially. We read Paul and the New Testament picture of church better when we read it as "*we* strengthen *us*." Who benefits when I give to a poorer brother or sister? Us. Who benefits when I preach? Us. Who benefits when I tolerate an annoying member of the church? Us. Who benefits when you are gentle to me? Us. For Paul, this is the meaning of fellowship in the church: "Therefore encourage one another and build each other up, just as in fact you are doing" (1 Thess 5:11). This has spiritual, relational, and material aspects. This way of life results from entering into God's grace, and when it happens, the body, and every part of it, is strengthened and protected.

DON'T THROW THE BABY OUT WITH THE BATHWATER, OR THE SYSTEM WITH THE PEOPLE

Earlier in the book, we saw how the Roman governor Felix misused the patronage system. Just as the taxi driver complained about his leader (patron) being a poor shepherd, fleecing his people and not caring for them, my Mediterranean friends often share a story of some patron abusing his or her power. So are we individualists right to condemn patronage because of the actions of patrons like Felix? What about the actions of Elisha and the Shunammite woman? Or Phoebe? Let's turn to another modern illustration. Amy, a Christian missionary, was sharing a ministry challenge from her life in the Middle East. While having coffee with her friend Muna, it became evident that Muna's husband had beat her again the previous night. Muna was wearing makeup, but Amy could see the bruises. Amy had been discipling women in the Middle East for over a decade, and she had seen this sort of thing before. Looking at Muna broke her heart.

Amy shared this story about Muna at a recent conference on patronage. There were about fifty people in the room. While she recounted Muna's plight, I was struck that no one in the room concluded that marriage as a system needed to go. They saw that the problem was the *people*, not the system. Yet, if our friend's story had been about a patron relationship that had gone sour, I was confident half the room would have concluded that the system was the problem and needed to go. Many of the individualists at the conference had negative impressions of patronage. One scholar, speaking on patronage in the New Testament, commented that Westerners often wonder why the New Testament didn't "condemn slavery or patronage." Why did he group those two items together, slavery and patronage? He might answer, "They both exploit people." My collective friends would beg to differ, asserting "Patronage helps people." In my individualist world, *patronage* carries negative connotations. By contrast, a panel of Lebanese leaders spoke on patronage, citing personal stories of successes and failures, but the system of patronage was never under assault. They critiqued the way people used and abused the system.

Our culture paints patronage in almost exclusively negative terms. When we paint these systems with negative terms, we hinder our ability to read some of the beauty in God's word. When we miss what is being said, or simply fit it into our own individualist framework, we can misread and thereby miss some of the wisdom that Scripture is bringing to situations related to patronage.

JESUS AS A BROKER

God is our patron, and we are his clients. So, why do we need Jesus? The New Testament frequently portrays Jesus as a broker. A broker bridges between the patron and the clients. Brokers establish *and maintain* relationships.

Only rarely is Jesus called a broker explicitly (Heb 9:15; 12:24; 1 Tim 2:5; 1 Jn 2:1). It usually went without being said. The New Testament writers talk about the ways Jesus acts as a broker and expect us to see it. This only became a challenge when we individualists who are not familiar with the system of brokerage began to read the New Testament. In John's Gospel, Jesus frequently speaks about being sent by the Father into the world (Jn 4:34; 5:30; 6:38). Jesus also speaks about going back to the Father (Jn 13:1; 16:5).[5] This is classic brokerage. Jesus is the Father's broker, sent to the other party, us.

John emphasizes how Jesus was very much of this world. Jesus is from Nazareth in Galilee (Jn 1:46; 7:42). He becomes tired (Jn 4:6). John is showing us that Jesus is connected to both God and humankind, making him the ideal broker. John tells us that Jesus was with God in the beginning (Jn 1:1-2) and also that Jesus was thirsty (Jn 4:7). John tells us both to show how Jesus is the ideal mediator or broker.

John isn't the only writer to portray Jesus as a broker. The Israelite high priest was the broker for Israel. The New Testament points out that Jesus is now our high priest. But he is a better one. But, if Jesus is perfect, how can he represent our side, as a broker should? While this objection may

---

[5]We are indebted to Jerry Neyrey for alerting us to the following ways Jesus is portrayed as a broker in John. See Jerome H. Neyrey, "'I Am the Door' (John 10:7, 9): Jesus the Broker in the Fourth Gospel," *Catholic Biblical Quarterly* 69, no. 2 (April 2007): 271-91.

not have occurred to us modern individualists, it did to the writer of Hebrews: "For we do not have a high priest who is unable to empathize with our weaknesses, but we have one who has been tempted in every way, just as we are—yet he did not sin" (Heb 4:15). Jesus is the unique broker between God and humankind. In Jesus, we have a bridge, a connection, to the Father.

Let's remember that brokers do not only connect the parties but *maintain* and *repair* the relationship. John writes to believers and encourages them not to sin. John immediately reminds us that we will at times fall into sin. He tells us not to deal with this by denying this fact, which would simply make us hypocrites and God a liar: "If we claim we have not sinned, we make him out to be a liar and his word is not in us" (1 Jn 1:10). Instead, John reminds us that, even when we do sin, the relationship is not broken because we have a broker: "My dear children, I write this to you so that you will not sin. But if anybody does sin, we have an advocate with the Father—Jesus Christ, the Righteous One" (1 Jn 2:1).

Jesus is the broker who connects us to God and who also repairs and maintains the relationship between us and God when we fall short. This is good news for John. He understands that Jesus as our broker is the means we have for remaining in God's love. Our hope and assurance lie not in ourselves but in our broker, Jesus. And Jesus has not only connected us to God but to one another. Our assurance of staying connected to one another also does not rest in ourselves but in our broker, Jesus.

Why Jesus is a better broker than Moses. God called Abraham and promised him a huge family. That family was soon enslaved in Egypt. God called Moses, an unlikely character, to be his broker to free them.[6] They exit Egypt to become God's people. They have a leader (Moses) and a powerful patron (God). Yet, no sooner are they free than they start complaining. They grumble against Moses because the water of Marah is bitter. Moses acts as a broker, and God uses Moses to miraculously make the

---

[6]A case can be made that God usually calls unlikely people, oftentimes the least worthy. Perhaps it is so God gets the glory, since the unworthy one cannot boast. The challenge is that God gifts whom he calls. After a time, the unworthy one begins to look pretty worthy. Temptation comes. Modesty in young ministers easily turns to arrogance in older ministers as giftedness begins to appear.

water sweet (Ex 15:22-26). In the next chapter, the people become hungry and again grumble against Moses and Aaron, "If only we had died by the LORD's hand in Egypt! There we sat around pots of meat and ate all the food we wanted, but you have brought us out into this desert to starve this entire assembly to death" (Ex 16:3).

God hears and miraculously responds again, providing quail and manna. Surely now they will trust God as their patron and stop being ungrateful. Yet in the very next chapter the Israelites complain about having no water, "Why did you bring us up out of Egypt to make us and our children and livestock die of thirst?" (Ex 17:3). We are supposed to be more than frustrated. We are supposed to be *scandalized* by their grumbling, because collectives think ingratitude a terrible vice. By missing the reason, we miss the lesson. We are supposed to marvel that, despite their ingratitude, God remains completely faithful to them. God is a patient patron par excellence. His mediator, Moses, continuously runs back and forth between the people and God to maintain the relationship. When Aaron and Miriam grumble against Moses, God rebukes them for disparaging their mediator:

> When there is a prophet among you,
> > I, the LORD, reveal myself to them in visions,
> > I speak to them in dreams.
> But this is not true of my servant Moses;
> > he is faithful in all my house.
> With him I speak face to face,
> > clearly and not in riddles;
> > he sees the form of the LORD.
> Why then were you not afraid
> > to speak against my servant Moses? (Num 12:6-8)

In the New Testament, the writer to the Hebrews is very much aware of Moses' role as broker. We have noted how collectives seem to always be looking for the best person to mediate for them with other parties, someone with a lot of honor and connected closely to both parties. Moses was clearly a very good option. He had a uniquely intimate relationship with God and had proven he could broker the covenant. Nonetheless, the author of Hebrews points out that Jesus is a better broker than Moses because "Moses was faithful as a servant in all God's house, bearing witness to what would be spoken by God in the future. But Christ is faithful as the Son over God's house. And we are his house, if indeed we hold firmly to our confidence and the hope in which we glory" (Heb 3:5-6). Jesus is a better broker than Moses, first, because Jesus is closer to God than Moses was. Moses was God's servant; yet Jesus is God's Son. There can be no better mediator than a son to his father. Second, Jesus is superior by having more honor and status than Moses. Jesus has authority *over* the house, while Moses served *in* the house.[7] The writer is combining brokerage and kinship to help us see the superiority of Jesus as a broker, even to Moses.

What about our brokerage connection to Jesus? Hebrews argues it couldn't be stronger: "Both the one who makes people holy and those who are made holy are of the same family. So Jesus is not ashamed to call them brothers and sisters" (Heb 2:11). Jesus is not just our broker but our brother. Because we are family, we can come to him for help without feeling embarrassed and ashamed. We can trust that Jesus will not be ashamed of us regardless of the issue and that he will broker for us to maintain our relationship.

We now have a Paraclete. When Jesus tells the disciples he is going to the Father, they are distraught at the thought of being alone. Who will broker for them? Jesus says he's sending them *another* broker: "And I will ask the Father, and he will give you another advocate [*paraclete*] to help you and be with you forever" (Jn 14:16).

The term *paraclete* has caused much confusion. In John *paraclete* is commonly translated "comforter" or "helper," but "advocate" is becoming more popular.[8] In an important study, Tricia Brown looked at how the

---

[7]We are indebted here to the work of Ekkardt A. Sonntag, "Jesus, the Good Wasta? Reading the Epistle to the Hebrews in Light of a Middle-Eastern Social Phenomenon" (PhD diss., Vrije Universiteit Amsterdam, 2015), 117-20.

[8]"Comforter," so KJV, ASV, Darby, GNV, TLB; "advocate," so NRSV, LEB, NET, NIV; "helper," so ESV, GNT, NASB, NCV; "counselor," so RSV, HCSB. *The Message* uses "friend," which might be

word *paraklētos* was used in Greek writings prior to the Gospel of John.
She discovered that the term was sometimes associated with courts of law,
but *paracletes* were never *in* the courtroom: "The *paracletes* are not portrayed as advocates in the court but as persons striving to use their connections and 'influence' to sway those involved in the formal court pro-
ceedings. . . . *Paracletes* denote powerful individuals among the crowd
striving to persuade the jurors to decide in favor of their client before the
trial has even commenced." For example, Demosthenes in the fourth
century BC, in a speech before some Athenian jurors, cautions them not
to be persuaded by any paracletes who might try to sway them by private
meetings and personal influence. When Demosthenes does refer to an
actual advocate in the courtroom, he calls that person a *syndikos* or *syne-
goros*, not a *paraklētos*. A hundred years later, Diogenes Laertius tells of a
man who is pestered by "an importune talker." The man responds to the
one annoying him: "I will satisfy your demand if you will only get a *paraclete* and stay away yourself" (*Lives and Opinions of Eminent Philosophers*
4.50.3-5). When Philo retells the story of Joseph in Egypt, Joseph's
brothers fall to the ground in fear when they realize who he is. Joseph replies: "Be not downcast. . . . I forgive and forget all that you did to me. Do
not ask for any other *paraclete*. Of my own free unbidden judgment I have
voluntarily come to make my peace with you" (Philo, *On the Life of Joseph*
239-40). Joseph is telling his brothers they don't need to find a broker. He
has already forgiven them. Brown concludes: "The word *paraclete* would
best be translated 'mediator' or 'broker.' "[9]

My collectivist friends find John's passage far more comforting than I ever
did. The disciples have been following Jesus, who multiplies bread, heals the
sick, deflects trouble from the authorities. He has provided protection and
provision, and now he says he's leaving them—but he is providing another

---

the preferred choice among collectives, but I am unsure Eugene Peterson meant "friend" in the way
collectivists do.

[9]Tricia Gates Brown, *Spirit in the Writings of John: Johannine Pneumatology in Social-Scientific Perspective*, Journal for the Study of the New Testament Supplement Series 253 (New York: T&T
Clark, 2003), 171-73, 181.

broker, who comes from the Father, the Spirit of truth.[10] Jesus doesn't explain it; the disciples don't need someone to explain what a broker does. What comforts them is that they are getting an amazing broker: one who will be with them forever. This passage has been cold comfort for me because I didn't really understand what a broker did. We should have no fear about an unknown future, about not being cared for, about being orphaned and left alone in the world. We have a Paraclete. Now that we understand better what John meant, we can be comforted.

WE ARE ALSO BROKERS, BUT NEVER PATRONS

My friend Bashar works at a university in the Middle East. There is a generous scholarship available for students, but one of the conditions of the scholarship is that students guarantee they intend to complete the full course of study. One of his students was a Syrian refugee. Halfway through the program, she was given the possibility of asylum in a Western country but did not know when it would happen. She informed Bashar that she needed the scholarship but that she could no longer guarantee she would complete the full course. It just wasn't in her hands anymore. A few weeks later, Bashar had the pleasure of telling her she would receive the scholarship despite the chance she would not finish the course. She was so grateful and began thanking him for his generosity. She expressed that she would not forget his generosity. My friend stopped her: "Actually, it wasn't my decision. I went to the donors and told them your situation, and they were willing to take the risk. They are generous and they are investing in you. I am simply telling you the news." The scholarship was still a very generous gift; that fact hadn't changed. But what did change was where the strings were attached. She was no longer tied to Bashar. He could have let her think it was his decision. He could have gained gratitude from her and a lasting relationship—and

---

[10]John speaks about the Spirit as the one who intercedes for us. Paul mentions Jesus interceding for us in Rom 8:32, but Paul also mentions the Spirit interceding for us (Rom 8:27). The New Testament portrays both Jesus and the Spirit as brokers. That seems confusing to us. We like clearly defined roles. We mentioned that collectives today often muddle all this up. It appears ancients were happy to do so as well.

the honor that comes from that. But he didn't. He was open about who the giver was. He was just the broker.

Paul writes to the Ephesians,

> But to each one of us grace [*charis*] has been given as Christ apportioned it ... So Christ himself gave the apostles, the prophets, the evangelists, the pastors and teachers, to equip his people for works of service, so that the body of Christ may be built up until we all reach unity in the faith and in the knowledge of the Son of God and become mature, attaining to the whole measure of the fullness of Christ. (Eph 4:7, 11-13)

God gives different gifts to his people so they can serve one another. Apostles, prophets, evangelists, pastors, and teachers are not patrons. God is the giver, and he has given these gifts to strengthen his community. We are the brokers of these gifts. We are to use what we have been given by God, our patron, for the purpose he intends us to use them, as his brokers. This purpose is to serve the body to build more strength and unity. As God's brokers, we are to be clear who the patron who actually provides the gift is: God.

Many Christians in Britain and the United States are wealthy compared to many other Christians in the Majority World. We often give generously to other Christians. Some Western missionaries, especially those serving in Africa and South America, have criticized this practice as creating an unhealthy patron-client relationship with national missionaries, arguing we are *patronizing* them, meant in the most negative way. "We are making them dependent on us," they argue. The solution to this problem is not to stop giving. The problem is that wealthy Christians have been acting as patrons and not brokers. Any wealth belongs to the Lord. We are merely his brokers. Like my friend Bashar, I need to make sure the strings attached are attached to the true patron. The solution is not for poorer Christians to avoid becoming dependent on a patron. The very concept of a patron is to create dependence, or, as my collective friends would term it, relationship. These Christians should be dependent on their patron, but their patron is God. We are just brokers.

Remembering we are brokers, not patrons, applies to the local level as well. Shepherding is a patronage motif. Peter writes to the elders: "Be shepherds of God's flock that is under your care, watching over them—not because you must, but because you are willing, as God wants you to be; not pursuing dishonest gain, but eager to serve; not lording it over those entrusted to you, but being examples to the flock" (1 Pet 5:2-3). Church leaders are to seek to serve, not to use their position and role to obligate or to gain dishonestly. Peter reminds these leaders that Christ is the chief Shepherd, who will reward them. They are not the ultimate patrons of the church but brokers of Jesus, placed by him to serve the church. It is easy for us to forget that we are just brokers. When we forget, then we begin to act as if we are the patrons, which obligates recipients to *us*, rather than to God.

Serving well as brokers. On the night before he is crucified, Jesus celebrates the Last Supper with his disciples. As Jesus prepares to lay his life down for sinners, the disciples begin arguing with one another about which of them is the greatest (Lk 22:24). Jesus rebukes them: "The kings of the Gentiles lord it over them; and those who exercise authority over them call themselves Benefactors. But you are not to be like that. Instead, the greatest among you should be like the youngest, and the one who rules like the one who serves" (Lk 24:25-26). This is the only time the technical term for benefactor or patron is used in Luke.[11] These patrons were giving gifts with strings attached in order to increase their own personal power. Jesus' disciples are not to be this way. Jesus says, "For who is greater, the one who is at the table or the one who serves? Is it not the one who is at the table? But I am among you as one who serves" (Lk 22:27).

Jesus' question isn't a trick. The one sitting at the table *is* more important than the servant who serves. Jesus is not encouraging a Christian leader to call himself a servant but still stand up at the front, to be thanked

---

[11]Classical scholars rightly nuance the difference between the Roman *patronus* and the Greek civic *euergetai*. See Myles Lavan, *Slaves to Rome: Paradigms of Empire in Roman Culture* (Cambridge: Cambridge University Press, 2013), 10. This nuance, though, is not significant for us here, nor likely for Jesus' audience. Jesus is contrasting a disciple with someone claiming an exalted status as the generous bestower of gifts.

by everyone, and to be honored. In the picture Jesus gives, the servant is not honored, not thanked, perhaps not even acknowledged. All too often "servant leadership" today is a euphemism. A true servant leader ensures the recipients of the gifts know the servant leader is just the broker, not the patron. In Jesus' story, the servant is Jesus, highlighting his role as our broker. As we imitate him, Christlike brokers use their skills, ability, and gifts to benefit others, without seeking to be repaid honor or gifts in kind, as if they were the patron. This is what Christ means by being a servant leader, a broker. It means taking the servant's status, those who aren't being honored when they serve.

Who can serve as leaders? The easy answer is those whom God has called and equipped. If God arranged his chosen leaders to be born with a big birthmark shaped like a checkmark on their foreheads, it would be easier. Instead we rely on "discernment." Here is a concern. In individualist cultures, it appears we allow leaders to "discern" on his/her own or we "discern" as leaders those who stand out, that is, those who have unique gifts or have new ideas, perhaps those who don't seem to need to depend on others. Are these qualifications to be a biblical leader or to be an individualist? Collectives seem to discern as leaders those who come from a strong family, who have status, who are honored by society. Are these qualifications to be a biblical leader or to be a collectivist? Do either of these reflect biblical values or merely cultural values?

Jesus thinks leaders are those who serve. They act to benefit those in their care, as generous brokers for a very generous patron. They don't do this to be honored or thanked or to burden people.

CONCLUSION

Biblical Collectivism in My Individualist World

WHY SHOULD I CARE ABOUT COLLECTIVISM? It is important because the world is becoming more global. My neighbors may be collectivists. But also it is important because I may serve here or abroad among collectivists. I can serve them better if I understand their worldview a bit better. Really, though, the most important reason is that the biblical stories occurred in a collective world. The biblical authors were collectivists. Their stories, illustrations, and, significantly, metaphors were all from their collective world. And their stories and metaphors had a lot that went without being said, because *everybody* knew those parts.

COLLECTIVISM IS BIBLICAL

For the sake of clarity, we have divided the social structures of kinship, patronage, and brokerage into neat, discrete categories. We have warned this can be misleading, as if kinship were entirely separated from patronage, or as if brokers were not patrons or kinfolk, or as if somehow these values worked independently from honor, shame, and boundaries. In practice, these dynamics often overlapped and complemented one another. In this chapter we want to draw out some of the ways the biblical writers drew on aspects of collective culture to teach us about God. We understand these themes, but we can at times intentionally squeeze them into our individualistic cultural framework. When we do this, it can limit our understanding of all that the biblical authors intended us to grasp from what they said.

One last time, let's imagine a common first-century Palestinian situation. A patron owns a large number of olive orchards, far too many for him and his sons to farm by themselves. His grandfather lived on the original farm. As the farm grew, his father moved down to the port town of Caesarea and rented out the land to tenant farmers. Many peasants farmed land, provided the landowner with the fruit, and lived off the excess.[1] Business continued to boom. Now, the grandson has moved to live in Corinth, where the olive oil is shipped. He enjoys life there and handles his import/export business from his villa.

Situations like this were not uncommon in the first century. Everyone involved in the business, from the family down to the tenants, was somewhat connected to the same household under the *pater*, the father, who ran the business and cared for the family. The family and clients honored the patron, who enforced the boundaries in order to define and maintain everyone's values.

In the temple, Jesus tells a story:

> A man planted a vineyard. He put a wall around it, dug a pit for the winepress and built a watchtower. Then he rented the vineyard to some farmers and moved to another place. At harvest time he sent a servant to the tenants to collect from them some of the fruit of the vineyard. But they seized him, beat him and sent him away empty-handed. Then he sent another servant to them; they struck this man on the head and treated him shamefully [literally dishonored him]. He sent still another, and that one they killed. He sent many others; some of them they beat, others they killed.
>
> He had one left to send, a son, whom he loved. He sent him last of all, saying, "They will respect my son."
>
> But the tenants said to one another, "This is the heir. Come, let's kill him, and the inheritance will be ours." So they took him and killed him, and threw him out of the vineyard. (Mk 12:1-8)

---

[1]Technically, the renters were required to pay a certain (often sizable) amount for the privilege of farming the land, since they didn't own it. From the harvest, first came the rent, and the excess belonged to the farmer. Good years meant sufficiency. Bad years could mean hunger, as all the harvest went to the owner.

We need to notice that Jesus' audience on this occasion are not tenant farmers in Galilee. Jesus is speaking to Jewish leaders in the temple. Nonetheless, his audience knows this social system well.

Jesus tells the parable of the tenants not to discuss ancient economic systems but to describe God, his prophets, his people, and the role of Jesus. It is how Jesus retells the story of the Bible, the story of God's salvation history. We hope you notice that this story is grounded in the key structures and tools of collectivism, but of course they went without being said: God is the patron (the owner), and Israel, his people, are his clients (tenants). The prophets were the servants sent to mediate/broker on his behalf. The best and final broker is his son. The owner says, "They will respect my son." The word translated "respect" is from *entropē*. This is the good kind of shame. It meant the clients should have a sense of shame, the kind of shame that knows the proper way to act in a situation. This kind of shame should prevent them from treating the son badly and to hopefully do the right thing (to call them back). They might beat a servant, but surely they will respect the son. Have they no sense of shame? Evidently not. They actually kill the son. Jesus uses the household, benefaction, and mediation (kinship, patronage, and brokerage) to summarize the Old Testament and God's saving plan for humankind. More than that, Jesus' story should create a sense of shame, *entropē*, in the Jewish leaders, to pull them back from crossing the lines in Jesus' day. He is calling them to repent. They don't. They kill Jesus (and throw him outside the city). If you were asked to summarize the Bible in one minute, how would you do it? This is how Jesus does it. The collectivist system of Jesus' day is the undercurrent of his story.

BUT AREN'T PATRONAGE AND SUCH THINGS THE PROBLEM?

As an individualist, though, it is hard for me not to think patronage is broken or to want to avoid kinship ties (nepotism) or to resist the use of a broker (the middleman). To me, somehow it seems like these structures are part of fallen creation. I notice that when individualists, even scholarly ones, talk about these structures, they are usually described in negative terms. At a recent international conference on patronage, a noted scholar remarked on "the oppressive expectations of reciprocity." It struck me. We had only been talking about reciprocity in patronage, not any particular abuses of it. His default assumption was that since patronage expects to be reciprocated, it is oppressive. We individualists love our independence. My Asian friends there may well have spoken of the blessings of reciprocity. Paul gives spiritual blessings to the Roman church and expects to be reciprocated with material blessings to pay for his trip to Spain (Rom 1:11; 15:28), just as he notes that the churches in Achaia and Macedonia received spiritual blessings from Jerusalem and Paul is expecting these churches to reciprocate with material blessings (Rom 15:26-27). Is Paul wrong to expect reciprocity? Is he being oppressive? His gifts have strings attached, and Paul glories in it.

These days half of marriages end in divorce, but we keep trying it. None of us is likely to conclude, "We need to jettison marriage. The institution is broken and the Christian world is better off without it." No. None of us blames the system of marriage. As we said in chapter four, it is the people, not the system. We live in a fallen world. Sin has warped the perfect world God has created. The church doesn't suggest tossing the whole system of marriage because it is abused by some. The solution is the good news of Jesus and the gifts he brings.

Individualist missionaries abroad often argue that national churches abroad need to eliminate patronage. We are happy to jettison these structures because they are foreign to us and we can live without them. Collectivists can't. At a recent conference, a community leader spoke of "the dance and . . . ," he paused, then continued, "management of patronage. The system is not good or bad. It is the people in it. It was this system that started our civil war. It was this system that ended it. It all depends on the goodness or badness of the person, not the system."[2] We would argue the same thing about marriage. It is not the structure of marriage but the

---

[2]Sheikh Mohammed, "Panel Discussion," International Patronage Conference, Beirut, Lebanon, October 4, 2018.

goodness or badness of the people involved. We would argue the same for these collectivist structures. God uses them in the biblical text, and we see them still at work today.

REDEEMING COLLECTIVISM WITH LOVE

Love is the answer. Are we being trite? No. This is the same thing we would say about failing marriages. In marriage, when the predominant value is love, the dynamics change. I have Christian friends who maintain a hierarchal view of marriage: wives should submit to husbands. They believe love is the answer to making this work. My friends who practice an egalitarian view of marriage have their own woes and believe love is the key to making it work. No matter the biblical model of marriage, when love pervades a marriage, the system works better. We argue that when love is what is valued, patronage works. Who is the ideal patron? The world might argue it is the rich one. No. The one rich in love. Likewise, brokerage, shame, boundaries, and other aspects of collectivism work when love pervades. When Paul faces the challenges in Corinth, he responds with love: "It always protects, always trusts, always hopes, always perseveres. Love never fails. . . . And now these three remain: faith, hope and love. But the greatest of these is love" (1 Cor 13:7-8, 13).

Christian love isn't just the solution to marriage problems. Paul argues it is the solution to all problems. When Paul wrote 1 Corinthians 13, he wasn't at a marriage retreat. The church at Corinth had problems. They had kinship problems: people were divided by ethnicity and valuing others over their brothers and sisters in Christ. They had patronage problems, even brokerage problems: people were trying to exploit their positions and obligate their fellow brothers and sisters by giving to them in a way that attached strings to themselves, not to God. They had problems with honor and shame: they honored those doing things that shame was supposed to be pulling them back from. Boundaries were in the wrong places, dividing the brothers and sisters on ethnic and economic lines. In other words, sin may show up differently among collectives than it does with individualists, but the problem is still sin. Paul doesn't solve these problems by suggesting individualism. Individualists who sin create individualist-type problems. Collectivists who sin create collectivist-type problems. Just as we use individualist structures and tools for the gospel among individualists, so also the structures and tools of collectivism are also to be used for kingdom work. We bring every thought and system captive to obedience in Christ (2 Cor 10:2-6).

When we bring Christian love into these collective systems, problems can be resolved. Missionaries shouldn't try to remove collectivism from national churches—it wouldn't work anyway. We are blaming a culture and its systems for a problem that goes back to Genesis 3. The problem is sin, not individualism or collectivism. The solution is the transforming power of the gospel of Jesus Christ: "A new command I give you: Love one another. As I have loved you, so you must love one another. By this everyone will know that you are my disciples, if you love one another" (Jn 13:34-35).

AUTHOR INDEX

SUBJECT INDEX

SCRIPTURE INDEX

ALSO AVAILABLE

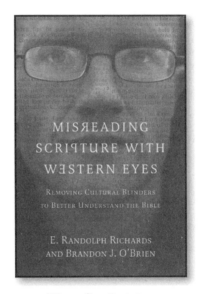

**Misreading Scripture
with Western Eyes**
*E. Randolph Richards and
Brandon J. O'Brien*
978-0-8308-3782-3